Art and
Human
Development

The Jean Piaget Symposium Series

Series Editor:

Ellin Scholnick
University of Maryland

Available from Psychology Press / Taylor & Francis

Overton, W.F. (Ed.): The Relationship Between Social and Cognitive Development.

Liben, L.S. (Ed): Piaget and the Foundations of Knowledge.

Scholnick, E.K. (Ed): New Trends in Conceptual Representations: Challenges to Piaget's Theory?

Niemark, E.D., DeLisi, R. & Newman, J.L. (Eds.): Moderators of Competence.

Bearison, D.J. & Zimiles, H. (Eds.): Thought and Emotion: Developmental Perspectives.

Liben, L.S. (Ed.): Development and Learning: Conflict or Congruence?

Forman, G. & Pufall, P.B. (Eds.): Constructivism in the Computer Age.

Overton, W.F. (Ed.): Reasoning, Necessity, and Logic: Developmental Perspectives.

Keating, D.P. & Rosen, H. (Eds.): Constructivist Perspectives on Developmental Psychopathology and Atypical Development.

Carey, S. & Gelman, R. (Eds.): The Epigenesis of Mind: Essays on Biology and Cognition.

Beilin, H. & Pufall, P. (Eds.): Piaget's Theory: Prospects and Possibilities.

Wozniak, R.H. & Fisher, K.W. (Eds.): Development in Context: Acting and Thinking in Specific Environments.

Overton, W.F. & Palermo, D.S. (Eds.): The Nature and Ontogenesis of Meaning.

Noam, G.G. & Fischer, K.W. (Eds.): Development and Vulnerability in Close Relationships.

Reed, E.S., Turiel, E. & Brown, T. (Eds.): Values and Knowledge.

Amsel, E. & Renninger, K.A. (Eds.): Change and Development: Issues of Theory, Method, and Application.

Langer, J. & Killen, M. (Eds.): Piaget, Evolution, and Development.

Scholnick, E., Nelson, K., Gelman, S.A. & Miller, P.H. (Eds.): Conceptual Development: Piaget's Legacy.

Nucci, L.P., Saxe, G.B. & Turiel, E. (Eds.): Culture, Thought, and Development.

Amsel, E. & Byren, J.P. (Eds.): Language, Literacy, and Cognitive Development: The Development and Consequences of Symbolic Communication.

Brown, T. & Smith, L. (Eds.): Reductionism and the Development of Knowledge.

Lightfoot, C., LaLonde, C. & Chandler, M. (Eds.): Changing Conceptions of Psychological Life.

Parker, J., Langer, J. & Milbrath, C. (Eds.): Biology and Knowledge Revisited: From Neurogenesis to Psychogenesis.

Goncu, A. & Gaskins, S. (Eds.): Play and Development: Evolutionary, Sociocultural, and Functional Perspectives.

Overton, W., Mueller, U. & Newman, J. (Eds.): Developmental Perspectives on Embodiment and Consciousness.

Wainryb, C., Turiel, E. & Smetana, J. (Eds.): Social Development, Social Inequalities, and Social Justice.

Muller, U., Carpendale, J., Budwig, N. & Sokol, B. (Eds.): Social Life and Social Knowledge: Toward a Process Account of Development.

Zelazo, P. D., Chandler, M. & Crone, E. (Eds.): Developmental Social Cognitive Neuroscience.

Milbrath, C. & Lightfoot, C. (Eds): Art and Human Development.

Art and Human Development

Constance Milbrath
University of British Columbia

Cynthia Lightfoot
Pennsylvania State University–Brandywine

Psychology Press
Taylor & Francis Group

New York   London

*Wall painting of bison, Niaux Cave (Ariège, France).
Courtesy of Dr. Jean Clottes.*

Psychology Press
Taylor & Francis Group
270 Madison Avenue
New York, NY 10016

Psychology Press
Taylor & Francis Group
27 Church Road
Hove, East Sussex BN3 2FA

© 2010 by Taylor and Francis Group, LLC
Psychology Press is an imprint of Taylor & Francis Group, an Informa business

Printed in the United States of America on acid-free paper
10 9 8 7 6 5 4 3 2 1

International Standard Book Number: 978-0-415-96553-8 (Hardback)

Library of Congress Cataloging-in-Publication Data

Art and human development / edited by Constance Milbrath, Cynthia Lightfoot.
   p. cm. -- (The Jean Piaget symposium series)
  Includes bibliographical references and index.
  ISBN 978-0-415-96553-8
   1. Creative ability. 2. Arts--Psychological aspects. I. Milbrath, Constance, 1943- II. Lightfoot, Cynthia.

BF408.A726 2010
153.3'5--dc22

2009025774

Visit the Taylor & Francis Web site at
http://www.taylorandfrancis.com

and the Psychology Press Web site at
http://www.psypress.com

IN MEMORIAM

These pages are graced by the inspiration of Terry Brown (1939–2005), a remarkable scholar and friend, who moved through this world as a dancer, confident in the generative intercourse of knowledge and art.

CONTENTS

PREFACE

This book is the culmination of a project that unfolded over the course of several years during which we sought ways to explore art, its development, and its role in the construction of knowledge. Two questions emerged from early discussions with our Jean Piaget Society colleagues, and with each other—questions that focused our efforts and galvanized our project. The first asked, "What are the origins of art, in an individual child, in a specific culture, and in the species as a whole?" And the second, "What is the epistemological status of creative, aesthetic activity in generating new knowledge?"

From these beginnings we fashioned the Jean Piaget Society annual conference, Art and Human Development, which convened in Baltimore, Maryland. Contributing to the invited program were luminaries—both scholars and artists—from the fields of archaeology, communications, education, psychology, and the performing arts. These contributors subsequently developed their conference addresses into the target chapters that compose this volume. In deference to our interest in anchoring our project to a constructivist epistemology, we invited commentary chapters from developmental scholars whose expertise uniquely positioned them to ground the main theses of the target chapters in constructivist developmental theory. The result of this organizational structure—target chapters followed by commentaries—is a rich dialogue flowing from the orienting questions of the origins and the epistemological status of aesthetic activity.

In addressing *the origins of art*, contributors to the volume explore the developmental, sociocultural, and evolutionary processes that make the creation and experience of art possible. In particular, they discuss how art emerges in individual development, in cultural groups (especially those that have been marginalized by virtue of age or ethnicity, or both), and in the species. In the context of addressing these issues, the contributors make reference to specific requisite developmental capacities, such as the child's developing theory of mind, empathy, and narrative reasoning, as well as a species-specific neurological substrate associated with consciousness. Speaking to the *epistemological status of art*, contributors examine art as a representational and sense-making enterprise that fixes meaning—for the artist, the spectator, the relations that hold between them, and the specific contexts within which meanings are culturally framed and inspired. In this respect, the contributors construe artistic activity as a process of self-expression or social commentary, or as otherwise related to the identity concerns of the artist-creator, thereby implicating creativity in the knowledge construction inherent to personal and cultural transformation.

The volume begins with an exploration in Part 1 of how cultures harness and exploit the arts to give expression to values, social practices, and traditions. This section traces the emergence of new art forms that arose during social unrest, including the symbolization of spiritual beliefs expressed on the walls of Paleolithic caves, and the racial identity and cultural values expressed in the media of the hip-hop generation. In Part 2 the journeys of a composer and a group of students are examined to highlight the process of becoming an artist and the role that education plays in its development. The third and final section focuses on the development of aesthetic appreciation and artistic activity in childhood and adolescence, including, for example, how a child's developing theory of mind affects appreciation for the arts, and how developing empathy and emotional regulation contribute to the cognitive and affective underpinnings of acting in adolescence. Intended for researchers and advanced students in both human development and the arts, this book will also serve as a textbook for advanced courses on psychology and the arts and/or special topics courses in cognitive and/or human development.

As with all creative endeavors, this book springs from the work of many hands. We are grateful to the Jean Piaget Society for providing a forum for exploring art and development and holding the line against the latest breed of "nativist and empiricist positions" that Piaget railed against in his book on the role of possibility in cognitive development.

We are especially grateful for the brilliant discussions on knowledge and art that we shared with our lost colleague Terry Brown, a Piagetian scholar and an artist to whom we dedicate these pages.

Cynthia Lightfoot
Constance Milbrath

CONTRIBUTORS

Jeanne Bamberger
Department of Music and Urban
  Education
Massachusetts Institute of
  Technology
Cambridge, Massachusetts

Theanna Bischoff
Department of Psychology
University of Toronto
Toronto, Ontario, Canada

Alan Costall
Department of Psychology
University of Portsmouth
Portsmouth, UK

Colette Daiute
The Graduate Center
City University of New York
New York, New York

Murray Forman
Department of Communication
  Studies
Northeastern University
Boston, Massachusetts

Norman Freeman
Department of Experimental
  Psychology
University of Bristol
Bristol, UK

Thalia R. Goldstein
Department of Psychology
Boston College
Chestnut Hill, Massachusetts

Carol D. Lee
School of Education and Social
  Policy
Northwestern University
Evanston, Illinois

Gerald Levinson
Department of Music
Swarthmore College
Swarthmore, Pennsylvania

Cynthia Lightfoot
Human Development and Family
  Studies
Pennsylvania State
  University–Brandywine
Media, Pennsylvania

Raymond A. Mar
Department of Psychology
York University
Toronto, Ontario, Canada

Constance Milbrath
Human Early Learning
  Partnership
University of British Columbia
Vancouver, British Columbia,
  Canada

Joan Peskin
Department of Psychology
University of Toronto
Toronto, Ontario, Canada

Margaret Beale Spencer
Department of Comparative
  Human Development
University of Chicago
Chicago, Illinois

Brian Tinsley
Graduate School of Education
University of Pennsylvania
Philadelphia, Pennsylvania

J. David Lewis-Williams
Rock Art Research Institute
University of the Witwatersrand
Johannesburg, South Africa

Shaunqula Wilson
Graduate School of Education
University of Pennsylvania
Philadelphia, Pennsylvania
and
Preservation LINK Inc.
Dallas, Texas

Ellen Winner
Department of Psychology
Boston College
Chestnut Hill, Massachusetts
and
Harvard Project Zero
Harvard University
Cambridge, Massachusetts

1

ART AND HUMAN DEVELOPMENT
Introduction

Cynthia Lightfoot and Constance Milbrath

The idea of the Boddhisattva, one who comes back and entices others on the journey, is to some degree the task of the artist.... This is where I began to appreciate an art that could be a non-vicarious act, a seeing whose subject was your seeing.

—**J. Turrell (1993, p. 18)**

Piaget (1987) wrote that the generation of "possibility in cognition means essentially invention and creation"; Vygotsky (1994), that "no accurate cognition of reality is possible without a certain element of imagination." It is a basic tenet of constructivist theory that supposing, speculating, and imagining are inherent to developing systems of knowledge and action: We reach *as if* objects can be grasped; we speak and gesture *as if* meanings can be shared. Notwithstanding the avowal that we live in and develop through conjectural worlds, traditional approaches to human development are more often concerned with "the real," the known, the salted-down-in-the-keg and actual. Rooted in a realist epistemology according to which a contingent environment becomes known and manipulated through processes of progressive adaptation, these approaches tend to view the products and processes of imagination as exotic or even frivolous departures from development's more serious course of adaptation and acquisition of "objective"

1

knowledge. The purpose of this volume, and the 2006 meeting of the Jean Piaget Society from which it sprang, is to contest this view. Our aim, in particular, is to examine stories, paintings, music, and myths—all marker buoys and trail signs of transparently creative human activity—in order to shed light on the developmental task of making sense of ourselves and our place in a world of other subjects.

Although our agenda is in many ways revisionist and intended to challenge what we perceive as a pervasive objectivism running through mainstream contemporary approaches to human development, its roots reach deeply into the history of developmental theory. James Mark Baldwin (1911), for example, whom many credit with establishing developmental psychology as a legitimate field of inquiry (e.g., Cairns, 1983; Valsiner & van der Veer, 2000), devoted the entire third volume of his seminal triumvirate, *Thought and Things*, to exploring the relationship between knowledge acquisition and the imaginative activities of art and play. According to Baldwin, the "mergings and reversals" between the actual and the imagined, between the "merely known" and the "playfully or aesthetically" known, show the "very nerve of the process of the development of knowledge" (pp. 3–4). In the less distant past, D. W. Winnicott (1971) traced a similar argument while defending his position that the activities and products of both science and art are analogous to the play of young children in that they serve to create a "transitional space" between a personal psychic reality and an objective shared reality—a space that constitutes the aesthetics of everyday life. "We experience life," Winnicott wrote, "in the exciting interweave of subjectivity and objective observation, and in an area that is intermediate between the inner reality of the individual and the shared reality of the world that is external to individuals" (p. 64).

Although our agenda is not new, neither is it narrowly circumscribed in the interest it holds for today's scholars. Novalis' famously expressed "making the familiar strange" has become a rallying cry for a growing number of modern theorists bent on arguing that development is as much a process of generating novelty and new ideas as it is a process of constructing order, truth, and knowledge out of disorder and the yet to be understood. Early insights of the sort voiced by Baldwin, and later by Piaget, Vygotsky, and Winnicott, consequently have been expanded in recent efforts to work out an understanding of how individuals undertake the fundamental task of creating and imagining possible worlds. There is, for example, a highly productive stream of current scholarship according to which our lives are storied; our minds literary; our identities aesthetic projects; and our art, music, and myths all instruments that confer meaning and value on who we are and what we do.

Thus, accounts both historical and contemporary have sought to narrow the divide between ordinary meaning-making folk and those artists, poets, shamans, and seers who impact our lives by interpreting our worlds. The purpose of this volume is to bring under one cover the work of scholars who share an interest in such world-making activities and whose work on aesthetic experience and artistic activity can be seen to have implications for understanding the course and processes of human development. Significantly, this shared interest is held aloft by distinct foci and occasionally conflicting tensions regarding how to theoretically capture why people paint, sing, dance, sculpt, and play music, and the effect these activities have on people. Such differences in foci and theory are hardly surprising given that the contributors to this volume work in relative isolation from each other across the disciplinary boundaries of archeology, psychology, communications, education, and the performing arts, as well as on vastly different time scales that range from the ontogenetic to the historical and the evolutionary. Although our authors may be perplexed and inspired in equal measure by matters concerning aesthetic activity and experience, they differ, sometimes subtly, sometimes radically, in the questions they ask regarding the emergence, function, and significance of making and understanding art, as well as how they set about answering those questions.

The primary chapters in the volume were contributed by the invited plenary speakers of the 2006 Jean Piaget Society meeting. A commentary chapter that exposes a fresh perspective on the material at hand follows each primary chapter. Chapters in the opening section, "Art in the Context of Culture," explore how cultures harness and exploit the arts to give expression to values, social practices, and traditions and in the process create new world-making activities. Both primary chapters in this section trace the emergence of new forms that arose out of social unrest; in the first case it constituted the first material expressions of what are interpreted as socially significant symbols, and in the second, the creation of a new multimedia art form that stands as a defiant symbol to the established order.

The volume begins with a chapter by David Lewis-Williams, a cognitive archaeologist, who describes the origins of image making amidst the complex social structures that marked the Upper Palaeolithic transition in Western Europe. He argues that the emergence of cave painting transformed naturally occurring labyrinthine caves into manifestations of a sophisticated supernatural realm that already existed in the minds of early humans. Early (cave) art was of deep religious significance, functioning to establish and maintain connections between two separate realities—that of the artist and that of the spirit world.

Interestingly, the spiritual functions of our earliest art may have had important social implications. According to Lewis-Williams, such image making expressed and deepened social schisms between those gifted with second sight and those more ordinary people whose knowledge of the spiritual realm was indirect and implicative. In addition to the cave art itself, Lewis-Williams draws from reports and analysis of hunter-gatherer communities around the world and recent neuropsychological studies of altered states of consciousness, in concluding that the spectrum of human consciousness and the way in which mental imagery is sometimes experienced in altered states give us insight into how early people first came to recognize and make two-dimensional imagery, that is, to think that small lines on a flat surface could stand for a huge, live, moving animal. Constance Milbrath's commentary on the chapter turns to methods from physical anthropology and developmental psychology to suggest that the *neurological bridge*, which forms the foundation of Lewis-Williams' interpretation, can be put on firmer foundation. She adds a more extended treatment of the social landscape of this culturally important transitional period by addressing the size, movements, and activities of Upper Palaeolithic human populations, and closes her commentary by remarking on the aesthetic aspects of these early images from the perspective of development of an art form.

Murray Forman brings the perspective of communication studies to the development in contemporary culture of a new multimodal art form, *hip-hop*, which he describes as "the modern lingua franca for the expression of racial identity, spatial politics, and the cultural values of black and Latino urban youth." Forman situates this new art form historically—in the specific social, economic, technological, and cultural influences that led to its naissance as an adaptive strategy for countering the hostile conditions of poverty and racism by way of providing a forum for representing the realities and dreams of inner-city minority youth. In discussing the new cultural identities for youth that have been forged globally since the inception of hip-hop, Forman observes that the notion of "hip-hop youth" has begun to unravel as it enters its fourth decade, undermined by the market-driven forces that have diluted the strength of both its founding themes of resistance and its association with poor, inner-city minority youth. Brian Tinsley, Shaunqula Wilson, and Margaret Beale Spencer take a developmental perspective in their commentary on Forman by critically exploring the relationship of hip-hop culture to adolescent identity formation. Although openly acknowledging the dark side of hip-hop culture, these authors focus on the potential benefits afforded to youth and explore how identifying with hip-hop culture can indicate a form of resiliency by serving to generate personal, group, political, and cultural forms of identity for many youth. In particular, they note that engagement with hip-hop is voluntary, giving a creative voice to the natural adolescent rebellion against authority and providing emotional and social support in contexts that are often hostile toward youth. The authors also starkly comment on how gender roles are both reflected in and influenced by hip-hop culture.

The second section of the volume, "Educating the Artists and Using the Arts to Educate," examines the personal journeys of a composer and of a group of students exposed to the arts. The first of these chapters reveals the key role formal education plays in scaffolding the development of a creative artist, whereas in the contrasting chapter, the arts become the decisive medium through which education can effectively take place.

Gerald Levinson, internationally recognized as one of the major composers of his generation, presents a compelling narrative of his own growth as a major creative talent. Validating other observations in the area of prodigious talent (e.g., Winner, 2006), Levinson acknowledges that for him, music was not a choice but a discovery and a compulsion. Beginning with his earliest memories, sounds and meter captured his attention, so much so that his early piano practices became a vehicle for improvising and reproducing pop music of the day rather than perfecting the assigned scales and pieces. Levinson credits this bent toward experimentation with leading him toward composition. His fascination with the perceptual exploration of sound became a model for composing that endured into his maturity. Studying with some of the most illustrious composers of the 20th century as a young adult, Levinson found his compositional voice gradually under their tutelage, which culminated in the important years he spent with Olivier Messiaen. Travels in Asia and further study of the music of Bali and India eventually resulted in integrating these unfamiliar scales and sonorities into a "composer's tool kit" upon which he still relies. Armed with a diverse tool box, Levinson approaches creating much like a painter, jotting down "primordial notions" as melodic motifs, rhythms, textures, chords, and musical images in a sketch book on which he later relies for developing a new piece. Jeanne Bamberger, a Piagetian scholar, an expert in musical development and an accomplished musician herself, gives us extraordinary insight into Levinson's developmental process in her commentary. Introducing us to a concept she calls the "dialectical spiral," Bamberger takes us through Levinson's development, pointing out instances in his narrative that mark his deep engagement with the sensuously sonorous moment and his subsequent reflective process, and cycling back to rework his initial perceptual experience. According to Bamberger, these "paired moments of direct sensory experience with related instances of reflective inquiry ... and the ongoing construction of inner and outer representations" both characterize the protracted work of the artist's development and his short-term enterprise of an emerging composition.

In contrast to Levinson's emphasis on art as a calling, something bred into one's bones that results in a special way of hearing the world, Carol Lee construes art as a means of connecting daily life and experience to formal, canonical knowledge. She suggests, in particular, that art can be used to further specific educational goals by bootstrapping "school work" to culturally framed, lived experience. She illustrates her "cultural modeling" approach with real cases of instruction that are built upon cultural repertoires of youth from ethnic minority and low-income communities. Using students' comprehension of fictional narratives as a case in point, Lee suggests that the knowledge generative capacity of the creative arts is to be found in the medium they provide for the "identity work" characteristic of adolescent life in general and the lives of low-income minority adolescents in particular. Colette Daiute, in her commentary, draws our attention to the growing number of youth surviving worldwide in other types of extreme environments as a result of armed conflict, major political transitions, and familial relocation. Daiute picks up the thread of "culture and identity across challenging contexts" as a productive approach to questions "about the interdependent nature of individual and societal development." Noting that adolescent identity work in contexts where engaging with society is threatening appears much more central than in relatively safer contexts, Daiute cautions that an interpretation of a universal identity crisis in adolescence appears unwarranted. She suggests further that the transformative power of "cultural tools" may lie not so much in the process of identifying with these symbolic tools but in the goals that are mobilized in the process of interpreting and engaging with them. She advocates foregrounding goals in the classroom and using cultural tools to mediate the gap between the actual and the ideal.

The final section in the book, "Artistic Development," focuses on the development of aesthetic appreciation and artistic activity in childhood and adolescence. In this context the authors make reference to particular requisite developmental capacities, such as the child's developing theory of mind or the developments in empathic ability and social cognition required by acting.

Norman Freeman argues that whenever children immerse themselves in a domain of knowledge, they quite naturally develop a theory about it, and art is no exception. In his chapter, Freeman grapples with how to characterize the development of a communicative theory of pictures, cross-comparing it with theory of mind and the end point of the art critique. Noting that at the very least, even the untutored readily pass judgments when looking at art, and so must children, the question becomes whether children can be considered naïve but developing art critiques. Drawing on his past research and that of others, notably Parsons (1987), Freeman presents examples of what children say about pictures to support the central claim that children do develop an increasingly articulated theory of pictures, and that their changing understanding of art maps the journey of their developing grasp of subjectivity. A prime task, however, is to work out how we would know whether what we regard as the child's theory is actually operative in the way that researchers suppose it to be, that is, whether the child's theory is, indeed, a theory. Clearly opposed to the "theory theory" of knowledge acquisition and its depiction of the child as a developing scientist or theorist, Alan Costall takes issue in his commentary with the idea that children must develop something like a theory about pictures. In particular, Costall appears to suggest that by endowing a child with early theory capacities, we strip away the historical significance of developments in fields such as physics, biology, or more broadly the sciences, replacing the long historical road to theory building with a set of domain "givens" that need only be discovered as the child's mind gains in sophistication. Although contentious, Costall's motives can be read as a desire to put "development" back into developmental psychology.

Despite the widespread involvement of humans in acting as either performers or audience members, Thalia Raquel Goldstein and Ellen Winner in their chapter draw our attention to the fact that psychologists know very little about the cognitive and affective underpinnings of acting. They suggest that this understudied art form may provide a powerful lens through which the mind can be better understood. In particular, studying acting and actors from a developmental perspective can shed light on three aspects of social cognition: (a) theory of mind, or the ability to read another's beliefs, desires, intentions, and emotions; (b) empathy, or the ability to congruously feel the emotion of another person; and (c) emotion regulation, or the ability to understand and exert control over one's emotions. A review of how actors are trained, as either Method or Technique actors, leads to the suggestion that these different forms of training may have differential effects on the individual's developing theory of mind, empathy, and emotion regulation. Joan Peskin, Raymond Mar, and Theanna Bischoff comment on the dearth of adequate measures for adolescents and adults in the areas of social cognition addressed by Goldstein and Winner's chapter. Methods more common to the study of expertise with contrasts between expert and novice are suggested as alternatives to more global social cognitive measures particularly because they are domain specific. These commentators note that although Goldstein and Winner only examined theatre, the issues they raised could be extended to other genres such as the writer or audience. They expand the frame to include these two genres, writer and audience, and discuss the different roles that aspects of social cognition have for becoming an "expert" in these genres.

We offer this collection of work as evidence for the generative scope of art and artistic activity and how it might be fruitfully explored to further our understanding of developing knowledge. Leaning on constructivist notions deeply embedded in the history of developmental theory, we sought to expose the knowledge construction process as fundamentally creative and imaginative—a process of making the familiar strange. In our expansively contracting postmodern world of raging and retracting information, identity possibilities, and systems of knowledge, beliefs, and values, meaning making can be a fraught affair. With this book, we hope to have taken some steps toward understanding how we manage to do it anyway, and do it so well.

REFERENCES

Baldwin, J. M. (1911). *Thoughts and things: A study of the development and meaning of thought, or genetic logic: Vol. 3. Interest and art being real logic.* London: Swan Sonnenschein.

Cairns, R. B. (1983). The emergence of developmental psychology. In W. Kessen (Ed.), *Handbook of child psychology: Vol. 1. History, theory and methods* (R. Siegler & D. Kuhn, Vol. Eds.) (pp. 41–102). New York: John Wiley.

Parsons, M. J. (1987). *How we understand art: A cognitive developmental account of aesthetic experience.* New York: Cambridge University Press.

Piaget, J. (1987) *Possibility and necessity: Vol. 1. The role of possibility in cognitive development.* Minneapolis: University of Minnesota Press.

Turrell, J. (1993). *Air mass.* London: South Bank Centre.

Valsiner, J., & van der Veer, R. (2000). *The social mind: Construction of the idea.* Cambridge: Cambridge University Press.

Vygotsky, L. (1994). Imagination and creativity of the adolescent. In R. van der Veer & J. Valsiner (Eds.), *The Vygotsky reader.* Cambridge, MA: Blackwell.

Winner, E. (2006). Development in the arts: Music and drawing. In W. Damon (Ed.), *Handbook of child psychology: Vol. 2. Cognitive language and perceptual development* (R. Siegler & D. Kuhn, Vol. Eds.) (pp. 859–904). New York: Wiley.

Winnicott, D. W. (1971). *Playing and reality.* New York: Tavistock.

I

Art in the Context of Culture

2

SCIENCE, RELIGION, AND PICTURES
An Origin of Image Making

J. D. Lewis-Williams

Picture making and picture using are central parts of Western life today. We can hardly imagine a world without pictures. Yet the Islamic world is next door to us. The existence of such a society shows that pictures cannot be said to be an intrinsic, inevitable feature of life. This chapter considers how image making became a part of so many human traditions without ever being an essential human attribute.

I argue that image making probably did not grow out of an innate aesthetic sense, as is often supposed. I realize that this is a rather radical departure. At the outset of our discussion, I therefore think it necessary to distinguish between image making and aesthetics. Here I am concerned with the problem of how people came to make images or "pictures" of various things—whether they considered them aesthetically pleasing or not. Recently, V. S. Ramachandran has advanced intriguing arguments to explain why people find certain pictures "beautiful" (Ramachandran, 1999, 2004; Ramachandran & Blakeslee, 1998). He lists 10 "universal laws of art" that, he claims, derive from human neurology (Ramachandran, 2004, p. 44). Whether Ramachandran is or is not correct in his explanation of aesthetic experience is a question that I do not address. The issue he considers differs from the one that I discuss. He asks why people find certain pictures more pleasing than others. I ask how it was that people first came to understand what an image, or a picture, is—how people came to realize that three-dimensional objects and animals could be represented in two dimensions on plane surfaces. I simply argue that aesthetics probably came after, not before, image making. And with image making came social consequences that are still with us today.

AN EVOLUTION OF "ART"?

One of Jean Piaget's enduring legacies has been—and continues to be—an interest in the mental development of children, including the ways in which they understand and make pictures. Out of this interest has grown a more specific question: Can we find out something about our evolving species by studying the mental development of children in a matter such as image making?

Understandably enough, some researchers interested in the origins of image making have wondered if the stages by which children today learn to draw illuminate the way in which, some 40,000 years earlier, *Homo sapiens* communities began to make their now famous cave art in France and Spain. Researchers, such as André Leroi-Gourhan (1968), proposed evolutionary sequences to account not only for the development of Upper Palaeolithic cave art but also for the exquisite pieces of mobile art—embellished pendants; carved spear throwers; small female figurines; some part-human, part-lion carvings; and stone plaquettes with engraved animals and lines. These small, portable pieces of art were believed to be the key to uncovering a sequence of styles in the wall, or parietal, paintings and engravings (Figure 2.1a and 2.1b). Preserved in stratified and relatively easily dated deposits, mobile art seemed to provide evidence for an evolution of styles both in its own sphere and, by extension, for the wall paintings in the deep caves (for more on mobile art and its relationship to parietal art, see Lewis-Williams, 2002, pp. 196–202). Mobile art, for the most part, is not found in the depths of caves but, significantly, where people lived in the entrances to caves. There therefore seems to have been a different kind of relationship between people and their mobile art and between them and the images in the deep chambers and passages. It is possible that deep cave art arose from a desire to actualize spiritual experiences of spirit animals, as I argue below, whereas mobile art used representations of those spirit animals in prophylactic ways and as reminders of spiritual realms and their relevance to daily life.

Rather confusingly interchanging "period" and "style," Leroi-Gourhan (1968) envisaged a sequence of four stages that have remained influential in Upper Palaeolithic art research. We need not describe

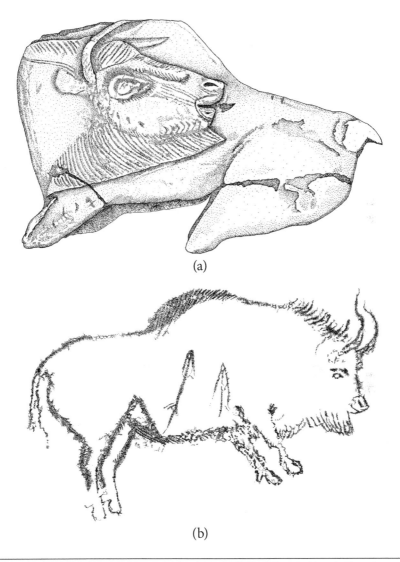

(a)

(b)

Figure 2.1 (a) Portable art: a bison carved on ivory. (b) Wall painting of a bison in Niaux. Images courtesy of Dr. Jean Clottes.

them now. It will suffice to note the underlying principle that Leroi-Gourhan believed he could detect:

> Evidences from before 20,000 B.C. are scanty, consisting of slabs decorated with extremely crude engraved or painted figures. In their content and style, however, these early finds prove to be the direct ancestors of works produced in the peak period—that is, between 20,000 and 15,000 B.C. After 15,000 B.C. a new phase seems to open up, marked by a profusion of decorated objects and stylistic developments in the representation of figures. By 8,000 B.C. the whole development seems to be over. (p. 205)

In essence, Leroi-Gourhan's conclusion was that our ancestors began by making simple, childlike outline drawings and later developed these into the stunning art that we find in the famous 17,000-year-old Lascaux Cave (Aujoulat, 2004; Leroi-Gourhan & Allain, 1979) and other Upper Palaeolithic sites in France and Spain. He and others thought that thousands of years of trial-and-error image making must have been necessary for our species to learn to draw so well. At the time when these ideas were popular, empirical evidence from dated caves seemed to support this conclusion. Lascaux with its complex, clearly composed, and balanced polychrome images stood in the middle of the Upper Palaeolithic period, not at the beginning, which was as much as 40,000 years before the present.

Over and above the supposed similarities between childhood development and evolutionary changes, researchers invoked a comparable parallel. Present-day artists, not just children, have to practice for many years before they can produce satisfactory results. An illogical inference from this observation was that our species must have needed a proportionately long period, to be measured in thousands of years, to achieve artistic maturity. The shaky analogy involved in this argument seems to have escaped its advocates.

A key absence from these evolutionary hypotheses needs to be identified. They do not take into account *the reasons why* people started, and continued, to make images on the walls of caves. This lacuna masks a dangerous assumption: Researchers assume that Upper Palaeolithic image making was similar in intention to image making in their own times and cultures and, moreover, that the picture-making urge was unproblematically part of being human. These writers think that Upper Palaeolithic people made images for a wide range of reasons that included pure aesthetic pleasure, recording memorable events such as a successful hunt, instruction of the young, marking the ownership that certain people exercised over specific caves, and recording their

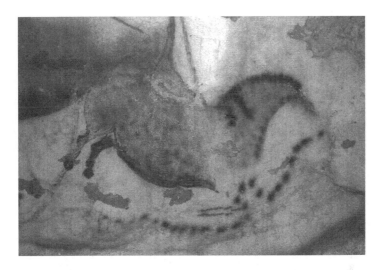

Figure 2.2 One of the so-called Chinese horses painted in the axial gallery of Lascaux. Image courtesy of Dr. Jean Clottes.

presence in them. Later, I shall argue for a departure from this position. The image of, say, a horse in Lascaux is, I believe, not a picture of an animal that the painter saw in the countryside around the cave, as those familiar with Western art too readily assume when they comment on the stunning aesthetic impact of the image (Figure 2.2). It is something altogether different, and this difference holds the key to an origin of image making. The prehistoric painters and engravers were aiming at something very different from the much later depictive art of the Western tradition.

Still, evolutionary sequences, such as Leroi-Gourhan's, seem eminently reasonable. At least they did until the 1994 discovery of the Chauvet Cave in the Ardèche region of France. Jean-Marie Chauvet and two of his friends, Eliette Brunel Deschamps and Christian Hillaire, were searching deep limestone caves for traces of early art. On December 18 of that year, they found a narrow tunnel behind a pile of rocks high up on a hillside. Eventually, by squeezing through this tunnel, they reached a series of large chambers. Despite their high hopes of success, they were unprepared for what awaited them: They found brilliant images that seemed to exceed in beauty and preservation even the greatest of the known Upper Palaeolithic caves (Figure 2.3). Lascaux, Niaux, Rouffignac, and other sites seemed to pale by comparison. A still more startling surprise awaited them and, indeed, the whole archaeological world: The sophisticated images they discovered in the Chauvet

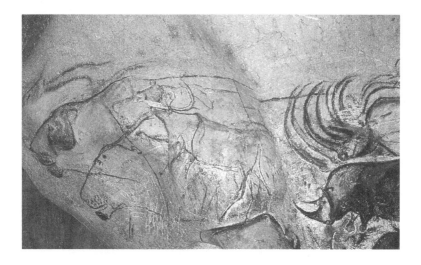

Figure 2.3 Black and white photo of lions in Chauvet. Image courtesy of Dr. Jean Clottes.

Cave were later dated to approximately 33,000 years before the present (Chauvet, Deschamps, & Hillaire, 1996; Clottes, 2001, 2003). These striking paintings and engravings—they are by no means childlike sketches—were made at the very beginning of the human artistic tradition in Europe. All the supposed evidence for an evolutionary sequence comparable to that found in children's drawings instantly evaporated. It now appears that art was born, like Venus emerging from the foam of the sea, fully formed.

Nevertheless, some writers still prefer to remain with the old idea that "art" evolved slowly from simple (childlike) forms to advanced degrees of complexity. Claire Golomb (2002), for example, got around the challenge of Chauvet by arguing that earlier evidence for image making has not been preserved. Indeed, archaeologists have long wondered if the earliest imagery was made on perishable materials, such as animal skins or in loose sand. This is, of course, arguing from an absence of evidence and then assuming that it did exist. It is doubtful if any scientifically minded archaeologists will accept this sort of thinking. Ultimately, we come back to the question of whether there is any explanation for the origin of image making that does not depend on hypothetical lost evidence. Postulating lost evidence may be unnecessary.

The evolutionary explanation of advance from simple beginnings has another problem. Even "simple beginnings," it should be borne in mind, imply that the actors had a fully developed concept of what a two-dimensional picture of something else *is*. Simple, childlike beginnings further imply that the actors were striving to attain a *standard* of representation (not just two-dimensional representation itself) that was already fully formed in their minds. They must have felt that their rather crude beginnings were not good enough; why else would they have striven to produce "better" pictures? Over the millennia, so the argument runs, they were trying to get closer and closer to what they thought a two-dimensional picture "should" look like. Here, advocates of this explanation are courting charges of teleology: An end product (here, a "perfect" two-dimensional picture existing in more or less everyone's minds) cannot explain an origin. In this case of teleology, we can ask: Where did that two-dimensional mental "end product" come from? So the question remains: How could a sudden (almost illogical) appearance have happened?

In answering this question, I shall argue that aspects of a current interest offer some insights. The science *versus* religion debate today seems to be caught up in a crescendo of intense emotions and violence. The nexus of *religion* (more broadly, beliefs in supernatural realms), *science* (empirical knowledge of the environment and the human brain), and *sociology* (the study of social forms and structures) is, I believe, a profitable starting point for understanding not only how people first came to make pictures but also how society came to be divided along lines that go beyond physical strength, sex, and age. I argue that scientific studies of the biology (or neurology) of the brain hold the key to the mystery of the early but nonetheless highly sophisticated Chauvet art. How could this be?

CONSCIOUSNESS

Students of human evolution place great emphasis on how *Homo sapiens* became more and more intelligent. They take it as a given that increasing intelligence enabled early people to overcome challenges that the environment (material and social) presented. They are doubtless correct, but their emphasis does not allow for the greater complexity that we find in human evolution. They hardly notice an associated factor that I think is crucial in understanding the evolution of human thought and art: consciousness. And with consciousness goes religion, as I argue in the next section. Scientists raised in a society that values intelligence above virtually all else are reluctant to consider the role of things as "irrational" as altered states of consciousness and religion. They miss a fundamental element, one that perhaps more than any other distinguishes human beings from apes and other hominids.

Consciousness is today a "hot topic." There is a vast and, it seems, exponentially increasing literature on the subject (amongst many others, see d'Aquili & Newberg, 1999; Donald, 1991; Edelman, 1992, 2004; Edelman & Tononi, 2000; Jaynes, 1976; Ledoux, 2002; Pinker, 1997). As in any developing field, there are disagreements; the problems of consciousness are by no means fully solved. But there is one overriding consensus: Consciousness is a function of neurology. Consciousness is not created by a separate "substance" that is nonmaterial or spiritual. There is no Cartesian duality. The wiring and electrochemical functioning of the human brain create the experience we call consciousness. Exactly how neurological wiring and functioning achieve that result is a separate issue. In tackling a question like the origins of image making, we can therefore explore the phenomenology of consciousness without having to explain how it comes about neurologically.

Briefly, human consciousness should be thought of as a spectrum, not as a state. If we examine our own daily experience of consciousness, we readily realize that we shift from states of acute awareness of our surroundings and problem solving to inner-directed states, such as daydreaming, and to dreaming in sleep (e.g., Martindale, 1981).

Then, if we add a further dimension—what we call altered states of consciousness (ASC)—we can extend the spectrum (for many neuropsychological descriptions of ASC, see, e.g., Eichmeier & Höfer, 1974; James, 1902; Klüver, 1926, 1966; Knoll & Kugler, 1959; Shanon, 2002; Siegel, 1977; Siegel & Jarvik, 1975). The number of stages (or phases) in the spectrum is not given—as I have said, the experience of consciousness involves subtle "drifts" from one state to another. But for the purposes of research, we may construct a three-stage model (Figure 2.4). This model can be discerned in phenomenological accounts of consciousness and ASC, even though the writers themselves do not speak in its terms (Lewis-Williams & Pearce, 2005).

The first stage comprises perceptions of what have been called *entoptic phenomena*, form constants and phosphenes (for fuller descriptions and references, see Lewis-Williams, 2002, Lewis-Williams & Pearce, 2005; on nomenclature, see Walker, 1981). These are bright, scintillating geometric forms. They include clouds of bright dots, zigzag lines (singly or in sets), parallel lines, concentric arcs, grids, and the so-called fortification illusion seen by migraine sufferers—an arc with a scintillating, castellated periphery and a "black hole" of invisibility within the arc. These forms are neurologically generated and are therefore universal; zigzags and the fortification illusion, for instance, may be experienced by people *whatever their cultural context*. By contrast, the meanings that they attach to them are culturally determined. The South American

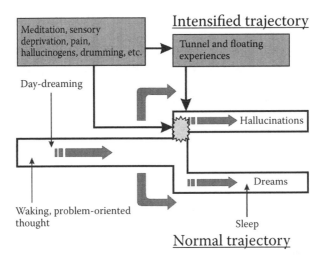

Figure 2.4 The three-stage model of altered states of consciousness.

Tukano, for example, take concentric arcs to mean "the Sun-Father's penis," whereas undulating lines of dots are said to represent the Milky Way, a celestial river that is the first goal of shamanic, hallucinogen-induced ecstatic experience (Reichel-Dolmatoff, 1978, p. 32).

In the second stage ("deeper" ASC), subjects try to make sense of the forms they are seeing. They may now say that they can see a snake rather than an undulating line. These construals of entoptic forms are culturally determined.

The third stage of ASC comprises what we may call full-blown hallucinations. They comprise animals, monsters, people, transformations, and so forth. The content of this stage is entirely cultural, though some entoptic forms may persist peripherally together with their culturally determined meanings. In stage 3, all the senses hallucinate, not just sight. Subjects see, hear, smell, feel, and participate in their hallucinations.

It is important to remember that the intensified spectrum (ASC) may be induced by a variety of means that include hallucinogens, sensory deprivation, pain, meditation, chanting, drumming, electrical stimulation of the brain, flashing lights, certain pathological conditions (e.g., schizophrenia and temporal lobe epilepsy), and so forth. The overall experience is much the same whatever the means of stimulation. Moreover, the three stages are not ineluctable. Some subjects move directly into stage 3 and therefore do not report seeing entoptic phenomena. If they do in fact experience them, they do not consider them important; consequently, they ignore them.

It is also important to realize that in speaking of shifting consciousness, I am not "dragging in" an unnecessary factor. People do not live by intelligence alone. The type of human consciousness I have described is a human universal. Every person has to deal with features of consciousness: Human behavior is therefore not always rational (Edgerton, 1992). To understand the role of consciousness in human evolution, history, and image making, we need to examine what I believe to be the three major, interacting elements of religion: experience, belief, and practice (Lewis-Williams, 2010; Lewis-Williams & Pearce, 2005). I consider each in turn.

ELEMENTS OF RELIGION

Religious Experience

Religious experience, the element to which we shall give most attention, derives from the shifts in human consciousness that I have described. All human communities have to come to terms with the spectrum of consciousness. They therefore have

- to divide it up into sections,
- to name at least some of those sections, and
- to place different values on them.

This last point is especially significant. Today, we do not place a high value on dreams. The answer to a scientific question may come to a researcher in a dream, but that is insufficient to persuade other workers to accept the answer. This has not always been so. We know that during the Middle Ages, dreams were highly valued as intimations from God or, on the other hand, feared as intrusions of the Devil.

General agreement within a society on values such as these may be called "the consciousness contract" (Lewis-Williams & Pearce, 2005). *All* societies have to reach their own common understanding of what shifts in human consciousness mean. It is, for instance, impossible to imagine a society that does not share some common understanding of what dreams and visions (hallucinations) mean. This common understanding is what I call the consciousness contract. It differs from society to society. But that is not all. Importantly, some people may challenge that contract (as they do with their "social contracts"), sometimes with disastrous results for themselves and others.

Disputes within a society over the significance that their consciousness contract allots to the introverted end of the spectrum become fiercer when we consider the intensified spectrum—altered states of consciousness. The content of stage 3 hallucinations is, as I have pointed out, culturally controlled: People "see" what they expect or hope to see. They "see" mental images of parts of their belief system and environment. Now we can begin to understand how it is that what passes as religious experience actually derives from the electrochemical functioning of the brain at the introverted end of the consciousness spectrum, intensified or not—from hallucinations (visions) and dreams.

In sum, human consciousness, in its shifting diversity, suggests different states, or modes, of being. And these states of being can easily be interpreted as events in and impingements by an alternative realm—in other words, a spirit world. Belief in supernatural realms derives, I argue, from the wiring and electrochemical functioning of the human brain (e.g., Hamer, 2004; Laughlin, McManus, & d'Aquili, 1992; Ramachandran & Blakeslee, 1998; Rolston, 1999; Strassman, 2001).

All religions have a "consciousness component." Not only do they postulate supernatural realms, but also all are, by one technique or another, concerned with moving human consciousness along the spectrum. Some religious experiences are mild and peaceful; others are more intense and ecstatic. One thinks of the almost hypnotic chanting, dim lighting, and incense in a cathedral and, by contrast, the shouting, swaying, and collapsing in a charismatic Christian church. Amongst religious experiences we may therefore include serene peacefulness, a sense of oneness with the universe, ecstatic visions, violent seizure by supernatural beings, and a sense of ineffable truth revealed. We should also allow what in some circumstances would be called a "bad trip": terrifying visions of Hell and punishment. Leaders, such as Joan of Arc, who act upon their own visions usually create havoc, yet somehow often retain the admiration of their followers; such is the power of the consciousness contract.

Religious Belief

Religious belief, my second component of religion, derives, *in the first instance*, from attempts to understand religious experiences. Religious dogma, recorded in scriptures or preserved in oral traditions, lays out

- the structure of the cosmos,
- the locations and natures of spiritual beings and forces, and
- the ways in which these beings or forces may be contacted or in which, uninvited, they may intervene in daily life.

That is not all. Religious belief often extends beyond a concern with spirit realms to explanations of the material world as well—where humanity came from, why the suns rises daily, how the big rock came to be in the middle of the desert, why people sicken and die, and so forth. This extension from essentially spiritual concerns to material conditions, so evident today, lies at the root of the science *versus* religion controversy: Religion trespasses on the territory of science.

Those who do not wish to acknowledge the importance of shifting consciousness sometimes argue that the existence of a spiritual realm can be inferred from the world around us. I believe that repeated or dramatic events in the material world do not *in themselves* suggest the existence of a spirit world; but for those who *already* believe in spiritual forces (for altogether other reasons), they may seem to be observable consequences of spiritual intervention. Thunder, for instance, does not, by itself, suggest a supernatural being living somewhere in the sky. But, if people already believe in such a being, they may think it reasonable to identify the rumbling sounds as his voice.

Let us now look more closely at certain features of intense, multisensory religious experiences (hallucinations and dreams) and the ways in which they relate to beliefs about a tiered cosmos and thus mediate between the spiritual and the material. Virtually universally, people believe in a tiered cosmos: the level on which they live and spiritual realms above and below—earth, Heaven, and Hell in the Christian tradition. Some religions develop multiple cosmological levels that may be related to social divisions on earth. Yet there is no observable evidence in the sky or below the earth to suggest such curious beliefs. How can this universal delusion be explained?

I argue that these irrational beliefs may be traced to two experiences that seem to be wired into the human nervous system. They are reported from all over the world and are, I argue, the reason why people of vastly different cultures believe in a tiered cosmos.

One is movement through a tunnel or passageway that has a bright light at the end (the well-known so-called near-death experiences are examples; Fox, 2003). This swirling vortex through which subjects believe themselves to be passing leads from mildly altered states to the stage 3 realm of vivid, overwhelming hallucinations. Now the person experiencing the altered state no longer merely "sees" hallucinations but also participates fully in a hallucinatory realm. Neurologically induced experiences of moving through this vortex or tunnel—together with a sense of physical constriction and, often, difficulty in breathing—creates a sense of being in an underground or underwater realm. Whether people interpret the vortex experience as subterranean or subaquatic movement is culturally determined.

The other experience that we need to note is a sense of floating above one's surroundings. Around the world, shamans, for example, talk about entering spiritual states and floating or flying (e.g., Hayden, 2003;

Pearson, 2002; Vitebsky, 1995). In some Eastern traditions the float-ing sensation is taken literally, and religious adepts are said to float as they meditate. The wiring and electrochemical functioning of the brain thus create experiences that can be interpreted as moving to a spiritual realm in the sky. Some societies combine subterranean, subaquatic, and aerial flight. The Ju/'hoansi San of the Kalahari Desert in southern Africa speak of traveling underground and underwater and rising into the sky. Old K'xau, a Ju/'hoan shaman, told Megan Biesele (1993) that a giraffe, his spirit guide, took him to "a wide body of water":

> I travelled like this. My sides were pressed by pieces of metal. Metal things fastened [to] my sides.... Then my protector told me that I would enter the earth. That I would travel far through the earth and then emerge at another place. When we emerged, we began to climb the thread—it was the thread of the sky. (pp. 70–72; see also Keeney, 2003)

Religious belief, meshed with neurologically generated religious expe-rience, thus bridges and formalizes the divide between a spirit realm and the material world in which people live. It does this by claiming that some people (shamans, priests) may visit the spirit world (in ASC). At the same time, spirit beings and forces are active in material circum-stances and are not confined to spiritual realms above and below.

Religious Practice

Religious practice, the third component of religion, is related to both reli-gious experience and religious belief. Some practices, generally called *rituals*, intentionally induce religious experiences of various intensities. They include meditation, communal singing, and chanting, as well as more bizarre practices, such as fasting, self-flagellation, and the inges-tion of hallucinogens. Other activities are more extensive and socially complex and may escape notice as religious practices. They include pilgrimages (e.g., Sumption, 1975) and the building of cathedrals and other monuments, such as the great Neolithic tombs of Newgrange in Ireland and Gavrinis in France (Lewis-Williams & Pearce, 2004a). These structures can have profound social, political, and economic consequences that splice religion into the apparently unbroken cable of continuing life.

A NEUROLOGICAL BRIDGE

If we are correct about the hard-wired nature of religious experiences and their universality, we can proceed to ask how Upper Palaeolithic people may have understood them. We concentrate on the mental vortex or tunnel. We need to recall that people probably believed in a subterranean realm independently of any experience they may have had of caves. It seems highly likely that, when people came across caves, they would have thought of them as entrances into the underworld in which they already believed—as, indeed, is still the case in a great many religious traditions worldwide. Because of the neurologically wired sense of moving through a tunnel or passage, people of that time probably believed that they were exploring a mysterious underworld when they ventured into the deep and totally dark caverns. They probably considered entrance into and movement through the caves to be virtually indistinguishable from entrance into the neurologically generated vortex that leads from "light" altered states to more intense hallucinations. As far as they were concerned, the underworld could be reached by means of ecstatic religious experiences and, perhaps (but not necessarily) less psychologically traumatically, by entering caves.

In the instance of the French and Spanish Upper Palaeolithic caves, we may add two further points. First, as people experience the mental vortex, they often find the sides of the "tunnel" to be dotted with pictures (Siegel, 1977). The embellishment of caves with paintings and engravings made them even more like the vortex of altered states. Second, the sensory deprivation afforded by the caves would have sometimes induced altered states of consciousness and attendant visions.

We can therefore say that researchers have a neurological bridge to certain Upper Palaeolithic religious experiences and beliefs: Like so many other societies, Upper Palaeolithic communities probably conceived of a tiered cosmos, and their religion was probably concerned, at least in part, with contacting cosmological levels other than the one on which they lived. This hypothesis makes sense of the varied ways in which Upper Palaeolithic people used the deep limestone caves of France and Spain.

But, because the content of stage 3 hallucinations is largely culturally controlled, we can go on to ask: What would those ancient people *expect* to see in their combined mental and geological caves? The framing of this question points to its answer. And that answer leads to an understanding that goes a long way to explaining the origin of image making.

AN ETHNOGRAPHIC EXAMPLE

If mental experiences such as those I have described (dreams and hallucinations) were part of Upper Palaeolithic life—and their neurological foundations strongly suggest that they were—may we call them "religious"? People of that time must have had a consciousness contract that was markedly different from the one to which we subscribe in our scientifically constructed cosmos. They probably placed much more credence on dreams and visions than we do today with our knowledge of neurology and science in general. Given that those ancient people were hunters and gathers and, moreover, noting a range of hunter-gatherer religions worldwide today, we can say that it is not too far-fetched to apply the word *religious* to their understandings of their own neurologically generated experiences. It also seems certain that animals would have featured prominently in their system of religious symbols and supernatural beings. Further, as world ethnography also suggests, Upper Palaeolithic people would have selected a handful of animals from all those around them to represent, or embody, beliefs about supernatural power and beings.

This point may be illustrated by reference to the southern African rock art made by the San, or Bushmen. The earliest southern African representational images have been dated to 27,000 years before the present (Wendt, 1976), but the tradition continued up to the end of the 19th century (Lewis-Williams, 1981, 2000a, 2003; Lewis-Williams & Pearce, 2004a). Southern African geometric "art" has been dated to as long ago as 60,000 to 70,000 years ago (Henshilwood et al., 2002). If these pieces of complexly engraved ochre may indeed be called "art," then this is the oldest art in the world.

Southern African rock art research has, however, concentrated on the much more recently made rock paintings found in open rock shelters in the more mountainous regions of the subcontinent. As it happens, there is abundant 19th- and 20th-century San ethnography that is relevant to an understanding of the images. The 19th-century verbatim records, made when the final artists were still at work, run to over 12,000 manuscript pages of accounts of rituals, myths, social life, and personal histories. Some of this material has been published (Bleek, 1924; Bleek & Lloyd, 1910; Hollmann, 2004; Lewis-Williams, 2000b; Skotnes, 2007).

The close "fit" between the ethnography and the rock art shows that the painters and engravers were *principally* concerned with the San's central and overwhelmingly important ritual—the trance, or healing, dance. The images show very few depictions of hunts (the popular conception of San rock art; the San rock painters were interested in something other than merely meat). Rather, the imagery comprises

- depictions of trance dances with participants in distinctive dancing postures,
- entities that can be seen only by shamans (such as supernatural potency and the spirit leaving the tops of dancers' heads),

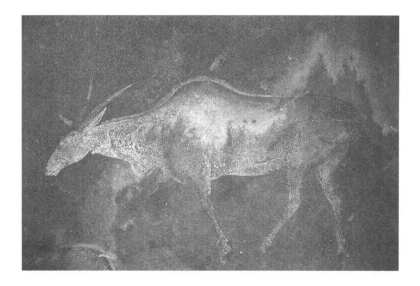

Figure 2.5 A San rock painting of an eland. Image courtesy of the Rock Art Research Institute, University of the Witwatersrand, Johannesburg.

- "fragments of the dance" (such as flywhisks that the San reserve for use in the trance dance) scattered through densely painted panels,
- "rain-animals" (hippo- or antelope-like creatures seen in trance and cut by shamans to allow their milk and blood to fall as rain),
- people performing a range of activities, and
- many animals, though with numerical emphasis on a small group of species, and especially on the eland (Figure 2.5), the largest and fattest African antelope; this antelope does not feature significantly in living site deposits.

The San sometimes used eland blood in the execution of their depictions of this animal. The supernatural potency (*n/om* or *!gi*) of the eland thus went into the images, which then became reservoirs of potency on which dancers could draw when they wished to increase their ability to enter trance (the spirit realm above and below the earth) and to cure the sick, make rain, travel to distant parts, and reach the realm of God and the spirits of the dead. They secured this potency by facing the image as they danced or by touching it (Lewis-Williams & Pearce, 2004a).

Some San images are derived from entoptic phenomena. In the Western Cape Province, for instance, there are paintings that were formerly taken to be depictions of boats (Figure 2.6). They are more

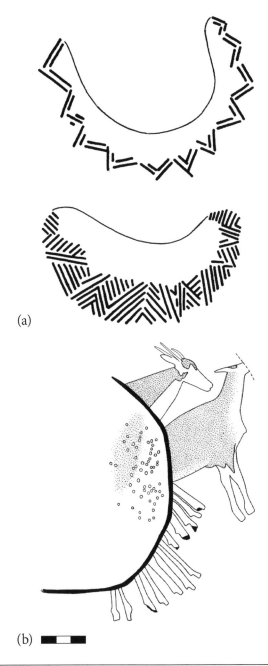

(a)

(b)

Figure 2.6 Rock paintings representing the fortification illusion seen in the first stage of altered consciousness. Image courtesy of the Rock Art Research Institute, University of the Witwatersrand, Johannesburg. *Continued*

(c)

Figure 2.6 *Continued.*

properly seen as representations of the fortification illusion, or entoptic phenomena. Sometimes antelope legs or other images are shown emerging from the fortification illusion, as they are from cracks and steps in the rock face. The subterranean spirit realm lay behind the rock wall, and it was the task of the painters to "draw" (in both senses of the word) spirit animals from behind this "veil" and to fix them there for everyone to see. The fortification illusion and cracks in the rock were, in effect, the vortex that, trance dancers themselves say, leads them to the spirit realm.

This very brief summary shows how, in the case of the San, neurology combines with specific lifeways and the environment to produce an art that is, in the phrase I have used, a bridge to tiered spiritual realms and a conduit for supernatural potency. San rock art also functions socially: The shamans in San communities were respected because they had been to the spirit realm and had met with God, though they did not flaunt any wealth (Lewis-Williams & Pearce, 2004a). Humility and modesty are cherished San values.

"INVENTING" PICTURES

Bearing these points about San rock art and neurology in mind, we can move on to consider a crucial feature of Upper Palaeolithic cave art. This feature confirms the presence of religious motivation and belief behind its making. It has been insufficiently acknowledged by researchers.

The earliest Upper Palaeolithic art, such as the images in the Chauvet Cave and the carved portable art from southern Germany (both belong to the Aurignacian period [±35,000 to 45,000 years ago], the first part of the Upper Palaeolithic), features a set of principal animals and a periphery of much less frequently depicted species (Clottes, 1996), as does San rock art. The central Upper Palaeolithic bestiary includes felines, horses, bison, aurochs, and mammoths; less commonly depicted species include owls, fish, human forms, and even, in one instance, a weasel. At different periods of the Upper Palaeolithic, image makers placed numerical emphases on certain species in the central bestiary (Clottes, 1996). There are, for instance, more depictions of felines in the early Chauvet Cave than in the later caves of Lascaux and Niaux. But, overall, the central bestiary of animals remained broadly the same from the beginning of Upper Palaeolithic image making to the end.

If, as is usually supposed, people in the early Upper Palaeolithic simply learned the techniques of making pictures, why did they make pictures of only certain animals? Why, we may ask, are there next to no depictions of human faces, snakes, mice, trees, and so forth? The answer is straightforward. There never was a time when early people made pictures of anything that took their fancy, perhaps prompted by some sort of innate aesthetic sense. The answer must be that the image makers were not freely depicting anything they wished: They were not "artists" in our sense of the word. Moreover, the subterranean locations of cave art and the focus on only certain species suggest that the image makers may not have been depicting the material world outside the caves—the hills and valleys where they hunted, gathered plant foods, and lived—but rather a set of creatures that was central to their belief system. Indeed, excavations in Upper Palaeolithic rock shelters where people lived and cooked show that the depicted animals did not constitute a menu; hunting magic cannot explain their limited range (such is also the case with San rock art). Rather, the image makers necessarily had to depict the animals that they believed inhabited the underworld, not the material world.

Upper Palaeolithic people must have believed in this set of symbolic or spiritually powerful animals *before they started making underground images*: There never was a time when they freely made images of anything that took their fancy. If we wish to explain the origins of Upper Palaeolithic art, we must therefore look for a connection between image making and the preexistent bestiary of animals. Beliefs about those animals must have contributed in some way to the making of images.

The next point that I want to make shows why I placed "inventing" in quotation marks at the head of this section.

REACHING OUT

Now we ask how people first came to understand that static marks on a two-dimensional surface could stand for, say, a horse. I argue that people have to learn certain conventions before we can see that a set of marks "means" a horse. This is a somewhat controversial point, though I believe that there is strong evidence for the answer I suggest.

For instance, the Abbé Henri Breuil (1952), the leading French prehistorian of the first half of the 20th century, recorded an interesting observation, the full implications of which he did not see. He reported that Salomon Reinach, the writer who first propagated the notion of sympathetic hunting magic, found that a Turkish officer whom he met was incapable of recognizing a drawing of a horse "because he could not move round it" (Breuil, p. 23). Being a Muslim, the officer was entirely unfamiliar with depictive art.

The anthropologist Anthony Forge (1970) discovered the same sort of thing while he was working with the Abelam in New Guinea. He found that these people make three-dimensional carvings of spirits and also paint bright two-dimensional, polychrome spirit motifs on their ritual structures. Although the motif is essentially the same in both cases, the two-dimensional versions arrange the elements in different ways. For example, the arms may emerge from below the noses of the figures, whereas the three-dimensional figures have the arms in the right place. Why do the Abelam not find this difference strange? The answer is that neither the two- nor the three-dimensional versions are representations. They do not show what the spirits *look like*; rather, they are avatars of the spirits. "There is no sense," Forge found, "in which the painting on the flat is a projection of the carving or an attempt to represent the three-dimensional object on two dimensions" (p. 281). The paintings are not meant to "look like" anything in nature. As a result, the Abelam had difficulty in "seeing" photographs. Forge had to outline human beings in the photographs so that the people could recognize them. As Forge puts it, "Their vision has been socialized in a way that makes photographs especially incomprehensible" (p. 287; see also Segal, Campbell, & Herskovitz, 1966). The Abelam were not inherently incapable of understanding two-dimensional representations of things in the material world. They easily learned to do so.

How, then, did people first learn to make and recognize two-dimensional representations? Three explanations are popularly advanced. One is that people noticed reflections in water and so found that three-dimensional things could be reduced to two dimensions. But there are problems with this simple explanation. If it were true, why did people not make pictures of their own and others' faces? Why did they make depictions of animals that they were less likely to see reflected in ponds? One should also notice that the static walls of caves are altogether different from the fluid surface of water: Transfer from one to the other, especially to cave walls deep underground, is not obvious.

Another popular suggestion is that shadows may have led to two-dimensional image making. At first glance, this explanation seems more plausible than the reflections-in-water explanation. It is easy to imagine people sitting around a fire in a rock shelter and their shadows moving on the rock wall behind them. But at least one of the previous objections remains: Why did people not start making pictures of themselves? They were more likely to see shadows of themselves than of wild animals.

The third and last explanation that we need to consider is that people accidentally discerned the forms of animals in natural marks on the mottled walls of caves or in random human-made marks. Once they spotted the likenesses, they could go on to make their own pictures. This explanation, unlike the first two more popular explanations, recurs in the literature (e.g., Breuil, 1952, p. 22; Davis, 1986, 1987). But we have an egg-and-chicken problem here. People could not have recognized accidental likenesses between, say, horses and natural marks on a cave wall without first having a notion of two-dimensional representation. How could they see representations of animals on the walls of caves if, like the Abelam, they had no notion of the necessary conventions? And then there is the same objection that we noted in relation to the two previous explanations that we have considered: Why did they make pictures of only a set of animals and not human faces, trees, and many other things?

The origin of two-dimensional representations is indeed a knotty problem. I argue that researchers have been tackling it from a wrong perspective. Let us rather start with the set of animals that Upper Palaeolithic people chose to depict, a set that, as we have noticed, must have existed in their belief system *before* they started making pictures and therefore very probably led in some way to the making of images of them. As I have pointed out, there never was a time when people made pictures of anything that they fancied. Picture making was closely restricted. The preexisting set of animals must have been closely associated with religious circumstances that generated image making.

The answer to the problem of image making lies in the wiring of the human brain, the spectrum of human consciousness, and religious experience, all of which I have briefly discussed. In the 1920s, Heinrich Klüver (1926) found that hallucinations appeared to be localized on walls and ceilings (pp. 505–506; see also Knoll, Kugler, Höfer, & Lawder, 1963, p. 208). This commonly reported experience has been described as "pictures painted before your imagination" (Siegel & Jarvik, 1975, p. 109) and as "a motion picture or slide show" (Siegel, 1977, p. 134). Klüver (1942) also found that "after-images" (hallucinations experienced spontaneously after a return to normal consciousness) recurred after he had awakened from an altered state and that they too were projected onto the ceiling (p. 179). These after-images may remain suspended in one's vision for a minute or more. Working in South America, Gerardo Reichel-Dolmatoff (1978) found not only that the Tukano saw their *yajé*-induced after-images (largely stage 1 entoptic phenomena) projected onto surfaces but also that they recurred for up to several months after ingestion of the drug (p. 8). We thus have a range of circumstances in which people in or after an altered state of consciousness see images on plane surfaces like "a motion picture or slide show." The images may be consciously induced and expected, or they may be uncalled-for after-images, flashbacks to earlier altered states of consciousness.

Here, I argue, is the answer to the enigma of the origins of two-dimensional image making. Early Upper Palaeolithic people did not "invent" the techniques and conventions of picture making. Their world (or at least the world of those who experienced ASC) was already invested with a set of animal visions. They saw these zoomorphic hallucinations in their dreams and visions, and were thus familiar with them. Given the right circumstances, these visions were projected onto the walls of caves and other surfaces. Those experiencing projected visions perceived them as "flat" because of their projected nature. Now here is the key point. These projected images contained within themselves the conventions needed to recognize two-dimensional imagery. "Images" were thus a function of the human nervous system, not an "invention."

The set of animals that constituted those early Upper Palaeolithic images suggests the next step. Those animals were probably spirit beings with supernatural power. People sought animal power, as shamanic communities, such as the San, around the world still do today. To secure contact with these spirit animals, they reached out to touch their projected visions of them and to trace, with their fingers or paint, their outlines on the rock face. This reaching out to power animals may have taken place during fairly lightly altered states or, later, after a person had returned to normal consciousness and was examining the rock face to find traces of the now-vanished images. To reestablish the vision on the rock surface—to "nail it down"—was probably a way of gaining some control over the spirit animal and retaining its power. They were thus not making pictures; they were touching what was (or had been) already there.

What of the rock surface on which the visions were projected? I argue that, for Upper Palaeolithic people, the walls of rock shelters were a kind of membrane between themselves and the creatures of the spirit world that lived behind it, deep in the nether world. Their projected visions seemed to materialize already existing spirit animals through the membrane, probably with accompanying aural hallucinations. The act of drawing them was an attempt to keep them there, to perpetuate contact with them, and perhaps even to make them available (assisted by appropriate explanation) to other people.

The first Upper Palaeolithic images were thus not representations of things that people saw outside the caves. Rather, they were "fixed" mental images. They probably did not "stand for" real animals. They *were* spirit animals, visions of power. Issues such as not being able to walk around a projected mental image simply did not apply. The images did not depict, or materialize, real animals but rather their spirit counterparts.

Further support for this explanation comes from Upper Palaeolithic imagery itself. The images have a number of features in common with the imagery of altered states:

- The painted images are disengaged from natural surroundings; there are no trees, grass, or hills.
- Only in a very few cases (e.g., the Rouffignac cave) is there any suggestion of a ground line (a natural stain on the rock).
- The images have what Halverson (1987) called their "own free-floating existence" (p. 66).

- The images are placed "without regard to size or position relative to one another" (Halverson, 1987, p. 67).
- Often, the images of animals have no hoofs, or the hoofs "hang" rather than being in a standing position.

I do not argue that *all* Upper Palaeolithic images are fixed visions. Once the initial step had been taken, Upper Palaeolithic image making probably took three courses:

- One stream continued to comprise fixed visions.
- A second stream derived from recollected imagery: People reconstituted their visions after they had returned to a normal state. They examined the rock face carefully by sight and touch; sometimes they needed to add only a few lines to natural features to make an image of an animal.
- A third stream derived from contemplation of the products of the first two streams. People who had never experienced visions could learn to make pictures, and people could unite to produce communally made images.

Because the repertoire of animals remained fairly constant, though with its temporal emphases on certain species and its periphery of seldom depicted creatures, we can feel assured that Upper Palaeolithic art remained religious in nature, though the significances of the images were probably not unchanging in their details.

RELIGION, ART, AND SOCIAL DISCRIMINATION

The practice of making images, almost certainly a religious activity, started at a specific time in Western Europe. Why it happened when it did is an issue I have tentatively addressed elsewhere: It may have been dependent on the contemporary presence of Neanderthals and on the availability of deep limestone caves (Lewis-Williams, 2002). For the present, I turn to one of the consequences—perhaps I should say "corollaries"—of image making. I argue that image making cannot be considered apart from this question; it helps us to understand something of how Upper Palaeolithic caves were used.

Today, numerous writers question the long-held benign view of religion and the deference that we are supposed to exercise when confronted with religious beliefs for which there is no evidence whatsoever (e.g., Dawkins, 2003; Dennet, 2006; Wolpert, 2006). In agreement with those who argue that religion is neither indispensable nor worthy of deference, I argue that it is intrinsically socially divisive. Belief in supernatural realms, beings, and forces, the foundation of religion, not only is false but also leads inevitably to strife and dissention. The history of the Christian Church, for instance, is a depressing tale of heresy, dissent, conflict, genocide, pain, and suffering. Church history does not bear out the organization's claim to be a bringer of peace and love. As the old hymn admits, "By schisms rent asunder, by heresies distressed."

When a society establishes a consciousness contract, it divides up the spectrum of human consciousness and allocates values to experiences at the introverted end. In doing so, it inevitably and simultaneously divides society. There are those who experience the spirit realm only through dreams, there are those who occasionally experience more vivid visions, and there are those who have mastered the techniques of altering consciousness and pronounce on the significance of visions. Those who routinely frequent the introverted end of the spectrum are believed to have special knowledge and insights. They have seen things that ordinary people can merely glimpse in their dreams. Their knowledge sets them apart from ordinary people and provides the basis for social power. Religion was, I argue, the first instrument to cut across the usual foundations for social discrimination that we see in the animal kingdom—sex, age, and brute strength. Even in societies such as the southern African San, a people renowned for their egalitarian spirit, there is social inequality. This inequality is not manifested in material goods, but in shamans' abilities to heal the sick, control the weather, and visit spirit realms where they valiantly face god and all his spirit animals. Social inequality among the San was entrenched and reproduced by image making (Lewis-Williams & Pearce 2004a, 2004b; see also Gulbrandsen, 1991).

Religious social discrimination was probably reflected in the ways in which Upper Palaeolithic caves were used (Lewis-Williams, 2002). The caves became templates of social divisions. The community at large congregated outside the caves. If a large chamber (such as the Hall of the Bulls in Lascaux) was available close to the entrance, it could be used for communal rituals. In it were striking, perhaps communally produced, images that prepared the minds of the few for their forays into the depths. Deep in the caves, in isolation, silence, cold, and darkness mitigated only by flickering lamps, they sought visions of the power animals about which they had been taught. Some of those visions they fixed to the walls with a few strokes (such as the felines in the small, remote Chamber of the Felines in Lascaux). Image makers were fully competent realm travelers and could emerge from the cave as changed people: They had seen what ordinary people could not see. Perhaps there was a distinction between those who saw the visions (paintings and engravings) of others and those who had the extra power to see and "fix" their own visions. Like those who have religious experiences today, Upper Palaeolithic people who ventured into the caves and had a variety of experiences probably considered themselves to possess ineffable insights, even though they may have been unable to explain those insights fully to other people.

The caves with their varied chambers and passages were thus adapted by the making of images in certain locations and by the performance of other rituals, such as chanting and dancing. They became frameworks of society: They physically divided people according to spiritually demarcated zones. Moving through them dramatized and reinforced social distinctions.

Ordinary people, of course, knew about the images—or rather fixed spirit animals—in the depths of the lower level of their tiered cosmos. If any were to be brave enough to enter the caverns, they would see the images and thus have what Othello called the "ocular proof" of spiritual things and the foundation of their stratified social structure.

CONSCIOUSNESS AND STRIFE

I do not claim that image making started in Western Europe and then spread to the rest of the world. On the contrary, there may well have been multiple origins of image making around the world. I have considered only the one that took place in Europe because the evidence is substantially richer there than anywhere else.

The origin of image making in the west European caves turns out to be much more than a narrative of how people first came to make pictures. If followed to its essence, it takes us to the heart of the fractious society that we know today. Any who believe that archaeology has little bearing on life as it is lived today are, quite simply, wrong. The questions with which we have here concerned ourselves are not dry, academic ruminations. Consciousness contracts that cause so much conflict and suffering can be challenged—as can other social arrangements. Religious strife that we seem to see everywhere today derives from the mistaken belief that certain groups have a monopoly on contact with the deity. If they could accept that their supposed contact derives from the spectrum of human consciousness, the absolutes that bedevil political negotiations would be diminished—not entirely eliminated, of course, but they would be seen to be insubstantial. Indeed, the future of the world will be bleak if people cling to ideas of divinities, spiritual realms, and guidance from "the beyond."

REFERENCES

Aujoulat, N. (2004). *Lascaux: Le geste, l'espace et le temps*. Paris: Le Seuil.

Biesele, M. (1993). *Women like meat: The folklore and foraging ideology of the Kalahari Ju/'hoan*. Johannesburg: Witwatersrand University Press.

Bleek, D. F. (1924). *The Mantis and his friends*. Cape Town: Maskew Miller.

Bleek, W. H. I., & Lloyd, L. C. (1910). *Specimens of Bushman folklore*. London: George Allen.

Breuil, H. (1952). *Four hundred centuries of cave art*. Montignac, France: Centre d'Etudes et de Documentation Préhistoriques.

Chauvet, J.-M., Deschamps, E. B., & Hillaire, C. (1996). *Chauvet Cave: The discovery of the world's oldest paintings*. London: Thames & Hudson.

Clottes, J. (1996). Thematic changes in Upper Palaeolithic art: A view from Grotte Chauvet. *Antiquity, 70*, 276–288.

Clottes, J. (Ed.). (2001). *La Grotte Chauvet: L'art des origines*. Paris: Le Seuil.

Clottes, J. (Ed.). (2003). *Return to Chauvet Cave: Excavating the birthplace of art: The first full report*. London: Thames & Hudson.

D'Aquili, E., & Newberg, A. B. (1999). *The mystical mind: Probing the biology of religious experience*. Minneapolis, MN: Fortress Press.

Davis, W. (1986). The origins of image making. *Current Anthropology, 27*, 193–215.

Davis, W. (1987). Replication and depiction in Paleolithic art. *Representations, 19*, 111–147.

Dawkins, R. (2003). You can't have it both ways: Irreconcilable differences? In P. Kurtz (Ed.), *Science and religion: Are they compatible?* (pp. 205–209). New York: Prometheus.

Dennet, D. C. (2006). *Breaking the spell: Religion as a natural phenomenon*. London: Allen Lane.

Donald, M. (1991). *Origins of the modern mind: Three stages in the evolution of culture and cognition*. Cambridge, MA: Cambridge University Press.

Edelman, G. M. (1992). *Bright air, brilliant fire: On the matter of the mind*. London: Penguin.

Edelman, G. M. (2004). *Wider than the sky: The phenomenal gift of consciousness*. London: Allen Lane.

Edelman, G. M., & Tononi, G. (2000). *Consciousness: How matter becomes imagination*. London: Penguin.

Edgerton, R. B. (1992). *Sick societies: Challenging the myth of primitive harmony*. New York: Free Press.

Eichmeier, J., & Höfer, O. (1974). *Endogene Bildmuster*. Munich: Urban and Schwarzenburg.

Forge, A. (1970). Learning to see in New Guinea. In P. Mayer (Ed.), *Socialization: The approach from social anthropology* (pp. 269–290). London: Tavistock.

Fox, M. (2003). *Religion, spirituality and the near-death experience*. London: Routledge.

Golomb, C. (2002). *Child art in context: A cultural and comparative perspective.* Washington, DC: APA.

Gulbrandsen, Ø. (1991). On the problem of egalitarianism: The Kalahari San in transition. In G. Reider, G. Haaland, & G. Henriksen (Eds.), *The ecology of choice and symbol* (pp. 81–110). Bergen: Alma Mater Forlag.

Halverson, J. (1987). Art for art's sake in the Palaeolithic. *Current Anthropology, 28,* 63–89.

Hamer, D. (2004). *The God gene: How faith is hardwired into our genes.* New York: Doubleday.

Hayden, B. (2003). *Shamans, sorcerers and saints: A prehistory of religion.* Washington, DC: Smithsonian Books.

Henshilwood, C. S., d'Errico, F., Yates, R., Jacobs, Z., Tribolo, C., Duller, G. A. T., et al. (2002). Emergence of modern human behaviour: Middle Stone Age engravings from South Africa. *Supplemental Data Science, 295*(5558), 1278–1280.

Hollmann, J. C. (Ed.). (2004). *Customs and beliefs of the /Xam Bushmen.* Johannesburg: Witwatersrand University Press.

James, W. (1902). *The varieties of religious experience.* New York: Mentor.

Jaynes, J. (1976). *The origins of consciousness in the breakdown of the bicameral mind.* Boston: Houghton Mifflin.

Keeney, B. (2003). *Ropes to God: Experiencing the Bushman spiritual universe.* Philadelphia: Ring Rocks Press.

Klüver, H. (1926). Mescal visions and eidetic vision. *American Journal of Psychology, 37,* 502–515.

Klüver, H. (1942). Mechanisms of hallucinations. In Q. McNemar & M. A. Merrill (Eds.), *Studies in personality* (pp. 175–207). New York: McGraw-Hill.

Klüver, H. (1966). *Mescal and the mechanisms of hallucinations.* Chicago: University of Chicago Press.

Knoll, M., & Kugler, J. (1959). Subjective light pattern spectroscopy in the encephalographic frequency range. *Nature, 184,* 18–23.

Knoll, M., Kugler, J., Höfer, O., & Lawder, S. D. (1963). Effects of chemical stimulation of electrically induced phosphenes on their bandwidth, shape number and intensity. *Confinia Neurologica, 23,* 201–226.

Laughlin, C. D., McManus, J., & d'Aquili, E. G. (1992). *Brain, symbol and experience: Toward a neurophenomenology of human consciousness.* New York: Columbia University Press.

LeDoux, J. (2002). *Synaptic self: how our brains become who we are.* London: Macmillan.

Leroi-Gourhan, A. (1968). *The art of prehistoric man in Western Europe.* London: Thames & Hudson.

Leroi-Gourhan, A., & Allain, J. (1979). *Lascaux inconnu.* Paris: Éditions CNRS.

Lewis-Williams, J. D. (1981). *Believing and seeing: Symbolic meanings in southern San rock paintings.* London: Academic Press.

Lewis-Williams, J. D. (2000a). *Discovering southern African rock art.* Cape Town: David Philip.

Lewis-Williams, J. D. (2000b). *Stories that float from afar: Ancestral folklore of the San of Southern Africa*. Cape Town: David Philip.

Lewis-Williams, J. D. (2002). *The mind in the cave: Consciousness and the origins of art*. London: Thames & Hudson.

Lewis-Williams, J. D. (2003). *Images of mystery: Rock art of the Drakensberg*. Cape Town: Double Storey. (*L'art rupestre en Afrique du Sud: Mystérieuse images du Drakensberg*. Paris: Le Seuil.)

Lewis-Williams, J. D. (2010). *Conceiving God*. London: Thames & Hudson.

Lewis-Williams, J. D., & Pearce, D.G. (2004a). *San spirituality: Roots, expressions, and social consequences*. Walnut Creek, CA: AltaMira.

Lewis-Williams, J. D., & Pearce, D. G. (2004b). Southern African San rock paintings as social intervention: A study of rain control images. *African Archaeological Review, 21*(4), 199–227.

Lewis-Williams, J. D., & Pearce, D. G. (2005). *Inside the Neolithic mind: Consciousness, cosmos and the realm of the gods*. London: Thames & Hudson.

Martindale, C. (1981). *Cognition and consciousness*. Homewood, IL: Dorsey.

Pearson, J. L. (2002). *Shamanism and the ancient mind: A cognitive approach to archaeology*. Walnut Creek, CA: AltaMira.

Pinker, S. (1997). *How the mind works*. New York: Norton.

Ramachandran, V. S. (1999). A neurological theory of aesthetic experience. *Journal of Consciousness Studies, 4*(5–6), 15–51.

Ramachandran, V. S. (2004). *A brief tour of human consciousness: From imposter poodles to purple numbers*. New York: PI Press.

Ramachandran, V. S., & Blakeslee, S. (1998). *Phantoms in the brain: Probing the mysteries of the mind*. New York: HarperCollins.

Reichel-Dolmatoff, G. (1978). *Beyond the Milky Way: Hallucinatory imagery of the Tukano Indians*. Los Angeles: UCLA Latin America Centre.

Rolston, H. (1999). *Genes, genesis and God: Values and their origins in natural and human history*. Cambridge: Cambridge University Press.

Segal, M. H., Campbell, D. T., & Herskovitz, M. J. (1966). *The influence of culture on visual perception*. New York: Bobbs-Merrill.

Shanon, B. (2002). *The antipodes of the mind: Charting the phenomenology of the ayahuasca experience*. Oxford: Oxford University Press.

Siegel, R. K. (1977). Hallucinations. *Scientific American, 237*, 132–140.

Siegel, R. K., & Jarvik, M. E. (1975). Drug induced hallucinations in animals and man. In R. K. Siegel & L. J. West (Eds.), *Hallucinations: Behaviour, experience and theory* (pp. 81–161). New York: Wiley.

Skotnes, P. (Ed.). 2007. *Claim to the country: The archive of the Lucy Lloyd and Wilhelm Bleek Collection*. Athens: Ohio University Press.

Strassman, R. (2001). *DMT: The spirit molecule: A doctor's revolutionary research into the biology of near-death and mystical experiences*. Rochester, VT: Park Street Press.

Sumption, J. (1975). *Pilgrimage: An images of mediaeval religion*. London: Faber and Faber.

Vitebsky, P. (1995). *The shaman: Voyages of the soul, trance, ecstasy and healing from Siberia to the Amazon*. London: Macmillan.

Walker, S. J. (1981). The amateur scientist: About phosphenes. *Scientific American, 255*, 142–152.

Wendt, W. E. (1976). "Art mobilier" from the Apollo 11 Cave, South West Africa: Africa's oldest dated works of art. *South African Archaeological Bulletin, 31*, 5–11.

Wolpert, L. (2006). *Six impossible things before breakfast: The evolutionary origins of belief*. London: Faber and Faber.

3

COMPARATIVE DEVELOPMENTAL AND SOCIAL PERSPECTIVES ON THE MYSTERY OF UPPER PALEOLITHIC ART

Constance Milbrath

There is a growing sense in the literature on Palaeolithic rock art of an epistemological crisis in archaeology (Bednarick, 2006; Montelle, 2007). As expressed by Montelle, traditional epistemology relies on a priori formulations that once constructed, act as unfalsifiable proofs "about the nature of human knowledge" (p. 35). In archaeology, this has contributed to interpreting early human models of reality in terms of the experiences and value-laden intuitions of those engaging in the inquiry rather than on "tangible artefactual evidence" that can be subjected to scientific falsification. This critical issue has been central to contemporary philosophical inquiry as well (Stich, 1988; Weinberg, Nichols, & Stich, 2001). The dilemma as to what counts as evidence looms especially large in evaluating the multiple and often conflicting interpretations given to the sparse artistic remains of Upper Palaeolithic societies.

Earlier in the 20th century, structuralism heavily influenced interpretation of cave images. A cave site was defined as a closed system, and interpretation focused on making sense of the relationship among images within the system. The stance was that of "anthropological humanism," which imposed a humanist preconception about man's universal nature and of art as a "universal essence" (Conkey, 1997; Soffer & Conkey, 1997). As a consequence, the meanings attributed to the sophisticated cave images were narrowly conceived, for example as metaphors for gender divisions, fertility magic, narrations of origin myths, and hunting magic, and as chronicles of man's universally evolving artistic style (e.g., Breuil, 1952; Laming-Emperaire, 1962, 1972; Leroi-Gourhan, 1968). Even contemporary authors, however, are prone to projecting their own "modes of thought," supported by their own individual experience, when interpreting Palaelolithic image-making societies. Guthrie (2005), for example, relied heavily on his own experience as a father of an adolescent, and his skills as a recreational artist and hunter, to bolster his conclusions about who the cave artists were and the meaning the images had for these artists.

The issue is indeed vexing because there is so little to go on. As Bednarik (2006) succinctly put it, "The problem, essentially, is that there is a gap between the reality of what really happened in the distant past, and the record of it *as perceived by the individual researcher today*" (p. 87; italics in original). To get beyond this seemingly impenetrable barrier, Bednarik (2006) proposed that archaeology move toward a "scientific alternative" and seek to understand both the taphonomic processes[1] that are related to what is preserved and the biases that shape the interpretative models of the researchers themselves, a sort of self-study that echoes the epistemological crisis. Conkey (1997), a decade earlier, made a similar point in calling for the "need to 'excavate' our own core concepts and the constitution of unquestioned background assumptions that set up evidential relations that, in turn, structure the selection of not just relevant data but what then constitutes relevant 'context'" (p. 358). In this regard, Conkey pressed for greater use of context, in particular through study of the *social geography* that comprised the lifeways of Upper Palaeolithic mobile societies. Included in Conkey's appeal for attention to the social geography is greater consideration (a) of "the referential contexts of social action," or those symbolic behaviors that relate to image making; and (b) to the inferences that can be made about the social relations extant at the time from the regional distribution of artifacts and sites. Below, I take up these two aspects of social geography largely to expand on the thesis and well-supported claims already advanced in Lewis-Williams' inspired chapter.

SYMBOLIC LIFEWAYS AND COGNITION: THE NEUROLOGICAL BRIDGE

In Chapter 2, Lewis-Williams focuses on the symbolic actions that led to the creation of these powerful and enduring images. Elsewhere he has elaborated the potential sociopolitical context for their appearance

(Lewis-Williams, 2002). Lewis-Williams' evidence for his interpretation of the origins and meaning of Upper Palaeolithic cave images rests on two critical, yet scientifically falsifiable, foundations: the universality of a set of basic human cognitive processes, and the validity of modern indigenous hunter-gatherer ethnographies as evidence of parallels in cognition and social practices. Both these cornerstones as applied by Lewis-Williams are hotly debated in the field of archaeology (see Helvenston & Bahn, 2003, 2004; Hodgson, 2006; Solomon, 2001).

My commentary takes up the first of these only.[2] Evolutionary biologists and paleoanthropologists agree that *Homo* (*H.*) *sapiens* or *anatomically modern humans* had the *potential* cognitive capacities of humans today (e.g., Deacon, 1997; Donald, 1991; Gibson, 1996). This general acceptance that humans crossed the Rubicon into modernity some 40,000 to 100,000 years ago, referred to as the *modern unity hypothesis*, however, lacks sufficient explanatory power (Renfrew, 1996). Soffer and Conkey (1997) noted that, if it was simply human capacity that was at issue, modern humans were present at least 60,000 years before the Cultural Transition of 40,000 years ago. What was "absent were the social and cultural contexts within which such material practice would have been efficacious and would have had appropriate meanings" (Soffer & Conkey, p. 6). Renfrew concurred and observed further that the significance of the Transition has been comprehended from the vantage of 40 millennia of cultural evolution. Renfrew eschewed the use of the unity argument, referring to it as the "sapient behavior paradox":

> If it is the case that genetically we today differ rather little from our sapiens ancestors of forty millennia ago, how does that genetic composition which emerged then explain the cultural differences between then and now? The usual answer is that from that time the human animal had the skill, the intelligence, the *potential* to achieve its later accomplishments. But what kind of explanation is it that lays such weight upon so apparently a teleological concept as *potential*? (p. 11; italics in original)

The question is, what can we know about the consciousness and cognitions of these early modern humans? Potential, after all, is not always realized or even achievable in all contexts. Methods, generally outside of paleoanthropology and Palaeolithic archaeology, are increasingly utilized to model the minds of early hominids and anatomically modern humans based on analysis of behaviors. Comparative studies of cognitive capacities and behaviors of living nonhuman primates, especially when combined with cladistic analyses, have provided intriguing insights into the emergence of modern cognition and consciousness and suggest the types of evolutionary channeling (Langer, 1993, 1998; Mithen, 1996; Parker, 1996; Parker & McKinney, 1999; Sherwood, Subiaul, & Zawidzki, 2008; Tomasello, 1998; Wynn, 1993) and social pressures that may have led to modern human capacities (e.g., Tomasello; Whiten, 1991; Whiten & Byrne, 1997).

Developmental frameworks that hark back to Baldwin's (1915/2001) interactive mapping of cultural history and ontogenesis and Piaget's approach to cognitive evolution and development (Piaget, 1971; Piaget & Garcia, 1989) have been used to better understand the minds of early hominids and *H. sapiens* (Damerow, 1998; Milbrath, 2005; Mithen, 1996; Parker & Gibson, 1979; Parker & Milbrath, 1993; Wynn, 1989, 1993). A strictly recapitulation hypothesis is not (and cannot be) entertained by these developmental analyses (but see Parker & McKinney, 1999, pp. 288–293, for a discussion that concludes that "hominoid stages of cognitive development are maintained both by selection [natural and social] and developmental constraints" [p. 292]). Yet, analyses of differences and similarities between ontogenetic and phylogenetic sequences for cognition support the utility of a developmental framework in making inferences about the intellectual capacities of early hominids (Parker & Gibson, 1979) and *H. sapiens*, and more importantly about the evolutionary history of human intellectual capacities (e.g., Langer, 1993; Parker & McKinney, 1999). It is perhaps these two routes, comparative and developmental, that can offer more support for some version of the unity hypothesis.

One example that relates directly to the symbolic abilities that evolved in modern humans is the comparative developmental approach of Langer. Langer and his collaborators have studied the comparative development of logical-mathematical and physical cognition in two (Old and New World) monkey species, two great ape species (Bonobo and common chimpanzees) (Langer, 1993, 1998), and human infants and young children (Langer, 1980, 1986) using a method that requires no instruction and allows for direct comparisons. The different primate species were presented with sets of objects that ranged from geometric shapes (e.g., a wooden cylinder) to realistic objects (e.g., a cup), and their spontaneous constructive interactions with the objects were recorded. Some object sets embodied class structures, for example by identity of color or shape of some objects in the set, but the procedure left it open as to what was to be done with the objects. A monkey, chimpanzee, or child was therefore free to interact causally and/or logically with the objects. Rolling a yellow cylinder is an example of an interaction that would be recorded as causal, whereas if the same yellow cylinder was placed adjacent to a yellow triangle, a logical class based on color could result.

Using these methods, Langer established a phylogenetic sequence that exposed a similar ontogenetically early onset for physical cognition in all primate species studies. The onset of the development of logical-mathematical cognition, however, was found to be increasingly delayed relative to physical cognition the farther back the primate tree one moved. For example, although monkeys mature more rapidly than apes and humans, their onset age of beginning classificatory behavior is relatively late, starting at the end of their developmental sequence in physical cognition; whereas in human infants, physical and logical cognition develop synchronously. A change in the developmental timing of a species as compared to that of an ancestral species (inferred from the study of close relatives) is referred to as *heterochrony*, and is one of several transformational mechanisms with long-lasting evolutionary consequences. In this case logical-mathematical development appears to be increasingly accelerated from monkeys, to apes, to humans with the result that two cognitive systems that formerly developed asynchronously in ancestral forms became fully synchronic in modern humans.

> This heterochronic reorganization of cognitive development opened up multiple cascading possibilities for full information flow between logicomathematical (e.g., classificatory) and physical (e.g., causal) constructions in human infancy (e.g., making it possible to form a "logic of experimentation"). These cognitive domains are predominantly segregated from each other in time and, therefore, in information flow in the early development of monkeys. They are partially segregated from each other in time and, therefore, in information flow in the early development of great apes. (Langer, 2006, p. 43)

Langer (1993, 1998) and his collaborators found as well that all primate species studied spontaneously constructed single-category classes, but the origins of classifying diverged not only in onset ages but also in offset ages, rate, and even sequence of development across the species. For example, in monkeys, in addition to the relatively late onset age of classificatory behavior, the extent of classification was limited to single-category classes of few objects, the rate of productive constructions was slower than for other primates studied, the stage sequence was unique for each monkey species, and the end point age of stage development was earliest of all primates studied. Chimpanzees stood somewhere between monkeys and human infants in the level of development of classifactory behavior, and their rate of classificatory development was slower than that of human infants. Significantly, the onset age in chimpanzees partially overlapped with still developing physical cognitions, whereas the stage sequence, although considerably more limited, was similar to that seen in human infants. The extent of classification, however, was confined to second-order classifying, that is, the construction of two overlapping classes, and did not appear until the fifth year with little subsequent development. Human infants developed three-category classifying during their second year, the minimum requirement for hierarchical inclusion (e.g., class A + A^1 = B), and by late infancy they mapped one set of cognitive constructions onto another (e.g., they create corresponding classes and then substitute objects in equal numbers to maintain equivalence between the two classes).

According to Langer (2004), mapping cognitions onto other cognitions forms the foundation of representational thought by allowing cognitions to be detached from the concrete objects that are the direct targets of their actions. Cognitions are no longer limited to concrete objects; "[p]rogressively, the referents of infants' cognitions become relations, such as numerical equivalence, and causal dependence, that are the products of other intellectual operations mapped onto objects" (Langer, 2004, p. 104). Cognition itself can now become the object of thought, opening the way for abstract and reflective thought. This revelation of intellectual and behavioral differences among primate species has implications for interpreting the fossil record and archeological record of our human ancestors when comparative brain size is used as a proxy for mental capacities (see Gibson, 2005).

THE DISTRIBUTION OF UPPER PALAEOLITHIC SOCIAL GROUPS IN EUROPE: SOCIAL NETWORKS

Nevertheless, like Soffer and Conkey (1997) and Renfrew (1996) cited above, Gibson (2005) concluded that modern mental capacity alone, which appears from studies of brain casts to have been in place even 150,000 or possibly more years ago, would not be sufficient to explain the "extraordinar[il]y rapid" cultural changes that occurred only 40,000 years ago. Instead, she proposed that the explanation for this cultural florescence lies in social and environmental circumstances. Gibson favored environmental instability as a major factor in *variability selection* (Potts, 1998), wherein ecological pressures would have selected humans with highly plastic and creative brains to withstand and adapt to ecological instabilities.

Dramatic climatic shifts represent one variable aspect of the environment that certainly played a role in human dispersal and corresponding social patterns, but it does not appear to have been the whole story. Gamble and colleagues (Gamble, Davies, Pettitt, Hazelwood, & Richards, 2005; Gamble, Davies, Pettitt, & Richards, 2004) in analyses using dates as data, based on archaeological site remains during the late glacial period in Western Europe, concluded that although climatic shifts in the form of repeated glaciations appear to have influenced population contractions, most notably to southern Iberian refugia, general climatic warming did not appear to have influenced demographic expansions. Estimates of numbers indicate that the population size of about 17,000, largely concentrated in southwestern France and Iberia, from 25,000 to 19,500 thousand years ago, swelled to 64,000 during subsequent northern expansion. Such population expansion, however, is apparently not directly linked with climatic warming; rather, the greatest northern expansion in Western Europe took place 17,600 to 14,900 years ago during a period in which the coldest sea surface temperatures in 70,000 years had been recorded off the Iberian coast (Gamble et al., 2004). Modern human population dispersal, therefore, appears to have taken place under conditions of wide climatic tolerance.

Furthermore, although counterintuitive, records of sea surface temperatures and of plant and animal fossils indicate that during such glacial periods, there existed local northern habitats where early warming was the response to glaciations (Gamble et al., 2004). As small refuges of limited duration, these areas may have attracted "human populations with an extensive settlement network" during cold periods. Archaeological evidence from site dispersals in fact suggests a saltatory settlement pattern in which preferred habitats were sought out by repeated forays that tested conditions for expansion. More significantly for the topic at hand is that the greatest northern expansion of H. sapiens in Western Europe during the Upper Paleolithic, a period spanning over 2,000 years, corresponds to the greatest number of dated Palaeolithic cave art sites. Gamble and colleagues (Gamble et al., 2005) speculated that the increase in artistic activity was an integral part of a new social process, "a new way of occupying and giving meaning to the land," representative of pioneer settlements that began to explore regions beyond refuge areas, "released from social proximity and globally distributed" (p. 203).

Gamble et al. (2004) emphasized that saltatory dispersal can occur only if prior population adaptations allow exploitation of local conditions. The *extended* social networks forged by these early moderns, those in which distant relationships were negotiated and maintained through *symbolic resources*, proved vital (Gamble, 1999). Earlier hominid populations in Europe, including Neanderthals, relied on less complicated social organizations; those that stressed small *intimate* networks of significant others or slightly larger *effective* networks that included friends and relatives (Gamble, 1999). Information and resource exchanges in these kinds of networks depended on *co-presence* and a landscape of habitual activities. According to Gamble (1999),

> [S]ocial life is negotiated and varies according to the resources—affective, material and symbolic—which individuals can mobilize to create their surrounding environment. The activities of attending and attention are essential to such an interaction model and in the earlier periods these aspects were both weakly developed and poorly preserved. (p. 413)

Evidence from Palaeolithic sites after about 60,000 BP suggests a change from a *landscape of habit* to a *social landscape*, one that brought people together to specific locales for social occasions and that required attention to objects and artifacts whose existence had value independent of their material utility and from the people who made or used them.

> These same artifacts now represent gestures which continue to live even though they are no longer animated by use or direct association with an individual.... For the first time they now serve the more complicated role of system integration beyond fact-to-face interaction. (Gamble, 1999, p. 415)

> The eventual use of artifacts as symbols, be they handaxes or carved horses, is an exaptation, available for use by reason of their form rather than designed by natural selection for that purpose (Gould and Vrba 1982). What makes them symbols is their contribution to integrating and structuring what people do when they are separated.... Rather than the familiar gestures, which empower an individual as an active social agent, being passed between parent and child and within intimate, or at most effective networks, they can now skip horizontally between networks.... Extended networks can be used by individuals to negotiate their social position as well as those of others who are bound into their intimate and effective spheres. Faithful transmission gives way to asymmetrical power relations that now fall along lines of age, sex and genealogy. (Gamble, 1999, pp. 425–426)

Significantly, the social relations that appeared to mark the social geography during the period that representational cave images emerged in Europe were ones in which extended social networks dominated the landscape and power ascribed to objects and artifacts through their associations could be symbolically transferred. Barton,

Clark, and Cohen (1994) took an information perspective, from which art as a vehicle of intra- and intergroup information exchange "had the potential to affect the replicative success ... of forager societies and, in turn, be acted upon by selective pressures" (p. 189). Following Weissner (1983), they made a potentially useful distinction between emblematic and assertive artistic styles. Emblematic style, epitomized by parietal art, identifies a material culture and carries information symbolically about the culture as a whole. In contrast, assertive style, identified with portable artifacts, is also associated with a material culture but functions idiosyncratically to identify individuals and reinforce personal identity.

In support of this thesis that considers art as a communication medium as well as a direct result of demographic pressures, Barton et al. (1994) charted the concentration of parietal and portable art in relation to population densities and geographical occupation throughout the three Upper and Post-Palaeolithic European temporal periods (*downturn*, 30,000 to 21,000 BP; *refuge*, 21,000 to 13,000 BP; and *upturn*, 13,000 to 7,000 BP) defined by Gamble (1986). They suggested further that the permeability of social networks covaries as a function of population density, such that when populations are at low density, network boundaries are relatively porous, whereas when densities are high, social networks become relatively impenetrable. Their analyses corroborate an information exchange perspective by demonstrating that assertive art in the form of portable artifacts and ornaments appeared irrespective of population density, apparently cutting across "identity-conscious social units ... unconnected to the relative degree of social network closure" (p. 193); whereas in contrast, emblematic art varied with population growth, flourishing during periods of highest population density and seemingly communicating across social unit boundaries during these periods of presumed network closure, perhaps enforcing spatial and social boundaries during times of potential conflict over resources. (See a similar interpretation for some geographically distinct regions in Australia containing rock art in Rosenfeld, 1997.)

The idea that demographic stress was an impetus for the development of parietal art in Western Europe is also embraced by Lewis-Williams (2002), but in his view the igniting spark emerged earlier and in relation to the relatively brief period (≈45,000 to 35,000 BP) in which modern humans and Neanderthals occupied the same landscape. In addition, rapid social differentiation of the Aurignacian modern human cultures, the first Upper Palaelolithic cultures to produce figurative artifacts, although fueled by immediate social pressures rested on broader foundations of previously evolved human capacities related to higher order

consciousness, memory, and creativity, and on a social and epistemological framework that already included the social practice of sharing
mental images (Lewis-Williams, 2002):

> It was, I argue, this distinction [higher-order vs. primary con-
> sciousness] between *Homo* sapiens and Neanderthals that was
> a pivotal factor … in triggering and driving the efflorescence of
> image-making that started at the Transition and, long after the
> Neanderthals had gone, spiraled through the rest of the Upper
> Palaeolithic. Homo *sapiens* communities saw that they had an
> ability that Neanderthals did not have: Neanderthals were con-
> genital atheists. *Homo sapiens*['] more advanced ability in this
> mental arena may have made it important for them to cultivate
> the distinction by (in part) manifesting their visions as two- and
> three-dimensional images. (p. 192)

Whatever the igniting spark, the emergence of parietal art in the Upper
Palaeolithic appeared in a social landscape that imparted value and
meaning to these images. Further, as Donald (1991) has suggested,
their appearance constituted a kind of technological hardware with
the advantage of off-loading knowledge to "external memory storage
devices" (symbolic representations) and the result, both potential and
actual, of rapidly accelerating the accumulation of cultural knowledge.

THE DEVELOPMENT OF AN ART FORM:
AESTHETIC CONSIDERATIONS
Can We Call It Art?

Lewis-Williams deliberately shies away from questions of aesthetics,
stating that his focus instead is on "*the reasons why* people started, and
continued, to make images on the walls of caves" and arguing that in
any case, an innate aesthetic sense did not lead to the development of
image making. Yet it is undeniable to modern viewers that the cave
walls of Chauvet and Lascaux contain some of the most extraordinarily
aesthetic images painted by humans in our more than 40,000-year history of image making. Nevertheless, archaeologists equivocate about
whether these images should be labeled as "art," particularly without
knowing the intentions of the image makers and the context in which
they were created. And if we, as most of us do off-handedly, refer to
these images as art, are we engaging in a form of cultural appropriation
that ignores the meaning these images had for the people who created
them (Clottes, 2005; Heyd, 2005; Lemarque, 2005)?

Notwithstanding, the realm of "rock art" has been brought into the aesthetic forum by taking an approach of "middle-road archaeology," to which Lewis-Williams also ascribes (Clegg, 2005; Lemarque, 2005). This route assumes human universals in basic cognitive process, that is, it relies on a version of the unity hypothesis referred to above. A corollary, which Clegg called "the aesthetic approach," proposes that one's own understanding of one's direct experience of viewing rock art becomes the basis for thoughtful exploration about the images, unfettered by some of the constraints imposed by the discipline of formal archaeology. In support of at least a perceptual unity hypothesis, Clegg as well as others (Lewis-Williams, 1986) have demonstrated several types of optical tricks found in ancient rock art, for example "shimmering," figure-ground reversal, and after-images in Australian Aboriginal rock art, that, although certainly subject to uniquely distinct interpretations across different cultural groups, produce similar visual effects in all viewers. Some of these, Clegg argued, lead to altered states of consciousness and may well have been used to enhance associated rituals or religious experiences.

Beyond these well-known optical illusions, many of the highly valued rock paintings have aesthetic features that are equivalent to those valued by modern art historians (Clottes, 2005), for example intrafigural proportions, visual balance of interfigural relations, creation of depth, dynamic and expressive use of line and color, and thematic narratives that enhance the compositional impact of the images. Clottes (2005) argued that if these features are evident to us, it is highly likely that the early image makers were also aware of and attended to them in the act of production. Heyd (2005) commented,

> [O]n the basis of the structural demands of making paintings and engravings (which require, for example, artistic and aesthetic judgment), one may argue that much rock art-making was likely to have been accompanied by the relevant attitudes, and hence, *prima facie*, should count as art. In order to *avoid merely identifying rock art with our categories*, and thereby evacuating it of its particular aesthetic meanings, though, attention to the specific features appreciable in rock art is called for. (p. 41, emphasis added)

Heyd cited these specific features as an appreciation for the integrity and identity of pictographs and petroglyphs as they are found, both as independent units or in relation to others that may have been made by different artists at a later or earlier time; a type of "multi-authored collage." Heyd also called attention to the substrate on which the images are painted and conditions under which these paintings were meant to be viewed, noting for example the aesthetic value of the rock surface as hard, colored, and/or textured, as opposed to other types of surfaces and the fact that some rock panels, for example those in the Laura region of Australia, are meant to be viewed by looking up from a prone position. Geographic location is an important additional feature that enhances the aesthetic as well as the potential sociopolitical significance.

Developing an Art Form

Elsewhere I have used a Piagetian framework to analyze the evolution of the Panel of Horses, which faces the entrance to a chamber in the deepest part of the Chauvet cave complex (Milbrath, 2005). I had the great fortune of capitalizing on the archaeological analysis of Fritz and Tosello (2003), who employed recent advances in dating and photographic technology to sequence the order in which the images of this panel were laid down. Yet even with these advances, we can know only very approximate dates for the order of the image sequences, not if these images were laid down over a period of months, years, or even thousands of years. Still it was startling to find that the evolution of the panel approximated developmental sequences described by Piaget and Garcia (1989) for the discovery and elaboration of the geometry of space, as well as closely fit the sequence noted by this author for developments in the drawings of talented child artists (Milbrath, 1998).

Unmistakable in the exposed sequence was an apparent shift in artistic concern for *intrafigural relations* by initially representing single animals, engraved with a stick in their clearest recognizable or canonical form and spatially unconnected to other images, to a concern for composing groups of animals in visual relationship to each other, that is, for treating the *interfigural relations* as paramount, including evidence for anticipation of figural placements and, later in the temporal sequence, evidence of concern for the relationships between units of figural groupings. This can be interpreted as a move from direct engagement in the immediate act or action of producing the image to a more studied and aesthetic engagement, marked at first by anticipating relationships between pairs of figures, and later culminating in planning for, at the very least, 3D spatial relationships between groups of animals on the two-dimensional surface. It becomes clear as well that at the same time, Palaeolithic artists were improving their technology with the use of charcoal, shading, and variations in color and line. Moreover, the final panel appears to have evolved through an aesthetic that took into account the existing compositional groupings as additions were made. To hark back to Lewis-Williams' theory, the content may still be tied to the image makers' shamanistic visions, but the compositional force of the panel strongly indicates that it developed toward planned actions that anticipated the end result as a whole.

In my opinion the revealed sequence stands as evidence of an entirely transformed image-making enterprise. The initial engraving techniques used for the first figures of the panel and likely for animal visions originally "fixed" with a stick on the ground were extensionally generalized to the cave walls and then seemingly evolved detached from the earlier technique and vision context as pictorial forms that began to stand in relationship to each other, with the eventual progression to compositional groupings (e.g., groups of aurochs and groups of horses), which could then themselves be composed in relation to each other and whose interrelationships became anticipated in the final phase of the panel. But rather than suggesting that this sequence indexed a broader evolutionary trend in the arts, I propose that the

> progression marks the emergence and development of an entire discipline, including artistic technique, style, and composition, which occurred *within a small group of individuals* over a relatively delimited period of time. The transformation from simple isolated "fixed" images to large composed panels emphasizing contrast, chiaroscuro, and color occurred as this novel practice was diversified and exploited by these gifted individuals. (Milbrath, 2005, p. 137; italics added)

The discovery and advances of cave painters in Western Europe may have been made on the foundations of existing artistic practices in portable art, but in my opinion, it is unlikely that they constituted a slowly evolving traditional style that was taught and transmitted across many generations. Rather, the evidence suggests that entry to many of the decorated caves was limited to a small number of individuals for relatively short but sometimes repeated periods (Clottes, 2003). It is more likely that these and similar discoveries in artistic practice were made anew repeatedly throughout the Upper Palaeolithic period as the social landscape and circumstances gave opportunity and meaning to the activity.

NOTES

1. Taphonomic processes are those that determine how plant and animal (as well as human) remains accumulate and are differentially preserved within archaeological sites. This is critical to determining whether these remains are associated with human activity. In addition, taphonomic pro-

cesses may alter biological remains after they are deposited at a site. Some remains survive better than others over time, and can therefore bias an excavated collection.

2. Treatment of a discussion of the validity of early ethnographies of hunter-gatherer societies is beyond the scope of this chapter. Lewis-Williams and T. A. Dowson (1999), however, have published results of their own ethnographic research on modern San readings of ancient San rock images that offer strong support for Lewis-Williams' interpretations as applied to Upper Palaeolithic images.

REFERENCES

Baldwin, J. M. (2001). *Genetic theory of reality*. New York: Putnam. (Original work published in 1915)

Barton, C. M., Clark, G. A., & Cohen, A. E. (1994). Art as information: Explaining Upper Palaeolithic art in Western Europe. *World Archaeology*, *26*(2), 185–207.

Bednarick, R. G. (2006). A unified theory for Palaeloart studies. *Rock Art Research*, *23*(1), 85–88.

Breuil, H. (1952). *Four hundred centuries of cave art*. Montignac, France: Centre d'Études et de documentation préhistoriques.

Clegg, J. (2005). Aesthetics, rock art, and changing states of consciousness. In T. Heyd & J. Clegg (Eds.), *Aesthetics and rock art* (pp. 159–176). Burlington, VT: Ashgate.

Clottes, J. (2003). The Horse Sector. In J. Clottes (Ed.), *Chauvet cave: The art of earliest times* (pp. 106–116). Salt Lake City: University of Utah Press.

Clottes, J. (2005). Foreword. In T. Heyd & J. Clegg (Eds.), *Aesthetics and rock art* (pp. xix–xxv). Burlington, VT: Ashgate.

Conkey, M. (1997). Beyond art and between the caves: Thinking about context in the interpretive process. In M. Conkey, O. Soffer, D. Stratmann, & N. Jablonski (Eds.), *Beyond art: Pleistocene image and symbol* (pp. 343–368). San Francisco: California Academy of Science.

Damerow, P. (1998). Prehistory and cognitive development. In J. Langer & M. Killen (Eds.), *Piaget, evolution and development* (pp. 247–270). Malwah, NJ: Lawrence Erlbaum.

Deacon, T. W. (1997). *The symbolic species: The co-evolution of language and the human brain*. New York: Norton.

Donald, M. (1991). *Origins of the modern mind: Three stages in the evolution of culture and cognition*. Cambridge, MA: Harvard University Press.

Fritz, C., & Tosello, F. (2003). The Horse Sector. In J. Clottes (Ed.), *Chauvet cave: The art of earliest times* (pp. 106–116). Salt Lake City: University of Utah Press.

Gamble, C. (1986). *The Paleolithic settlement of Europe*. Cambridge: Cambridge University Press.

Gamble, C. (1999). *The Paleolithic societies of Europe*. Cambridge: Cambridge University Press.

Gamble, C., Davies, W., Pettitt, P., Hazelwood, L., & Richards, M. (2005). The archaeological and genetic foundations of the European population during the late glacial: Implications for "agricultural thinking." *Cambridge Archaeological Journal, 15*(2), 193–223.

Gamble, C., Davies, W., Pettitt, P., & Richards, M. (2004). Climatic change and evolving human diversity in Europe during the last glacial. *Philosophical Transactions, Royal Society of London B, 359,* 243–254.

Gibson, K. R. (1996). The biocultural human brain, seasonal migrations, and the emergence of the Upper Palaeolithic. In K. Gibson & P. Mellars (Eds.), *Modelling the early human mind* (pp. 33–46). Cambridge: McDonald Institute for Archaeological Research.

Gibson, K. R. (2005). Human brain evolution: Developmental perspectives. In S. T. Parker, J. Langer, & C. Milbrath (Eds.), *Biology and knowledge revisited: From neurogenesis to psychogenesis* (pp. 123–144). Hillsdale, NJ: Lawrence Erlbaum.

Gould, S. J., & Vrba, S. (1982). Exaptation—a missing term in the science of form. *Paleobiology, 3,* 4–15.

Guthrie, D. (2005). *The nature of Paleolithic art.* Chicago: University of Chicago Press.

Helvenston, P. A., & Bahn, P. G. (2003). Testing the "three stages of trance" model. *Cambridge Archaeological Journal, 13*(2), 213–224.

Helvenston, P. A., & Bahn, P. (2004). Waking the trance-fixed: Reply from Halvenston & Bahn. *McDonald Institute for Archaeological Research, 14*(1), 96–100.

Heyd, T. (2005). Rock art aesthetics: Trace on rock, mark of spirit, window on land. In T. Heyd & J. Clegg (Eds.), *Aesthetics and rock art* (pp. 37–50). Burlington, VT: Ashgate.

Hodgson, D. (2006). Altered states of consciousness and Palaeoart: An alternative neurovisual explanation. *Cambridge Archaeological Journal, 16*(1), 27–37.

Laming-Emperaire, A. (1962). *La signification de l'art rupestre paléolithic.* Paris: Picard.

Laming-Emperaire, A. (1972). Système de pensée et organisation sociale dans l'art rupestre paléolithique. In *L'homme de Cro-Magnon: Anthropologie et archéologie.* Paris: Arts et Métiers Graphiques.

Langer, J. (1980). *The origins of logic: Six to twelve months.* New York: Academic Press.

Langer, J. (1986). *The origins of logic: One to two years.* New York: Academic Press.

Langer, J. (1993). Comparative cognitive development. In K. R. Gibson & T. Ingold (Eds.), *Tools, language and cognition in human evolution* (pp. 300–313). New York: Cambridge University Press.

Langer, J. (1998). Phylogenetic and ontogenetic origins of cognition: Classification. In J. Langer & M. Killen (Eds.), *Piaget, evolution and development* (pp. 33–54). Malwah, NJ: Lawrence Erlbaum.

Langer, J. (2004). Constructive manipulatory action and the origin of cognition in human and nonhuman primates. In I. J. Stockman (Ed.), *Movement and action in learning and development: Clinical implications for pervasive developmental disorders* (pp. 93–116). San Diego, CA: Elsevier Academic.

Langer, J. (2006). The heterochronic evolution of primate cognitive development. *Biological Theory: Integrating Development, Evolution, and Cognition, 1*(1), 41–43.

Lemarque, P. (2005). Palaeolithic cave painting: A test case for transcultural aesthetics. In T. Heyd & J. Clegg (Eds.), *Aesthetics and rock art* (pp. 21–36). Burlington, VT: Ashgate.

Leroi-Gourhan, A. (1968). *The art of prehistoric man in Western Europe.* London: Thames & Hudson.

Lewis-Williams, D. (1986). Cognitive and optical illusions in San Rock Art research. *Current Anthropology, 27,* 171–178.

Lewis-Williams, D. (2002). *The mind in the cave.* London: Thames & Hudson.

Lewis-Williams, D. J., & Dowson, T. A. (1999). *Images of power: Understanding San rock art* (2nd ed.). Johannesburg: Southern Book Publishers.

Milbrath, C. (1998). *Patterns of artistic development in children.* New York: Cambridge University Press.

Milbrath, C. (2005). Creativity and epistemology. *Journal of Cultural and Evolutionary Psychology, 3*(2), 121–142.

Mithen, S. (1996). *The prehistory of the mind.* Cambridge: Cambridge University Press.

Montelle, Y.-P. (2007). Naturalized epistemology, human models of reality, salience and cave iconography. *Rock Art Research, 24*(1), 35–45.

Parker, S. T. (1996). Using cladistic analysis of comparative data to reconstruct the evolution of cognitive development in hominids. In E. Martin (Ed.), *Phylogenies and the comparative method in animal behavior* (pp. 361–398). New York: Oxford University Press.

Parker, S. T., & Gibson, K. R. (1979). A model of the evolution of language and intelligence in early hominids. *Behavioural and Brain Sciences, 2,* 367–407.

Parker S. T., & McKinney, M. L. (1999). *Origins of intelligence: The evolution of cognitive development in monkeys, apes, and humans.* Baltimore: Johns Hopkins University Press.

Parker, S. T., & Milbrath, C. (1993). Higher intelligence, propositional language, and culture as adaptations for planning. In K. R. Gibson & T. Ingold (Eds.), *Tools, language and cognition in human evolution* (pp. 314–333). New York: Cambridge University Press.

Piaget, J. (1971). *Biology and knowledge.* Chicago: University of Chicago Press.

Piaget, J., & Garcia, R. (1989). *Psychogenesis and the history of science.* New York: Columbia University Press. (Original work published in 1983)

Potts, R. (1998). Variability selection in hominid evolution. *Evolutionary Anthropology, 7,* 81–96.

Renfrew, C. (1996). The sapient behaviour paradox: How to test for potential? In K. R. Gibson & P. Mellars (Eds.), *Modelling the early human mind* (pp. 11–14). Cambridge: McDonald Institute for Archaeological Research.

Rosenfeld, A. (1997). Archaeological signatures of the social context of rock art production. In M. Conkey, O. Soffer, D. Stratmann, & N. Jablonski (Eds.), *Beyond art: Pleistocene image and symbol* (pp. 289–300). San Francisco: California Academy of Science.

Sherwood, C. C., Subiaul, F., & Zawidzki, T. W. (2008). A natural history of the human mind: Tracing evolutionary changes in brain and cognition. *J. Anatomy, 212,* 426–454.

Soffer, O., & Conkey, M. (1997). Studying ancient visual cultures. In M. Conkey, O. Soffer, D. Stratmann, & N. Jablonski (Eds.), *Beyond art: Pleistocene image and symbol* (pp. 1–16). San Francisco: California Academy of Science.

Solomon, A. (2001). What is an explanation? Belief and cosmology in interpretations of Southern San rock art in southern Africa. In H. P. Francfort & R. N. Hamayon (Eds.), *The concept of shamanism: Uses and abuses* (pp. 161–178). Budapest: Akadémiai Kiadó.

Stich, S. P. (1988). Reflective equilibrium, analytic epistemology and the problem of cognitive diversity. *Synthese, 74*(3), 391–413.

Tomasello, M. (1998). Social cognition and the evolution of culture. In J. Langer & M. Killen (Eds.), *Piaget, evolution and development* (pp. 221–246). Malwah, NJ: Lawrence Erlbaum.

Weinberg, J., Nichols, S., & Stich, S. (2001). Normativity and epistemic intuitions. *Philosophical Topics, 29*(1/2), 429–460.

Weissner, P. (1983). Style and social information in Kalahari San projectile points. *American Antiquity, 48*(2), 253–276.

Whiten, A. (1991). *Natural theories of mind: Evolution development and simulation of everyday mindreading.* Cambridge, MA: Basil Blackwell.

Whiten, A., & Byrne, R. W. (1997). *Machiavellian intelligence II: Extensions and evaluations.* Cambridge: Cambridge University Press.

Wynn, T. (1989). *The evolution of spatial competence.* Urbana: University of Illinois Press.

Wynn, T. (1993). Layers of thinking in tool behavior. In K. R. Gibson & T. Ingold (Eds.), *Tools, language and cognition in human evolution* (pp. 389–406). New York: Cambridge University Press.

4

HIP-HOP CULTURE, YOUTH CREATIVITY, AND THE GENERATIONAL CROSSROADS

Murray Forman

Cultural expression is an important site of social and political reproduction. How we imagine, reproduce, and define ourselves, and how we are imagined, reproduced, and defined through culture, are critically linked to (and often sustain) struggles for change and freedom.

—Tricia Rose (1997, pp. 259–260)

For all of its pop culture ubiquity, hip-hop culture remains a widely misunderstood facet of creative activity. It is certainly seen and heard by many, yet its creative processes—the real labor behind its production—are hardly evident. Though it is a factor in the lives of millions of people around the world, detractors abound, denying the legitimacy of hip-hop even as it garners billions of dollars in the culture industries and ascends to the level of art and cultural heritage. This latter point is evidenced by the display of graffiti canvases in private gallery exhibitions and in some of the world's most esteemed modern art museums, break-dancing- and hip-hop-inspired plays in the world's more prominent theatres, and rap music on concert stages around the globe. Over the years hip-hop exhibits have been mounted at important cultural centers (including the Brooklyn Museum of Art in 2000), and the Smithsonian Museum has initiated a special hip-hop collection in recognition of its cultural importance.

Of course, how and where we encounter art matters. If, for example, one turns a city street corner and is suddenly confronted with the unique and awesome spectacle of abstract swirls of aerosol color sprayed across a mural-scale brick wall, the impression is inclined to be rather different than if a canvas of similar scale and vibrancy is hanging on a gallery wall. Similarly, in the realm of popular music the overall effect will differ if a dynamic rap track is embedded between raucous radio commercials or if it is received favorably among a crowd in a performance context.

Art and creativity allow humans to imagine various and alternative futures. It is therefore appropriate to ask what futures are imagined in and through hip-hop. Is there something about hip-hop's cultural practices that foster or enable particular kinds of creative expression? What does hip-hop *do* that makes it so relevant to so many people, both young and not so young? The fact remains that the arts and media are mobilized in the vibrant articulation of what can be described as hip-hop sensibilities, aesthetics, and politics. Hip-hop exists today as a multimedia phenomenon, unconfined by any single form or mode of expression. It is actively experienced in material and physical form (CDs, films, fashion, music, comedy and poetry performances, literature, and photography)[1] as well as in the immaterial forms of the electronic virtual realm, whether this includes online retail sites, fan blogs, artists' MySpace websites, or YouTube video webcasts. Hip-hop is also now global in scope, a facet of transnational postmodern media flows. The creative dialogue among hip-hop artists has, thus, transcended traditional boundaries of race, space, and place, and the aesthetic and political outcomes are unique in each new cultural locale in which they emerge.

HIP-HOP'S CREATIVE ORIGINS AND THE FOUR (OR MORE) ELEMENTS

It is important to first establish what hip-hop culture is. In the discussion of hip-hop, we are not simply talking about the music, though music is generally where the discussion ends up. Rap music is but one form, albeit the most popular and accessible form, of artistic and cultural expression within hip-hop. Rap's popularity is mainly a result of a particular evolution with the entertainment industries facilitating our exposure to recordings and film soundtracks. Media-induced celebrity adulation fixates on bankable rap performers enhanced by the commercial circulation of ancillary texts such as music magazines or videos.

Seeking a thumbnail definition, MC (rapper) and self-appointed keeper of the hip-hop flame KRS-1 makes the distinction that "rap is something you do, hip-hop is something you live." For him, rappers excel only at rhyming in time to a musical beat; they may be clever or aurally pleasing, but their primary role is in the domain of entertainment. MCs, on the other hand, employ the rap form to innovatively articulate cultural values and ideals, serving as carriers of news and information in ways akin to the traditional griots of Western Africa. Within KRS-1's definition, hip-hop might be understood in relation to British cultural studies theorist Raymond Williams' (1981) notion of culture. Williams famously pronounced that culture consists of "a whole way of life" encompassing intellectual knowledge, material practices, affect, and the ostensibly lowbrow or inconsequential aspects of everyday existence. As in hip-hop culture, Williams identified a unique set of cultural sensibilities inflected by various daily forces that fully permeate the subjective self.

Mark Runco (2004) also isolated the everyday-ness of creativity: "Creativity is useful; it can be applied each day to many aspects of our lives.... Creativity does not just play a role in the arts, invention and innovation; it is also a part of our everyday lives" (p. 660). Thus, one does not simply consume or produce hip-hop's artistic or expressive forms; rather, one fully inhabits hip-hop at various geosocial scales of mobility and according to ever-shifting affective intensities. Hip-hop is experienced as "a whole way of life" to the extent that one can often hear the proud and defiant identity claim "I am hip-hop" asserted in the streets of urban centers around the world.

Initially born in the Bronx and rapidly expanding throughout New York City, hip-hop is forged in the genius innovation of urban Black and Latino youth. The cultural forms of hip-hop are bound in complex ways to the creative and artistic legacies of African and Afro-Caribbean traditions, but they are not simply reducible to these traditions. Rather, hip-hop accommodates a range of hybrid practices that are historically resonant *and* highly attuned to the contemporary condition.

Hip-hop is generally seen as a cultural culmination involving four core creative elements: graffiti (or aerosol art), b-boying/b-girling (or break dancing), deejaying, and emceeing. Each of these is quite familiar by now, having been featured in film, television, and recordings, and hyped and profiled in the press. The famous four elements have been part of the collective urban reality on the streets in front of us for roughly 30 years. Hip-hop began to display the characteristics of a cohesive culture by the mid- to late 1970s and throughout the early 1980s, when the combination of the foundational elements began to show relative consistency and when the individuals or groups affiliated with one or another of the foundations—rap and DJ "posses," b-boy or graffiti "crews," "cliques," or "squads"—congregated in the shared settings of streets, community centers, or nightclubs, uniting under hip-hop's common banner. These small, localized group amalgamations (usually, but not exclusively, fraternally bound) also serve as a creative cohort among which innovation is discussed and, whether through collaboration, mutual encouragement, or intense in-group competition, expertise is honed.

Although the rhymed exclamation "Hip-hop, it don't stop" might have seemed like a casual boast or wishful thinking over 25 years ago, the conditions within which hip-hop simmered were perfect for the creation of a delicious and enduring cultural gumbo. But hip-hop did not simply rise magically. It emerged from very specific social, economic, technological, and cultural influences. Michael Eric Dyson (2007) asserted, "The metaphysical root of hip hop is connected to the ghetto whether or not many of its artists grew up there" (p. 11). Although Dyson's assessment is beyond dispute, the ghetto is itself a fluid and fluctuating construct, shifting discursively as well as in concrete, material terms as, for example, gentrification and "urban renewal" initiatives redefine urban locales and alter the social flows.

It is therefore significant that hip-hop emerged from the particular urban terrains that it did. The Bronx of the 1970s was in severe depression, an urban wasteland in the eyes of many outside observers but home to those who dwelled within its borders. Daily life was fraught with challenges, and although the surrounding environment lacked many standard infrastructural services, love abounded and, despite everything, hope persevered. The four elements of hip-hop were initially conceived as an outlet for the human expression of joy, pleasure, and presence while also providing a mechanism for the public articulation of *self* in adverse conditions that reduced the potentialities of the individual, conspiring to crush expectations and ideals. In somewhat different contexts, hip-hop was also a catalyst for the decline of organized gang activity among New York youths, offering alternative models of group affiliation and creative mechanisms through which to assert dominance and to articulate identity.

It is a curious aspect of human psychology that in the midst of the harshest conditions, humans will commonly employ creative and artistic means to weave a fabric of hope, in the process redefining the issues at hand, reframing their own relations to crisis conditions, and recasting collective responses to a callous world that is not of their making. Creativity is, I believe, essential to human existence, and it must be regarded in a dialectical framework where the conditions that restrict or limit actual possibilities of individual or collective action can also harbor hidden or less orthodox means of overcoming such barriers. Hip-hop is, then, a product of its times, reactive to conditions even as it is a creative force of conditional change, radically intervening in and transforming the cultural landscapes in which it is forged.

According to David Edwards (2008), "[C]reativity flourishes outside our institutions.... Disaffection with contemporary institutions is the story of famous technology innovators" (p. 15). The story of one of the pioneering DJs, Grandmaster Flash (Joseph Saddler), tells us about the son of Caribbean parents (from Barbados) living in the Bronx, training in the repair of electronic appliances. Through serendipity and a process of unorthodox experimentation, Flash and others at the time developed an exceptionally effective method of manipulating two turntables simultaneously, not only enhancing efficiency for standard disk jockey work but also creating an entirely new set of aesthetic possibilities that immeasurably changed the character of popular music, providing a new soundtrack that converged with the physicality of break dancing and the visual forms of graffiti.

That these innovations occurred when and where they did is pertinent: At hip-hop's inception, the New York borough of the Bronx was a renowned environment that was cemented in the popular imagination as a zone of chronic despair, danger, and social disease. Foundational institutions in the Bronx (perhaps with the exception of the church) were often undermined by unemployment, drugs, gang activity, poverty, and other forces, leading to the severe disruption of families and to the erosion of the education system. Schools were grossly underperforming, and, due to raw economics, various areas of the educational curricula—notably, music programs—were often dissolved. Young people in the Bronx faced reduced prospects at every turn, yet in the midst of hardship, some thrived. Flash was among the latter with his skills as an electronics repairman, displaying the proud can-do spirit that seems fundamental to many Caribbean immigrant families.

Adopting Edwards' (2008) concept of "artscience,"[2] we might speculate momentarily: Was Flash an electronics repairman who had learned new musical practices, or was he a musician whose applied electronics training opened a world of technical knowledge? In fact, it is likely a bit of both, and Flash's innate creative talents and his facility with the inner workings of record turntables and sound mixers allowed him to forge the connection between these two dimensions of his identity and interests. But there is another element at play here, for it would be irresponsible to ignore Flash's Afro-Caribbean heritage in this story. Many will speak of the importance of the drum in the various musics of the African diaspora, and this is indeed a critical aesthetic force in hip-hop.

Rhythm helps to demarcate the character and distinctions between, say, the deep bass culture of Jamaican reggae music or the percolating sound of soca and calypso. But the sound system, too, stands as a major facet of modern popular music throughout the Caribbean, with DJs providing the core rhythmic components for the all-important dancehalls where many Caribbean cultural practices are enacted. The rhythmic and overall aesthetic elements of African American music circulated widely throughout the Caribbean via recordings or powerful U.S.-based radio broadcast stations as well (Toynbee, 2007), fusing various dispersed musical forms while facilitating creative conversations within the African diaspora.

Flash's creative labor, then, was positioned within a matrix of heritage, technology, location, and mobility, and the material conditions of postmodern society. It is not reducible to any single factor but must be conceived within this complex array of influential forces. Perhaps the final thing to say about this is that Flash was not the only one embarking on these musical experiments at the time. Others, such as New York–born Afrika Bambaataa and the legendary DJ Kool Herc (Clive Campbell, who also claimed Caribbean origins, having migrated to the Bronx from Kingston, Jamaica), were working a similar creative vein, producing very similar results. In this light, the Bronx might be regarded as a creative crucible, a fascinating urban cultural laboratory where transformative cultural experiments were underway. Or, it might also be speculated that hip-hop was simply an idea that was ready to happen, consonant with myriad swirling factors, producing dynamic changes to the cultural landscape of the Bronx and, soon after, to every major urban locale in the United States and beyond.

Runco (2004) identified the importance of "flexibility" as a factor in human creativity. He wrote that "the flexibility of creative persons is what gives them the capacity to cope with advances, opportunities, technologies, and changes that are part of our current day-to-day lives" (Runco, p. 658). Scholars and hip-hop historians repeatedly cite the flexibility inherent in the practices of early hip-hop artists who demonstrated uncanny skills in the appropriation and reinvention of everyday technological objects and social spaces. Postmodern practices and sensibilities figure prominently, aided by new technological possibilities. In hip-hop, the past is powerfully resonant. History offers a repository to be raided (for example, via the use of old records and sampled sounds from classic recordings or obscure tracks), whereas the present is defined within an apparently limitless flow of information from vastly diverse sources and moments in time. Images in mass circulation overlap wildly in a mostly unorthodox palimpsest, obscuring original sources and producing unforeseen hybrids. In this historical context, information and ideas, as well as such "things" as images and sounds, are deterritorialized and reterritorialized continually, wrenched from one setting or situation and recast in another. This can be a matter of haphazard decontextualization, or it can be a highly focused and carefully conceived matter of creative juxtaposition. Either way, it fuels new perspectives, affecting our aesthetic sensibilities.

In the early days of hip-hop, electricity was pirated from street poles and channeled toward the DJ sound systems, reconfiguring the city block with booming bass and gyrating teen bodies ... at least until the police arrived. Urban space was, in these instances, reconfigured and reconceived according to localized patterns of sociality. The tools of musical *reception,* such as the record, turntable, or sound mixer, were also transformed into instruments of musical performance and *production*, recast as rhythmic instruments in the hands of the DJ. As Dyson (2007) explained, this creative innovation reflects *bricolage,* "using what is literally at hand to create something—a style, an approach, a practice" (p. 73). This postmodern electronic transmutation can be equated with Afro-Caribbean practices involving the redesign and reassignment of 45-gallon oil drums (otherwise destined for disposal) to create the gorgeously musical steel pans that are essential to Trinidad's calypso tradition. In rap music, the artist must win the audience's attention, and the cacophony of sound and the sheer density of audible snippets sampled from myriad sites and sources are simultaneously a complex and alluring collage *and* a provocation of sorts. Chuck D, MC and leader of the influential hip-hop group Public Enemy, cites the seemingly endless capacity to make "something out of nothing" as one of hip-hop's important characteristics.

HIP-HOP, SPATIALITY, AND THE GLOBAL-LOCAL NEXUS

As I have stressed above, hip-hop did not arise out of thin air in the mid- to late 1970s but emerged from very specific social, economic, technological, and cultural influences. Hip-hop is a product of its times, reactive to conditions even as it is a force of conditional change, radically intervening and altering the cultural landscapes in which it is forged. Yet there is an imperative localism attached to hip-hop in its nascent moment because the various cultural phenomena associated with the foundational elements were (and remain) closely aligned with specific neighborhoods and zones of identification that bear deep affective meanings for their inhabitants.

The early history of hip-hop, perhaps best detailed in Jeff Chang's excellent historical exegesis *Can't Stop, Won't Stop* (2005), describes the way that the Bronx was divided into sections, first organized according to neighborhood structures and, with more sinister implications, gang turf, but gradually yielding to what might be regarded as a mobile DJ party circuit with specific public housing units or community halls as the key social centers. The emphasis on local attachment and locally defined identities is clearly part of hip-hop's lore, yet it remains one of hip-hop's more interesting characteristics; it can still be heard clearly in the music, seen in the videos and films, and read in the graffiti murals and in the printed materials that emanate from hip-hop's cultural producers.

Elsewhere I have isolated the spatial element of hip-hop, especially as it is framed or conceived within the discourse of "the 'hood" (Forman, 2002). The 'hood is a highly localized space—a place—distinct from and less abstract than the earlier notions of the ghetto and encompassing the primary locus of one's operations, where one is from and where one has the highest degree of affective affiliation and social capital. More narrowly circumscribed than the ghetto, the 'hood is a highly concentrated locus of creativity. Moreover, the 'hood can be regarded almost like a studio of sorts, as an incubator for the ideas and artistic tendencies that inform hip-hop practices.

Enunciating locale and one's point of origin or affiliation has evolved as a pervasive hip-hop convention with artists touting their home spaces, amplifying the "sites of significance" (Forman, 2002) that shape their art and identities. In rap, locally resonant signifiers are commonly employed, and place-based references (including natural or built markers, postal zip codes, or telephone area codes) proliferate. This tendency is evident in myriad cases; for example, entrepreneurial rap music production and promotion companies frequently employ the regional telephone area code as their corporate moniker. MCs and rap artists adhere to a lyrical convention by citing their neighborhood affiliations and, in their videos, by featuring footage of their actual home sites and their extended neighborhood entourage. Graffiti affixed to transport train boxcars (most urban subway cars have been, since the late 1980s, buffed clean and graffiti-free) generally include geolocational signs such as place names or area codes alongside the artist's name. In another specific instance, New Orleans producers merge the city's famed second-line marches and brassy choruses with hip-hop beats and a characteristically slow "N'Awlins" vocal flow, creating a distinct aural statement that enunciates the city of its origins. Such proud and explicit localism is displayed in New Orleans artist Juvenile's video "Get Ya Hustle On" that features him and his posse in and around the

Hurricane Katrina–ravaged neighborhood of the lower Ninth Ward in New Orleans.

Along with this urgent localism, we are also subject to shifting world conditions, repositioned within what Roland Robertson (1992) called "glocality" or what Kevin Robins (1991) termed "the global-local nexus." This concept addresses diverse and fluid cultural influences and sensibilities that are exerted at the level of scale. As Robins wrote,

> Globalization is, in fact, also associated with new dynamics of re-localization. It is about the achievement of a new global-local nexus.... It is important to see the local as a relational, and relative, concept. If once it was significant in relation to the national sphere, now its meaning is being recast in the context of globalization. (pp. 34–35)

Geocultural scales converge in unprecedented ways today due to both human endeavor (i.e., travel and migration) and electronic technological capabilities. The pronounced emphasis on the local, expressed in celebratory or defensive modes, is matched by equally assertive emphases on global phenomena. We seem to exist simultaneously in two realms, fully conscious of our place in the local environment and increasingly cognizant of our status within the larger global frame.

Hip-hop has been harnessed in the construction of new cultural identities within this global-local nexus. This can be witnessed in countless cases, such as when Somali refugee and immigrant teens (Forman, 2001), Ghaniain youths, or Cape Verdean youths arrive in the United States. These youths generally claim limited "cultural capital" in relation to international media and artistic repertoires, yet they are instantly exposed to a complex range of ideas and experiences that require radically different cultural maps from those of their homeland or those presented by their parents, teachers, or other adult authorities.

These youths generally have no historical sense of North American cultural politics and lack familiarity with race, identity, and difference in North American contexts. Moreover, they have never explicitly conceived of themselves as *Black youth*, yet the institutional forces of North American society rapidly locate them within this racialized identity position. They are forced to engage in the self-aware processes of renegotiating their individual and collective identities, and they do so by many means: watching television and music videos, carefully observing the sartorial codes of their classmates and neighbors, developing new "westernized" cultural tastes and consumer patterns, or even developing new linguistic and rhetorical abilities, including a facility with the hip-hop slang of the day.

It can be observed, however, that hip-hop constitutes a hegemonic influence; there is no other cultural form that competes with it for authority in relation to teen expression or taste among Black and Latino youth. It is the unchallenged cultural dominant. Demonstrating a creative approach that is consistent with hip-hop practice, teen refugees from around the world engage in extensive "sampling" of cultural forms and commodities once in the United States, learning to read and interpret the codes and signs through which their Black and Latino peers communicate. They subsequently observe with great care the myriad performative modes of other youths, experiencing the dynamics of teen culture and the codified distinctions of subcultural difference.

Identifying the importance of performativity, Manthia Diawara (1993) suggested that the creative element of identity performance "involves an individual or group of people interpreting an existing tradition—reinventing themselves—in front of an audience or public; and that black agency in the U.S. involves the redefinitions of the tools of Americanness" (p. 265).

Taking cues from those surrounding them, these teens develop creative strategies of identity performance and transformation, working within the systems of youth-oriented style and meaning as a method of fitting in while drawing on their unique and unfortunate experience of the world. This corresponds with Arjun Appadurai's (1996) suggestion:

> Electronic mediation and mass migration mark the world of the present not as technically new force[s], but as ones that seem to impel (and sometimes compel) the work of the imagination. Together, they create specific irregularities because both viewers and images are in simultaneous motion ... both persons and images often meet unpredictably, outside the certainties of home and the cordon sanitaire of local and national media effects. (p. 4)

As I have already indicated, hip-hop's most vital and creative minds show an impressive propensity with what I call the *re*: This covers the *re* in concepts like *re*mix, *re*wind, *re*contextualize, *re*invent, *re*iterate, and *re*peat, and perhaps even *re*consider and *re*spond. In a discussion of immigrant and refugee youth, this emerges within a complex and rapid process of identity *re*vision, a process of cultural *re*definition or *re*newal, for as Dyson (2007) noted, "[H]ip-hop is able to renew its intellectual identity when it begins to forge alliances with the cultural expression of degraded and oppressed people around the world" (pp. 49–50).

African immigrant and refugee teens quickly recognize that hip-hop establishes many of the norms and values currently defining "authentic" Black identity among youths, and, moreover, they quickly determine that these informal (i.e., noninstitutionally grounded) articulations of blackness are organized alternatively and often in radical opposition to the formally structured discourses of race and nation. Through hip-hop, these youths adopt the mantle of blackness, consciously and unconsciously adapting the dominant codes of North American Black youth culture in the formation of their own evolving teen identities (Forman, 2001).

Style and the body are obviously essential facets of this creative transformative process. Herman Gray (1995) observed that "within the mediascape of contemporary consumer culture, black youth constantly use the body, self-adornment, movement, language, and music to construct and locate themselves socially and culturally" (p. 149). Visual style produces interesting cultural hybrids: African Muslim teenage girls, for example, display a sartorial blend of traditional garb (such as the hijab or clan robes) and hip-hop street wear. Among Somali males who are most explicitly aligned with the hip-hop culture, rugged camouflage sportswear, commonly displayed in hip-hop magazines and music videos, is very popular. Yet for these young men, camouflage has dual significance: It allows them to conform to the style statements of other hip-hop-identified teens who wear similar gear, but it also maintains a continuity with the military attire that is common among fighting men in the militias and clan forces of the Somali capital, Mogadishu. These sartorial tendencies are part of a highly creative and symbolically loaded performance—what British cultural studies theorist Paul Willis (Willis, Jones, Canaan, & Hurd, 1990) referred to as "symbolic creativity" and Dick Hebdige (1979) described as "semiotic guerilla warfare"— that is enacted within the global-local nexus and that cannot easily be dismissed as a mere fad.

Though it was a slow process (due to clear linguistic barriers), immigrant and refugee youths from around the world have also gradually taken up the microphone in their new cultural environments, articulating their transnational and hybrid identities through hip-hop and rap's unique cadences. John Shepherd (1993) suggested that music is particularly well suited to such creative expressivity:

> Music is ideally suited to coding homologously, and therefore to evoking powerfully yet symbolically ... because music can enter, grip, and position us symbolically, it can act powerfully to structure and mediate individual awareness as the ultimate seat of social and cultural reproduction. (p. 52)

Among the very few successful Somali MCs is Toronto-based artist K'naan, whose work (such as the track "Soobox") deftly navigates his status as a refugee from a war-torn country while asserting his reputation as an engaged citizen and rising artist in Canada and on the world stage. He laments the fact that militia and warlords have forced him and thousands of other Somalis into a state of global wandering and unchosen refugee status, and he seeks to reconcile his hopes for peace within the contexts of seemingly enduring violence in his homeland and in the tough neighborhoods of his new nation of residence. K'naan consequently exists as a dispersed subject, but hip-hop has transformed the character of his trek while providing both a creative source of inspiration and a powerful mode of articulation. Now, through international concert tours, CD sales, and an Internet presence, his words and ideologies circulate in the global mediascape, continuing in a kind of motion that reflects his own human trajectory through deadly war-torn territories, refugee camps, and safe nations.

CREATIVITY AND THE CULTURE INDUSTRIES

Discussion of professionalization leads inevitably to the issue of creativity and the culture industries. American cultural critic Greg Tate (2004) suggested that, with hip-hop entering its fourth decade of existence, we are witnessing "the marriage of heaven and hell, of New World African ingenuity and that trick of the devil known as global capitalism … what we call hip-hop is now inseparable from what we call the hip-hop industry." Tate's jaundiced view is not rare among hip-hop's most ardent aficionados (or perhaps among artists more generally) who perceive the commercialization of culture as a worrisome development. Capital is indeed a powerful force, and like so many cultural and artistic movements before it, hip-hop and its cultural producers have struggled to find a balance between commercial success and cooptation.

The issue is generally framed in a relatively simple way between the poles of incorporation and resistance, where exploitative commercial enterprises (of the media and entertainment sectors) are said to exert a negative influence on hip-hop's character and direction, steering it away from its ostensibly "authentic" and organic roots in the street or in the 'hood toward the social mainstream and the market.

Notwithstanding claims to an idealized moment when hip-hop was said to exist outside of the commercial realm and was, thus, more "pure," the fact remains that hip-hop has essentially been commodified from the very beginning, when savvy entrepreneurs and artists first realized that there was a market for their labors and their wares; ghetto commerce remains active commerce. Still, it matters greatly whose vision is guiding hip-hop's artistic, commercial, and corporate development and who the primary beneficiaries are. One of the biggest crises articulated by critics who speak out against hip-hop's commercialization focuses on corporate indifference to Black cultural traditions and the willingness to ignore hip-hop's status within a deep and meaningful cultural legacy. In this argument, commercial or corporate hip-hop is derided as being inauthentic or tainted, subject to the whims of an industry populated by White executives and a market that is dominated by White consumer tastes—the common estimate being that 70% to 80% of all hip-hop product is sold to White consumers who have no direct stakes in Black culture.

In the late 1980s and early 1990s, an era often termed the "golden era" of hip-hop by those in their mid-30s or older, multiple musical subgenres coexisted and succeeded in the hip-hop market, often produced and distributed by independent, Black-owned record labels. In this period, the industry and artists alike benefited from a generic diversity and broad aesthetic creativity. In this same general period, we also saw the rise of a new generation of young Black filmmakers, such as Spike Lee and John Singleton, who were deeply influenced by the hip-hop culture surrounding them, directing now classic hip-hop films such as *Do the Right Thing* (1989) and *Boyz 'N the Hood* (1991) that reflected the hip-hop way of life among youth in Brooklyn and South Central L.A., respectively. For a brief moment, the collaborative relations between independent and major entertainment corporations actually nurtured and reinforced the conditions of hip-hop's artistic creativity.

At this same general time, however, global media, entertainment, and fashion conglomerates stepped into hip-hop with new rigor, accelerating the processes of mainstreaming the music, style, and attitude that had, to this point, been mostly incidental to mainstream society. This trend had several unusual effects; for example, after we had encountered a rapping Pillsbury doughboy or a break-dancing Ronald McDonald on late-1980s television, the media helped to amplify new hip-hop terminology and style among various social groups. Suddenly investment bankers or demure schoolteachers could be heard describing their middle- or upper-middle-class neighborhoods as "the 'hood," and, more recently, *bling* exploded in the mainstream as a term used to describe expensive watches, jewelry, and other bright, shiny accessories.

Perhaps the most explicit comments on the subject declare that commercial enterprise has delimited hip-hop's creativity, narrowing the range of expression and cultural articulation due to formulaic market-directed demands. There is ample evidence of the power of the market to establish dominant artistic forms and content. Yvonne Bynoe (2004) wrote,

The record companies encourage these young people to tell their ghetto tales (real or imagined) in the crudest fashion for predominantly White rap CD buyers…. What the music industry has done through rap music is to frame the "authentic" Black American not as a complex, educated or even creative individual, but as a "real nigga" who has ducked bullets, worked a triple beam, and done at least one bid in prison. (p. 149)

When commercial and corporate forces dictate that particular subgenres (such as gangsta rap) are easiest to promote and sell, there will undoubtedly be a creative contingent that will produce exactly that. It is folly to disregard the ways that commerce and the allure of economic rewards can influence and at times alter or dilute hip-hop's artistic output. That said, artists, especially those who emerge from adverse conditions or abject poverty, are not to be simply castigated for pursuing the economic rewards that can accrue in the market; for a unique and important dose of reality, I point to Beanie Siegel's "I Can't Go on This Way," a heart-wrenching description of a man's stress and anxiety about incarceration and tribulations with the criminal justice system, the efforts to support his children, his lack of health care insurance, as well as his difficulties with debilitating hypertension and asthma. We might regard this as the flip side to the glorification of ostentatious consumption and "bling" excesses.

It is not that creativity has stalled or that hip-hop has become monolithic (despite the title of the 2007 CD release by Nas proclaiming *Hip-Hop Is Dead*), but the current outcome of this market-driven trend, especially concerning rap music and the recording industry, is a reduced aesthetic. It is not insignificant that, since the early 1990s, the once prominent expression of radical political ideology, pro-Black cultural themes, and communitarian ideals have been seriously displaced (though not absolutely replaced) by narratives and images associated with "gangstas," "pimpin'," or "thug life." Those artists in the United States who are most explicitly identified with the more prosocial and politically engaged themes of the "conscious rap" subgenre (including Bahamadia, Common, the Coup, Dead Prez, Mos Def, the Roots, or Talib Kweli) are generally relegated to the underground or noncommercial, nonmainstream realm. They are, however, very popular among White audiences on university and college campuses, much to their own dismay.

This is not to outright invalidate the expressive and artistic qualities of gangsta rap or the southern party subgenre associated with Atlanta, Houston, or New Orleans, but it does require careful analysis to determine how this should be understood within the larger frame of hip-hop's cultural creativity. It also begs the question of what other forms of artistic expression, what other themes and modes of cultural imagination, are being marginalized. The artists' continual alignment with hip-hop as a culture—and as a whole way of life—is essential here. If success is achieved in the commercial mainstream, then the "true" hip-hop artist must always ensure that he or she maintains and furthers the influences of hip-hop's foundational elements, sacrificing nothing in the exchange "between the street and the executive suite" (Negus, 1999). Additionally, authenticity in hip-hop is associated with a focused critical perspective and the unyielding articulation of themes of resistance.

One positive aspect of the mainstreaming of hip-hop and the intervention of major transnational corporations is that the sounds and images of U.S. hip-hop have, over roughly the past 15 years, circulated to youth worldwide. Today, hip-hop is as much a part of daily 'hood life and everyday experience for youths in the favelas of Rio de Janeiro, the barrios of Bogotá or Caracas, or the cinderblock housing throughout Europe's major urban centers as it is in our cities here in the United States. From a creative and artistic standpoint, the global diffusion of hip-hop has also presented myriad opportunities for cultural cross-pollination and the intermingling of indigenous art with global forms and style. For instance, the Orishas, a Cuban rap group now based in Paris, prominently merge standard hip-hop beats with the rhythms of Latin son and salsa, lyrically invoking Cuba's religion and politics and employing snippets of English and French with their Spanish. Brazilian rap acts have been known to include the sonic boom of the samba drum in their composition, and Canadian Aboriginal MCs accommodate the Indian heartbeat drum that is at the core of their tribal gatherings. In these cases, postmodern digital technologies produced by transnational electronics firms are strategically deployed by hip-hop's organic intellectuals, facilitating both collision and correspondence with deeper cultural traditions.

Of further interest are the ways in which hip-hop has evolved as the lingua franca of social protest and struggle around the world. Chuck D of Public Enemy refers to the deliberate creative objectives to produce "noise," "turbulence," "chaos," and "rage" as a means of cultural-political disruption. These are not empty or idle concepts for the politicized MC but stand as a fierce call to consciousness. Politicized and culturally "conscious" hip-hop seeks to awaken an ostensibly complacent constituency via the creative expression of challenging ideological concepts. In many national contexts, this is among the first applications of hip-hop aesthetics, strategically mobilized as a component of wider social protest movements by disenfranchised youth.

In another compelling example, according to Usama Kahf (2007), "Hip hop is appropriated and transformed by local artists in different parts of the world who are searching for emancipatory and empowering avenues of expression in the midst of a reality that continues to shut doors in their faces" (p. 359). Kahf, who has written about hip-hop and social protest among Arabic youth in Palestine and Israel, has seen hip-hop as a nontraditional yet highly effective force in the articulation of political and cultural identities among Middle Eastern youths whose voices are often marginalized within rigid old-guard political structures. As the 2003 documentary film *Channels of Rage* (directed by Arotzim Shel Za'am) or *Slingshot Hip-Hop* from 2006 (directed by Jackie Salloum) each reveal, Middle Eastern youth protest and the rhetoric of conflict and resistance are increasingly arrayed within the forms and patterns of hip-hop. Israeli and Palestinian MCs rap in their native tongues, addressing political tensions from regional and local perspectives, and winning support and respect from their peers for their capacity to frame conflict in powerful discursive frameworks.

No corporate opportunist or capitalist exploiter could ever have predicted such an outcome. It seems that the forceful images and discourses of radical political opposition that were started in the United States have been sustained in the global context in ways that they have not always been in the United States, despite the efforts of chronically underfunded and struggling North American "'hood workers," those hip-hop-identified men and women who attempt to reach disenfranchised, gang-affiliated, or "at-risk" youth through hip-hop after-school programs at community centers or teen agencies. Let us not forget that hip-hop provided the soundtrack to the social protest enacted by immigrant and other disenfranchised youths in the *banlieues* of France in 2005. Similarly, the development of teen centers and community action networks that actively resist police harassment and state violence in the urban favelas in Brazil is also commonly organized in direct consultation with the local hip-hop or Afro-Reggae crews, as depicted in the 2005 documentary film *Favela Rising* (directed by Jeff Zimbalist and Matt Mochary). These locally resonant and highly politicized developments are an indirect result of the commercialization and global distribution of hip-hop art and culture.

HIP-HOP CREATIVITY: NOT JUST A YOUTH ISSUE

The majority of North American youth today know only a world where hip-hop exists as a viable means of cultural expression and a robust facet of the commercial entertainment industries. The shifts and changes in creative orientations, approaches, and aesthetics are primarily generationally driven as new artists synthesize hip-hop's past traditions, building on the foundations and expanding the contours of what can be done and, more importantly, what can be imagined within a hip-hop sensibility. In Boyd's (2002) assessment,

> [W]e have a generation of Black people, now defined by the many strands that emerge most visibly through hip-hop culture, who have decided to take what they want from the mainstream, while leaving behind what they do not care to embrace. (p. 10)

Yet the parent generation continues a disheartening tendency to invalidate the creative talents and pursuits of the young. Encompassing social elders in his assessment of contemporary hip-hop, Greg Tate observed that "people are still very much afraid of this culture and who it represents, no matter how commodified and blinged-out it seems to have become" (Tate, Prashad, Neal, & Cross, 2006, p. 36).

Age in hip-hop, thus, emerges as a factor that creates an interesting turbulence and warrants some discussion in relation to creativity. The term "generational 'playa hatin'," or *player hating* (Boyd, 2002, p. 12), has been coined to describe the condescending attitudes exhibited by parents, teachers, cultural critics, and even veteran musical artists (such as Dionne Warwick) who deride hip-hop's artistic innovations and its popularity, dismissing it somewhat nonchalantly as a mere case of collective poor taste among undiscriminating and impressionable youth.

Politicians and other civic leaders frequently criticize members of the hip-hop generation for abdicating their responsibilities as engaged citizens, for discounting many of the political lessons they learned from their elders who struggled in the Civil Rights Movement, and even for their ostensibly slovenly and disrespectful sartorial preferences (Bill Cosby is noteworthy, though not unique in this latter regard, taking particular umbrage at the hip-hop style of low-slung "sagging" pants). Style and the sounds and practices of the culture have led to instances of race and youth profiling by police, school authorities, and others who harbor unfounded assumptions of nefarious activity associated with hip-hop.

Many youths affiliated with hip-hop culture and politics defy these perspectives, however. Todd Boyd (2002) asserted that we are now witnessing "the death of civil rights and the reign of hip-hop," adopting the general themes of Bob Dylan's influential 1964 track "The Times, They Are A-Changin'" when he argued that "we cannot live in the past forever. Civil rights had its day; now it is time to move out of the way" (p. 152). It is with urgency that I state: Adults simply must come to terms with the practices, values, and ideals of this youth generation if they ever hope to recognize the political and cultural stakes involved and take pleasure in the creative production that occurs within the hip-hop culture. In this regard, it is worth quoting hip-hop analyst and cultural commentator Bakari Kitwana (2002), who wrote at length about what he termed "the hip-hop generation":

> Young Blacks, like most Americans, when given the opportunity to work, have demonstrated their willingness to do so.... Many ... work more than one job. Some supplement their low-wage, no-benefits job with some sort of underground economy hustle, adding even more hours to an already long workday.... Rappers from working-poor backgrounds often work long hours in recording studios, giving concerts, making music videos, and so on. Aspiring and self-published rappers selling their CDs in local and regional markets do the same. With rap music as a concrete and legitimate employment option, they have something to believe in and are working in an area where they receive a sense of personal worth and satisfaction. (pp. 46–47)

Still, even within hip-hop culture itself, there is undeniable evidence of generational dissonance creeping between those who are now in their late 30s, 40s, or early 50s and those in their teens and 20s, some of whom already have their own children (giving rise to the reality of the hip-hop grandparent). To give a sense of this age gap, consider for a moment that among hip-hop's so-called founding fathers, Grandmaster Flash was born in 1958 and DJ Kool Herc's birth date is 1952. Gray hair tinges the domes of many an elder hip-hop "head." For the elder contingent there is an unfortunate tendency to romanticize and valorize hip-hop's early years or its "golden age," referring longingly to conditions "back in the day" when things were supposedly more exciting, when creativity was at its peak, and when there was more peace and unity across the hip-hop culture. Of course, with time, the meaning of "back in the day" becomes less fixed and certain, sliding along the scale of age and experience as each generation reimagines its own past. Hip-hop's veterans and pioneers consistently seek to recuperate the values and practices from this earlier moment (often, but not always, nostalgically), whereas the youths ostensibly operate according to the powerful dictates of the market and within the cultural dynamics of the moment, of a pervasive and encompassing "now." There may be inbuilt truths in such perspectives, but it is equally true that such perspectives capture only a portion of the story.

Sheila Whitely (2005) noted that "age is critical to the identity of both performers and musical genres" (p. 16), and we can easily see how the varied entertainment and media sectors explicitly summon age and temporality when they identify cultural texts in generic terms as classics, oldies, and standards, creating chronological subgenres into which creative output is slotted. Even as place and spatiality are powerful inflections throughout hip-hop culture, the past is also increasingly marked as a distinct factor within the definitional term *old school*. The term is slapped onto reissued catalogue material recorded by pioneering rap acts and applied to their "old-school" concert tours; it is used to describe certain aesthetic styles or is employed in artistic retrospectives of graffiti artists, b-boy demonstrations, or public lectures by members of the original breaking crews, and for screenings of such now "classic" hip-hop films such as *Wildstyle* (directed by Charlie Ahearn) or *Style Wars* (directed by Harry Chalfant and Tony Silver), each produced in 1982.

In these situations, the original creativity associated with the artistic output of earlier historical moments is isolated, recontextualized, and repackaged for sale and consumption among both old and young hip-hop aficionados. At their best, however, and sidestepping simple nostalgia, they can also serve as educational tools, facilitating a deeper understanding among today's youth about how various creative practices evolved, what the struggles among hip-hop's cultural workers entailed at specific moments and within particular conditions, and how the past continually informs the hip-hop practices of the present.

According to age theorist Margaret Morganroth Gullette (2004), in today's society "ageing equals decline" (p. 7). "Humans," Gullete asserted, "are aged by culture" (p. 12). She cited the influence of what she termed "decline narratives" that are widely circulated and, in their diffusion, function within a powerful discourse of ageism. In hip-hop, as young creative artists working within the various elements develop both skill and confidence, they often employ the derogatory expression "falling off" to describe the corresponding notion of decline in creative innovation and skill, expressive capability, or market clout among older veteran artists. This age-oriented critique mobilizes an unambiguously dismissive discourse of decline, addressing the perceived inability of older cultural workers to stay abreast of current trends and practices. In the specific case of b-boys and b-girls, we might also include the reality of age-related physical limitations that curtail the capacity to perform sensational athletic break-dancing moves.

Deployed by younger hip-hop artists, the discourse of decline is wielded as a challenge to those who came before, the young lions confronting the "O.G.s," who may once have been idealized in hip-hop parlance as *original gangstas* but are now derisively scorned as *old goats*. We are seeing older hip-hop artists taking their age seriously, however, articulating their status as adults through the various hip-hop elements not only as a method of defining a transitional process in their own life cycles but also as a means of distinguishing themselves from the crop of "new jacks" who are emerging onto the hip-hop scene in significant numbers. In many of these cases, the discourse of age is intended to positively demarcate experience and professionalism and to separate the veterans from those hopefuls who are new to the game, whose skills are unproven, and who have no claim on career longevity.

This creates some interesting and entertaining results, especially in hip-hop's time-honored tradition of the "battle"; the popular upstart Nelly, for instance, explicitly criticized veteran MC KRS-1 within the discourse of age and decline when he uttered, "[Y]ou the first old man who should get a rapper's pension / no hit since the cordless mic invention." KRS-1's appropriately dismissive reply maintained the theme of age, creativity, and experience, inviting Nelly to come back and challenge him when he also has 10 albums under his belt, explaining that flavor-of-the-month commercial rap hits do not automatically equate with cultural status and respect in the hip-hop culture.

In another instance, Cam'ron, a relatively minor figure in the rap industry, assailed the hip-hop superstar Jay-Z for his age, improbably accusing him of "pushing forty." He then attacked Jay-Z for dressing like the 37-year-old man that he is, ridiculing him for wearing fashions that indicate a "falling off" and, in masculine terms, a softening of the veteran's macho urban edge. Yet Jay-Z embraces the ageing process, repeatedly referring to himself as "a grown man" who, having ascended the celebrity and economic ranks, no longer feels comfortable wearing the casual sports gear associated with his youth. He is frequently pictured in expensive designer suits, and his successful fashion line, Roca Wear, also reflects this new grown-up attitude with the introduction of stylish button-down shirts and men's suits designed for an ageing hip-hop consumer base. On his track "My First Song," Jay-Z exclaims, "I'm about to go golfing man, I might even have me a cappuccino," admitting with typical humor and self-awareness that he has evolved as a man and is subsequently attuned to a quite different set of bourgeois options and adult priorities.

Established Houston MC Scarface, a contemporary of Jay-Z and KRS-1, makes a preemptive statement on the track "Big Dog Status" where he recounts his longevity as a hip-hop innovator, declaring his experience and professional bona fides as both a statement of fact and as a challenge to younger rappers. In his more recent creative oeuvre, Scarface urgently testifies to his age and personal development, citing his origins and sustained alignments with his urban 'hood formation while reflecting in a staggeringly revealing manner on issues ranging from fatherhood to success, age, and mortality.

CONCLUSION

This chapter is an attempt to provide some insight onto this unwieldy set of cultural practices and attitudes called *hip-hop* and the ways that it is implicated in creativity, art, and human development. There are stakes involved, and I would argue that the stakes are quite urgent. In the United States and, increasingly, in many other international urban contexts, hip-hop constitutes a prominent cultural realm where themes of racial politics, social identities, and issues of equal rights and justice are addressed head on and without compromise. It is in and through hip-hop's creative forms of expression that the guiding ideologies of an entire generation are being established, tested, and defined, for better and, at times, for worse. The artistic and creative labor of hip-hop's core producers exceeds mere entertainment, and it surpasses the negativity for which hip-hop is often most aggressively castigated and challenged.

It is essential that hip-hop's elaborated qualities and its progressive potentials be understood and acknowledged by cultural authorities and members of the parent population if we expect to fully comprehend the actions and mode of being among many urban youths today. There is really no stage in its entire history when this country could afford to ignore the voices and creative cultural expression emanating from its Black citizenry or from the socially disenfranchised; many of hip-hop's wily young innovators are both. As hip-hop is taken up and fiercely defended by Turkish youth in Germany, by Arab and North African youth in France, by Maori or Aboriginal youth in New Zealand and Australia, by ethnically disenfranchised Roma-Gypsy youth in the Czech Republic, and by the urban poor everywhere, it is evident that it offers a powerful and effective means for the articulation of hope and fear, and of struggle and victory, and the declarations of hate and of profound, enduring love. Let that last word, *love*, resound if for no other reason than it is so infrequently associated in the public sphere with hip-hop and its creative minds. Hip-hop: Can't stop, won't stop.

NOTES

1. For a thorough and enlightening monograph detailing hip-hop and the creative arts, see Chang (2006).

2. Defining "artscience," Edwards (2008) wrote, "There may be aesthetic aims that require application or understanding of the scientific method.... Or there may be scientific aims that require application or understanding of the aesthetic method.... Either way, the fused method that results, at once aesthetic and scientific—intuitive and deductive, sensual and analytical, comfortable with uncertainty and able to frame a problem, embracing nature in its complexity and able to simplify nature in its essence—is what I call *artscience*" (pp. 6–7).

REFERENCES

Appadurai, A. (1996). *Modernity at large: Cultural dimensions of globalization.* Minneapolis: University of Minnesota Press.

Boyd. T. (2002). *The New H.N.I.C.: The death of civil rights and the reign of hip hop.* New York: New York University Press.

Bynoe, Y. (2004). *Stand and deliver: Political activism, leadership, and hip hop culture.* Brooklyn: Soft Skull Press.

Chang, J. (2005). *Can't stop won't stop: A history of the hip-hop generation.* New York: St. Martin's.

Chang, J. (Ed.). (2006). *Total chaos: The art and aesthetics of hip-hop.* New York: Basic Civitas.

Diawara, M. (1993). Black studies, cultural studies: Performance acts. In *Border/ Lines: Canada's Magazine of Cultural Studies, 29*(30), 21–26.

Dyson, M. E. (2007). *Know what I mean? Reflections on hip hop.* New York: Basic Civitas.

Edwards, D. (2008). *Artscience: Creativity in the post-Google generation.* Cambridge, MA: Harvard University Press.

Forman, M. (2001). Straight outta Mogadishu: Prescribed identities and performative practices among Somali youth in North American high schools. *Topia, 5,* 33.

Forman, M. (2002). *The 'hood' comes first: Race, space, and place in rap and hip hop.* Middletown, CT: Wesleyan University Press.

Gray, H. (1995). *Watching race: Television and the struggle for "blackness."* Minneapolis: University of Minnesota Press.

Gullette, M. M. (2004). *Aged by culture.* Chicago: University of Chicago Press.

Hebdige, D. (1979). *Subculture: The meaning of style.* New York: Methuen.

Kahf, U. (2007). Arabic hip hop: Claims of authenticity and identity of a new genre. *Journal of Popular Music Studies, 19*(4), 359–385.

Kitwana, B. (2002). *The hip-hop generation: Young Blacks and the crisis in African-American culture.* New York: Basic Civitas.

Lee, S. (Dir.). (1989). *Do the right thing.* New York: 40 Acres & a Mule Filmworks.

Negus, K. (1999). The music business and rap: Between the street and the executive suite. *Cultural Studies, 13*(3), 488–508.

Robertson, R. (1992). *Globalisation, social theory, and global culture.* Thousands Oaks, CA: Sage.

Robins, K. (1991). Tradition and translation: National culture in its global context. In J. Corner & S. Harvey (Eds.), *Enterprise and heritage: Crosscurrents of national culture.* New York: Routledge.

Rose, T. (1997). Cultural survivalisms and marketplace subversions: Black popular culture and politics into the twenty-first century. In J. Adjaye & A. Andrews (Eds.), *Language, rhythm, and sound: Black popular cultures into the twenty-first century.* Pittsburgh, PA: University of Pittsburgh Press.

Runco, M. (2004). Creativity. *Annual Review of Psychology, 55,* 657–687.

Salloum, J. (Dir.). (2005). *Slingshot hip-hop.* Farmington Hills, MI: Fresh Booza Productions.

Shel Za'am, A. (Dir.). (2003). *Channels of rage.* Tel Aviv: Anat Alachmi Film.

Shepherd, J. (1993). Difference and power in music. In R. A. Solie (Ed.), *Musicology and difference: Gender and sexuality in music scholarship.* Berkeley: University of California Press.

Singleton, J. (Dir.). (1991). *Boyz 'N the Hood.* Los Angeles: Columbia Pictures.

Tate, G. (2004, December 28). Hip-hop turns 30: Watcha' celebratin' for? *Village Voice.*

Tate, G., Prashad, V., Neal, M. A., & Cross, B. (2006). Got next: A roundtable on identity and aesthetics after multiculturalism. In J. Chang (Ed.), *Total chaos: The art and aesthetics of hip-hop.* New York: Basic Civitas.

Toynbee, J. (2007). *Bob Marley.* Malden, MA: Polity.

Whitely, S. (2005). *Too much, too young: Popular music, age and gender.* New York: Routledge.

Williams, R. (1981). *Culture.* London: Fontana.

Willis, P., Jones, S., Canaan, J., & Hurd, G. (1990). *Common culture: Symbolic work at play in the everyday cultures of the young.* Boulder, CO: Westview Press.

Zimbalist, J., & Mochary, M. (Dirs.). (2005). *Favela rising.* New York: All Rise LLC.

5

COMMENTARY

Hip-Hop Culture, Youth Creativity, and the Generational Crossroads From a Human Development Perspective

Brian Tinsley, Shaun Wilson, and Margaret Beale Spencer

INTRODUCTION AND HISTORY

Music is an essential component of life for many and represents a critical vehicle for meaning making and self-representation. As a specific art form, it communicates thoughts, feelings, reactions, and perspectives about noteworthy issues. For many, it allows for the relief of stress; it encourages celebration among others; and for some, it serves as the soundtrack for social and political protest. People from various nationalities, cultural traditions, and ethnic backgrounds may connect through music even though not sharing the same language (Crozier, 1997). The functions of music are endless and, in fact, include and contribute to the identity formation process of individuals as well as groups of people (e.g., a society's youth). Since its emergence in the 1970s, hip-hop music has amassed an international and significant following. Created in the musical underground of the South Bronx, the genre began capturing broad recognition throughout the mid-1980s and continues to grow in popularity (Chang, 2005). Still, many criticize this powerful musical entity for its mainstreamed explicit misogynistic lyrics and suggestive romanticizing of violence. Frequently, the whole of hip-hop is accused of downplaying the importance of family, community, and formal education. These charges abound, whereas others note the complexity and diversity within the genre and acknowledge its popularity among young people across the globe. Thus, for many, this is the basis to take a deeper look at what hip-hop means and represents for adolescents and those concerned with positive youth development.

A critical exploration of hip-hop culture's relationship to youth development provides an important insight concerning why and how youth co-construct and interpret their identity as a function of their experiences. In addition, these experiences are marked by a period of development during which changes in cognitive abilities, social awareness, and physical makeup influence how adolescents interpret feedback from and engage with others. Although this engagement may include a preoccupation with others' perspectives, it can also include a great deal of introspection, reflection, construction, and general analysis of how one fits into the world as both a local and global citizen. According to Spencer and Markstrom-Adams (1990), the idea of identity—and by extension citizenry—may prove especially difficult for some ethnic and racial minorities who differ by national origin, skin color, or other physical features and often confront unique context-associated challenges and biases. However, Spencer (1995) asserted that it is insufficient to focus narrowly on environmental effects and youth outcomes without also examining *how* youth process attitudes expressed and evaluative beliefs communicated about their ethnic and racial groups.

In his review of hip-hop's bidirectional links with cultural identity, Forman underscores the character of these links by highlighting the experiences of many youth of the African diaspora (e.g., Ghanaians and Cape Verdeans) who arrive in the United States and are quickly exposed to ideas imposed about themselves based primarily on their phenotypic traits. Forman asserts that many of them are unfamiliar with North American policies and the racial dynamics therein. Although this may be true for some who lack access to broad forms of media in their nations of origin, global access to the Internet has influenced exposure to the United States' racial dynamics and introduces many immigrants to the nation's cultural idiosyncrasies before they arrive on American soil. Nevertheless, for the two groups specified, a renegotiation of identities takes place as they are inundated with cues from television, videos, magazines, and peers. Thus, many experience a forced classification as "Black," often without regard to their unique ethnic backgrounds. The psychosocial dilemma unavoidably prompts a measure of self-reflection. Accordingly, it is not coincidental that many of the youth noted, in fact, belong to the very ethnic groups who contributed to hip-hop's inception. Experiences of dual or multiple ethnic-cultural identities continue to manifest through the lyrics of hip-hop artists of immigrant descent such as Wyclef Jean. Thus, the underexamined yet salient experiences with ethnicity, race, and cultural influences suggest the need to critically examine hip-hop's potential to empower youth.

Personal identity is an individual's unique qualities, attributes, and values, reflecting one's personal history cumulatively accrued in multiple settings. It develops throughout life and is influenced by numerous social messages concerning what constitutes normalcy. Music, therefore, provides an outlet for youths' examination and expression of personal identity. This may be achieved through composing, playing, or simply listening to and valuing a unique music genre generally independent of adults' appreciation. Zillmann and Gan (1997) maintained that it is during adolescence that individuals develop their strongest bond with music and become serious consumers of it. Some researchers have further asserted that the ability of music to address pertinent developmental issues adds to its appeal (Bleich, Zillmann, & Weaver, 1991; Larson & Kubey, 1983). These developmental themes include youths' acquisition of beliefs, values, socially responsible behaviors, and emotional independence. According to Erikson (1968) and Marcia (1980), adolescence is a time during which youth consider beliefs and explore possible identities for the *self*. Although Erikson might have characterized this process as an identity crisis, Forman asserts the period's function as one of identity exploration (i.e., in this case, through role performance and transformation). Each continues to serve a unique function in the complexity of what is known as hip-hop. When discussing what constitutes normalcy, it is impossible to ignore and not recognize the fact that the very experiences considered by most as deficit laced have contributed to the richness of hip-hop. Nevertheless, hip-hop may assist youths' efforts to take ownership of their identity processes and challenge inconsistencies frequently associated with life in their communities (e.g., structural inequality or oppressive conditions).

Fundamentally, Forman's chapter effectively relays the widely accepted idea that hip-hop is an exemplar illustration of human artistic expression. It, indeed, manifested in response to specific social, economic, technological, and cultural influences, which were largely presented as obstacles to the positive development of *self* for many youth. Evoking the prominent four elements that compose hip-hop artistry (graffiti, break dancing, deejaying, and emceeing), Forman notes that hip-hop is largely used to transmit messages that promote mutual encouragement, in-group competition, and praise of expertise (i.e., contributors to positive youth development). Forman explicates the idea that youth are "fully conscious of [their] place in their local environment and increasingly cognizant of [their] status with the larger global frame" while also recognizing that hip-hop is a means of establishing an individual's identity relative to the surrounding environment.

Efforts made to understand the experiences of our youth allow for greater levels of communication, particularly intergenerational exchange. Additionally, it is imperative to understand how to address these experiences in nondemonizing ways and to highlight normal human development–promoting factors in hip-hop that stand to facilitate positive youth experiences and development. In many ways, given the often underacknowledged and hostile climates of youths' developmental context as poignantly and classically described by Chestang (1972), hip-hop may, for some, facilitate resiliency (i.e., good outcomes achieved in the face of significant challenge; see Spencer, 1995, 2005, 2006b, 2008; Spencer, Fegley, & Harpalani, 2003). That is, although there may exist particular consequences for a subset who infer too literally, hip-hop may afford intended proactive coping responses for many young people struggling under chronically harsh socio-politico-emotional climates around the globe. Thus, in this chapter as approached from a normal human development point of view, we frame the components used to construct hip-hop as well as illuminate the impact of hip-hop on its audience(s) from a youth coping and identity formation perspective. This exercise is designed to further explain and interpret the attractiveness of hip-hop and its potential benefit to the many youth who seek to be a part of it and, thus, benefit from the identification.

A DEVELOPMENTAL PERSPECTIVE

When thinking about the complex situations that youth face, important factors that influence perceptions and provide sources of support are frequently ignored. For example, contextual experiences, distinguishing cultural or physical characteristics (e.g., skin color) and associated stereotyping, in addition to available supports (e.g., socioeconomic status, including both levels of privilege as well as varied representations of risk) can influence not only how individuals are perceived but also, as a response, how humans perceive the world around them. Acknowledging and taking into account diverse points of view and experiences can improve one's ability to understand youths' evolving sense of purpose, achievement motivations, varied social behaviors, coping needs, and aesthetic tastes.

As a form of art, hip-hop serves as a forum by which individuals can actively express various dimensions of creativity. Thus, for many youth who come of age in environments riddled with social challenges and inadequate supports, hip-hop may provide a means of coping with the various elements that impact their development. For others, hip-hop allows for positive adaptive coping and a potential deterrent from involvement with other environmental elements that many consider negative. That is, the music genre may provide an adaptive, productive, and creative response to uncontrollable and socially constructed adverse conditions.

Unfortunately, there are a number of maladaptive coping mechanisms that have come to be associated with hip-hop that are not indigenous to its intended artistic contribution. Activities such as drug use, gang involvement, and so on are not elements in which hip-hop was founded, nor do they consume all who choose to affiliate with the genre. Still, many of those involved at the pinnacle of the hip-hop industry— for varied reasons—have chosen to promote the commercialization of such activities and convey them as a significant component of their lives. Most unfortunately, the music industry—alongside mainstream media, most likely as a "product-branding" enhancing strategy—has chosen to highlight individuals who seemingly glorify such activities in particular ways that have both created and projected a skewed and stereotypic view to many naïve observers. Accordingly, for those generally unfamiliar, the shortsightedness has further sustained perceptions of the congruity between hip-hop and those activities that mainstream society deems illegitimate. Furthermore, the conundrum facilitates the demonizing of youth who use hip-hop for developmentally relevant and coping purposes.

As Forman and others note, generations of individuals continue to redefine and reinvent their own meanings and definitions of hip-hop. Thus, it appears important to understand the complexity, impact, and psychosocial (i.e., identity formation) significance of hip-hop as a strategy for determining and understanding its present and future potential impact on young people. In many ways, its divisive generational impact is no different from those of earlier genres such as rock and roll and youths' preoccupation with it beginning in the 1950s. Forman cites multiple individuals and suggests that hip-hop is something that you live. The statement is highly salient in that it both directly and indirectly illuminates the potential role of hip-hop in the lives of youth and hence its degree of influence. Elements of hip-hop are a constant part of the lives of many who participate in its various expressions. Similar to its originators, participants of hip-hop use it as a medium to reflect their own lives and experiences in settings that range from family to neighborhood, vocational, social-relational, and academic contexts.

For many, the various elements of hip-hop represent voluntary engagement despite the potential stark contrast with one's own neighborhood context. In recent years, as a case in point, the majority of retail consumers of hip-hop are not urban African American youth, though figures depicted in the industry most often belong to this demographic. Thus, the largest consumers of hip-hop music and its byproducts are those who may not necessarily experience the life events represented in the lyrics of what has come to be mainstream hip-hop.

Remaining aware of these phenomena potentially contributes to a better understanding of the impact that the lyrics and images can have on youth. We posit that youth sharing both psychological and contextual histories with those depicted in the videos would appear to be significantly more likely to comprehend—and internalize—the implicit messages offered by such artists. Otherwise stated, many adolescents live out existences that are reflected in mainstream's version of hip-hop and may infer the content (money, cars, etc.) to be accurate and perhaps enviable compared to the lived experiences of those in their own neighborhood contexts. As a result, youth might infer from the art form tangible options and thus attempt to emulate them. Indeed, the successes of some hip-hop personas encourage young people to realize their own potentially successful experiences and their attainability given some parallels between the lives of mainstream performers with their own lives. In fact, many adolescents may be likely to model themselves after those they admire in an effort to achieve social stature that they perceive to be otherwise improbable and generally out of reach.

Conversely, adolescents for whom contextual hardships can easily be avoided may perceive the images conveyed in mainstream hip-hop as nonsalient issues. Accordingly, the elements of hip-hop as they know them may merely be overtly romanticized and dramatically pictured forms of entertainment. Thus, they are less likely to be influenced by the negativity that is present in the mainstream representation of hip-hop.

The social groups mentioned by Forman reinforce a sense of "mutual encouragement," "intense in-group competition," and the honing of skills in an effort to achieve expertise; thus, the perspective acknowledges the importance of environments in which youth can maintain healthy peer support and a motivation to learn. A key component of this environment is safety as adolescents need to perceive situations as minimally threatening and, at least, safe. For some, hip-hop provides such an atmosphere. Youth need to feel a sense of physical well-being and emotional belonging in order to achieve successful outcomes (Spencer et al., 2003). Involvement in hip-hop may provide some measure of safety that is not experienced elsewhere. When youth lack trust or do not receive what they perceive to be sensitive responses, they may infer negative feedback and, in response, disconnect from intended resources (e.g., schooling "opportunities"). Unfortunately, assumed and tendered social supports are infrequently perceived by youth as providing actual sustenance for confronting normative developmental tasks (e.g., achievement or healthy relationships; see Havighurst, 1953). Too frequently, this dilemma denies their alleged or intended functionality as a much needed protective factor. Consequently, for some youth, hip-hop has become synonymous with rebellion against authority figures (e.g., parents, teachers, and law enforcement).

A common interest in hip-hop often serves to provide social and emotional support to adolescents who may not receive it from the generally expected socializing figures (e.g., parents and teachers). Youth desire and benefit from the approval of such authority figures. Hence, beyond traditional activities such as sports, it is worth investing attention and supporting the interests of youth as one strategy for providing needed validation. In accord with Eriksonian notions concerning identity formation processes, youths' recognition of minimal approval and their frequent limited access to mainstream power may fuel their desire to seek approval from an alternative source (Erikson, 1968). Hence, youths' normal and expected desire for acceptance—observed across the globe—may be particularly salient for those growing into adulthood under especially hostile or challenging situations (Chestang, 1972).

For many, hip-hop offsets the angst associated with daily challenges—however small—that are experienced in their environments, including the aforementioned frustrations with authority figures. Though these challenges may include a range of experiences from relational problems with parents to involvement in criminal activity, the engagement in the artistic genre may represent a means of diminishing the impact of life's hardships. To deal with such difficulties, hip-hop provides a coping strategy, which frequently represents exponential creativity. Recognizing and utilizing its developmental import may beget, bolster, and parallel effective coping strategies. Considered together, the scaffolding potential of the artistic outlet potentially increases the capacity to cope with the large number of influences and pressures acting on youth. That is, because many youth frequently develop in severely underresourced contexts, the need to create something of value from minimally resourced contexts, in effect, demonstrates an adaptive creativity. Hip-hop provides opportunities for demonstrating adaptive functionality. Regrettably, a continuing shortcoming is society's unwillingness to move from the stereotyping of youth culture to the universal promoting, framing, and supporting of youthful creativity as an adaptive strategy for countering underacknowledged hostile environments and chronic conditions of inequality. Hence, the creative nature of hip-hop has the potential for contributing to the design of social supports actually experienced by young people as, indeed, supportive. It provides an instrumental expression of youths' adaptive creativity and, thus, can assist in the design and implementation of critically needed social supports for maximizing youthful outcomes in response to normal developmental tasks (e.g., forming a positive identity, achieving literacy and higher cognitive skills, preparing for adult work, establishing healthy intimate relationships, and preparing for competent parenthood). We suggest that social supports are helpful and a good utilization of tax dollars and human capital outlay only if they are actually perceived and, more importantly, experienced by young people as psychologically supportive. In sum, without the sensitivities and youth culture considerations noted, all labeled supports proffered as policy and implemented as practice are not necessarily supportive and effective for reducing youths' level of extraordinarily high human vulnerability (see Spencer, 2006b, 2008).

Although one's involvement in hip-hop as a suggested protective factor may also represent a need for validation and respect (e.g., for the perfection of a skill), it also has the potential for a degree of psychological ownership and source of self-esteem, given that meaningful opportunities and resources remain unavailable to many young people. With the acquisition of a particular skill that is admired by one's peers, thus, psychosocial development may be buttressed; that is, one's identity is solidified, self-esteem internalized, and confidence surfaced. More important, of course, is youths' emergent sense of ownership of the environment that frequently serves as a significant source of threat. The conceptual and practical links with the local environment recognize its salience as the context of struggle requiring resistance. Despite the recognition of local barriers, there is recognition of global similarities. Hence, for this reason, many ethnic minorities living in low-resource enclaves across the globe and struggling with normal identity formation needs, at the same time, share a pronounced identification with the art forms of hip-hop regardless of land and language barriers.

HIP-HOP AND CONTEXT-RELEVANT IDENTITY DEVELOPMENT

As Forman states, hip-hop is often used as a medium for dissuading youth from becoming involved in gang activities and, thus, providing a forum to establish an alternative means of individual and/or group identity. Not unlike other forms of artistic expression, hip-hop may serve to generate a number of identity forms (i.e., personal, group, political, cultural, etc.). These emergent identities are infrequently associated with the "culture of hip-hop." Alternatively, mainstream media have emphasized identities that incorporate the artistic style of hip-hop, yet project counterproductive and oppositional messages that some adolescents particularly deem appealing as a function of their identity formation status and coping processes (e.g., see reviews of adolescent coping processes: Spencer, 1999, 2006b, 2008).

For some, hip-hop becomes a means of "agency" in a society in which youth may not otherwise feel empowered by messages that constantly challenge their sense of worth and, in many instances, discount their experiences and their ability to contribute adequately to the fabric of their respective contexts. Hip-hop not only provides a means to renegotiate their individual and collective identities but also endows them with a belief that they can have an impact on the physical and social world around them. Consequently, a sense of purpose, self-worth, and effectance motivation emerges that has implications for competence formation (see White, 1959, 1960).

The misinterpretation of one's cultural context can lead to challenges that require coping and for which hip-hop provides functional support. One's pattern of coping with these challenges is linked to identity formation (Spencer, 2006a), and the consistency of one's identity process lends itself to the development of stable coping responses. The "challenges encountered and coping response" cycle represents a process, which unfolds over the life course as each stage of development comes with its own unique set of challenges (e.g., achievement during the school years, job seeking during the adolescent and early adult years, and starting and raising a family during the adult years). Cultural contexts can be made meaningful through rehabilitation and restructuring. These changes can potentially improve human adaptation and provide opportunities for growth and development. Bronfenbrenner's ecological systems theory highlights how this occurs by examining different levels of the environment that deserve significant attention as lives unfold and specific challenges are confronted (Bronfenbrenner & Morris, 1998).

At various levels of social and environmental contexts, as described by Bronfenbrenner and Morris (1998), characteristics such as ethnicity and socioeconomic status have a large impact on an individual's status and experiences. One aspect of this complexity comes from the ways that youths' perceptions of situations evolve due to the normal changes in their thinking. However, their social experiences, physical growth, and emotional status also serve as increasingly complex factors. It is because hip-hop allows for the adequate expression of coping in response to these experiences that adolescents may find the genre appealing. For a more detailed reading on the development of coping mechanisms given one's perceptions of and sensitivity to neighborhood settings and context features, more generally, see Spencer's (2008) *Phenomenology and Ecological Systems Theory: Development of Diverse Groups.*

HIP-HOP AND THE MAINSTREAM

Mainstream society indeed continues to indulge and benefit from the industry of hip-hop while simultaneously maintaining and spreading sweeping remarks on its worth and location in the lives of both youths and adults. The fear that the whole of hip-hop evokes misogyny and violence is problematic. These beliefs represent an ever-present phenomenon that is often overlooked and continually legitimized as a rational analysis. Unjustly, other visual arts (e.g., movies and print media) appear exempt from parallel misogyny-promoting accusations perhaps due to their portrayal as legitimate members of a nation's business elite. Because of hip-hop's automatic association with gang involvement and violence, many of those who consider themselves part of the hip-hop culture are viewed as involved in such negative activities. This fear is sustained by unfamiliarity with hip-hop and can only be overcome, in part, if those who are "unaware" become more cognizant of the intricacies of the culture and the overlooked potential benefits of its influence. As previously mentioned, especially evident beginning in the 1950s, youth managed to communicate their own unique musical style, which, too, was pathologized by parents and other socializing adults currently representing the "generativity-relegated (baby-boomer) generation."

It appears that the agency desired by adolescents is sometimes found in the annexation of hip-hop culture. For some, the inferred agency indicates a level of active control of one's life that can be exercised. The practice of exercising one's agency is too often determined to be problematic if the resulting behavior does not fit within the confines of the dominant culture's social norms. Hence, whereas one's peers and acquaintances may find a set of actions to be productive, the dominant social order deems them as unproductive—and, in many cases, counterproductive—to the social agenda.

Consistent with Eriksonian thought, it is not surprising that youth retain "problematic" identities rather than adopt feelings that might suggest a lack of an identity altogether. An achievement-based self-concept as a source of esteem is not possible in mainstream society if that culture is perceived to be harboring a lack of respect for one's own forms of expression (Spencer, 1999). For African Americans, in particular, for whom hip-hop is most impactful, Stevenson (1997) suggested that coping strategies used by African American adolescents may be misconstrued due to a failure to take into account the context and purpose in which a particular identity has been constructed. Thus, youth may not intend to function or be perceived as "defying" authority; rather, they may be developing what they perceive to be the necessary identity that will yield the most success when navigating structural conditions and underresourced settings such as urban neighborhoods and schools.

HIP-HOP AND HYPERMASCULINITY

The acquisition of fast money, fast cars, and fast women is not a concept narrowly indigenous to hip-hop, nor is it a native idea to those living in the harsh neighborhoods that mirror the birthplaces of hip-hop's origins. Instead, these ideas reflect the ideals that have existed for decades. Though unfortunate, they have just more recently been the focus of many young males who have chosen to join and consume the industry that is now hip-hop.

The participation of some males in the hip-hop music industry reflects the hypermasculine realities of their neighborhood contexts. This is because hypermasculine behavior within many low-resourced urban neighborhoods may yield temporary but favorable responses, including "safe passage" through difficult and underresourced terrain. Males coming of age in urban environments, particularly African American males, report significant concerns as they look forward to adulthood status and activities that promote success (Chestang, 1972; Diemer & Blustein, 2006). However, the coping strategies required for successful navigation outside of one's neighborhood might compromise their expectations to have a successful future. In essence, as a survival response for walking through dangerous, underresourced neighborhoods, male youth may frequently exhibit hypermasculine behavior. Unfortunately, when used consistently over time and across contexts, this coping behavior becomes difficult to curb outside of the environment in which it is most successful (Spencer, 1999). Too frequently, youths' seemingly inappropriate coping responses (e.g., involvement in the hip-hop lifestyle) are associated with less than ideal situations, and hypermasculine behavior is often construed as hyperaggression by many in positions of authority, including teachers and police officers.

When coping strategies are repeated with enough frequency and perceived success, they become stable coping responses used at various times and across many situations and represent stable identities. At this stage, youth begin to assume an identity that is synonymous with the coping they have adopted. For instance, hypermasculine behavior as an effective coping strategy in one's neighborhood can serve as a source of protection and admonition for respect. Accordingly, a young person may use it in other contexts.

HIP-HOP AND FEMALES

Universally, music serves as a form of exploration of the various roles in society, and hip-hop music has been no exception. In addition to the roles related to economic status, ethnicity, and geography, the role of gender remains a point of contention. When discussing hip-hop and human development, gender has to be addressed due to the unique role of "one's image" in hip-hop. Although a number of assertions have been made about males and hypermasculinity, there exist distinct differences in the development of females as a function of race and subsequent experiences. Interpersonal relations play a significant role in the identity development of females, as they often judge themselves according to others and frequently face issues prompted by the depiction of women in society (Chae, 2001–2002). African American females often experience unique challenges as they must not only contend with their status as women in a patriarchal society but also cope with group membership as members of a racial group experiencing a history of policies and social mores used to subjugate the broader group's status. Risk factors such as low-income status and an underrepresentation of diverse and positive Black female images have made identity development especially challenging for some females as they struggle into womanhood. The socialization of many African American females has included a myriad of dichotomous and simplistic depictions that are often characterized as good versus bad or embracing Black versus rejecting Black characterizations (e.g., kinky vs. straight hair, short vs. long hair, dark vs. light skin, and "thick" vs. thin lips). This quandary has left many African American girls with few positive representations of their own image, leading many to opt for images that reflect European ideals of beauty and/or images that reflect those of the scantily clad women in many modern hip-hop videos.

Although such early female hip-hop artists as Roxanne Shantee, MC Lyte, Queen Latifah, and Salt-N-Pepa have become hip-hop legends in their own right, the number of female artists is meager when compared to the number of their male counterparts who have reached mainstream hip-hop status. The 1990s ushered in such hip-hop artists as Missy Elliot, Bahamadia, and Lauryn Hill, followed by more recent artists like Eve, Mystic, and Jean Grae. Although these artists have conveyed personas that rely heavily on their lyrical abilities, such artists as Trina, Foxy Brown, and Lil Kim—all of whom rose to fame as "protégées" of male rappers—have chosen to use overtly sexualized imagery to gain prominence. Many view the aforementioned artists as a response to hypermasculine male figures in hip-hop as these women coopted bragging, "playing the dozens," and sexually aggressive personas to the acclaim of some and chagrin of others. Unfortunately, the developmental experiences of many young girls have been marred by this belief that their display of sexual aggression is, in fact, also related to themes of control.

In an industry dominated by male influence—both in front of and behind the camera—many female artists may view the displays of sexuality and use of their femininity as tools to obtain significant stature in the industry. Although it may not be the most desired means of achieving success according to mainstream positive youth development standards, it is a practice that is widespread and broadly accepted in the mainstream United States. Without a doubt and quite unfortunately, the topic continues to be underexplored by the human development research community as an identity and normative development issue in the development of girls. Hence, the problem of the overly sexualized female image—though exacerbated by hip-hop's mainstream industry—is symptomatic of mainstream American societal practices, more generally.

Although female artists with the extraordinary lyrical prowess of Lauryn Hill and Jean Grae are not given due attention, their music may be viewed as a protective factor for some because many of their messages serve to inspire and empower young Black girls through an establishment of positive self-concepts and coping mechanisms to deal with the disproportionate hardships that they face. Furthermore, the significant role that body image plays in developmental experiences— and, more specifically, in the marketing strategies used in promoting hip-hop—warrants an in-depth look and general exploration as to why industry support has existed for only a small enclave of female artists given the plethora of male hip-hop artists.

CONCLUSION

This chapter takes a much needed look at the complexity that is hip-hop and what it means for understanding and promoting the positive outcomes of human development. The imagination that circumscribes hip-hop encourages individuals to convey life as they see it. Moreover, historic events such as the Civil Rights Movement, Jim Crow laws, the Reagan era, and massacres in Mogadishu and Rwanda provide backdrops as they influence what is created and make it appropriate, according to Forman, to ask "what futures are imagined in and through hip-hop." Countless opinions about hip-hop's influence and continuing viability thrive. Although we grapple with the concept of defining *hip-hop*, many youth the world over continue to create song, dance, art, speech, and fashion that represent their realities as well as their dreams. The expansion of amateur production tools and Web access has afforded many youth opportunities to take on roles that have been traditionally assumed by adults. The proliferation of peer-to-peer sharing and virtual community sites has played a key role in helping young people produce, promote, and distribute hip-hop. In turn, the multimedia packaging that is current hip-hop ensures its travel to unchartered territories and across boundaries that were once thought to be impenetrable. Thus, the potential of hip-hop is the power and affordance it offers to advocates of positive youth outcomes for tapping into the lived experiences of those who use it as a means of identity expression and positive youth development.

REFERENCES

Bleich, S., Zillmann, D., & Weaver, J. (1991). Enjoyment and consumption of defiant rock music as a function of adolescent rebelliousness. *Journal of Broadcasting and Electronic Media, 35*, 351–366.

Bronfenbrenner, U., & Morris, P. A. (1998). The ecology of developmental processes. In W. Damon & R. M. Lerner (Eds.), *Handbook of child psychology: Theoretical models of human development* (5th ed., Vol. 1, pp. 993–1028). New York: Wiley.

Chae, M. H. (2001–2002). Gender and ethnicity in identity formation. *New Jersey Journal of Professional Counseling, 56*, 17–23.

Chang, J. (2005). *Can't stop won't stop: A history of the hip-hop generation.* New York: St. Martin's.

Chestang, L. W. (1972). *Character development in a hostile environment* (Occasional Paper No. 3, pp. 1–12). Chicago: University of Chicago Press.

Crozier, W. R. (1997). Music and social influence. In D. J. Hargreaves & A. C. North (Eds.), *The social psychology of music* (pp. 67–83). Oxford: Oxford University Press.

Diemer, M. A., & Blustein, D. L. (2006). Critical consciousness and career development among urban youth. *Journal of Vocational Behavior, 68*(2), 220–232.

Erikson, E. H. (1968). *Identity: Youth and crisis.* New York: Norton.

Havighurst, R. J. (1953). *Human development and education.* New York: McKay.

Larson, R., & Kubey, R. K. (1983). Television and music: Contrasting media in adolescent life. *Youth and Society, 15*, 13–31.

Marcia, J. E. (1980). Identity in adolescence. In J. Adelson (Ed.), *Handbook of adolescent psychology* (pp. 159–187). New York: Wiley.

Spencer, M. B. (1995). Old issues and new theorizing about African American youth: A phenomenological variant of ecological systems theory. In R. L. Taylor (Ed.), *Black youth: Perspectives on their status in the United States* (pp. 37–70). Westport, CT: Praeger.

Spencer, M. B. (1999). Social and cultural influence on school adjustment: The application of an identity-focused cultural ecological perspective. *Educational Psychologist, 34*(1), 43–57.

Spencer, M. B. (2005). Crafting identities and accessing opportunity post *Brown. American Psychologist, 60*(8), 821–830.

Spencer, M. B. (2006a). Commentary. *Research in Human Development, 3*(4), 271–280.

Spencer, M. B. (2006b). Phenomenology and ecological systems theory: Development of diverse groups. In W. Damon & R. Lerner (Eds.), *Handbook of child psychology* (6th ed., Vol. 1, pp. 829–893). New York: Wiley.

Spencer, M. B. (2008). Phenomenology and ecological systems theory: Development of diverse groups. In W. Damon & R. Lerner (Eds.), *Child and adolescent development: An advanced course* (pp. 696–735). New York: Wiley.

Spencer, M. B., Fegley, S. G., & Harpalani, V. (2003). A theoretical and empirical examination of identity coping: Linking coping resources to the self process of African American youth. *Journal of Applied Developmental Science, 7*(3), 181–188.

Spencer, M. B., & Markstrom-Adams, C. (1990). Identity processes among racial and ethnic minority children in America. *Child Development, 61*, 290–310.

Stevenson, H. S. (1997). "Missed, dissed and pissed": Making meaning of neighborhood risk, fear, and anger management in urban Black youth. *Cultural Diversity and Mental Health, 3*, 37–52.

White, R. (1959). Motivation reconsidered: The concept of competence. *Psychological Review, 66*, 297–333.

White, R. (1960). Competence and psychosexual development. In M. R. Riley (Ed.), *Nebraska symposium on motivation* (pp. 3–32). Lincoln: University of Nebraska Press.

Zillmann, D., & Gan, S. (1997). Musical taste in adolescence. In D. J. Hargreaves & A. C. North (Eds.), *The social psychology of music* (pp. 161–187). Oxford: Oxford University Press.

II

Educating the Artists and Using the Arts to Educate

6

"WHY SHOULD I WRITE?" SAID THE PENCIL. "WHAT ELSE CAN YOU DO?" SAID THE KNIFE.

Or, Why I Can't Tell You Why I Am a Composer

Gerald Levinson

The only thing I know is that I paint because I need to, and I paint whatever passes through my head, without any other consideration.

—Frida Kahlo[1]

All my life I am waiting. Like an insect I am waiting.

—Igor Stravinsky[2]

Any writer beginning a story might well say to himself: "Keep your hat on. We may wind up miles from here."

—Kurt Vonnegut, *Palm Sunday* (p. 153)

It may seem marvelous and strange, but it is an experience common to creative artists that one doesn't *decide* to be a composer or poet or sculptor but rather *discovers* this about oneself; that a creative vocation isn't something willed or chosen, but somehow is innate in one's essential makeup. It has also been said that artistic inspiration is nearly indistinguishable from obsessive-compulsive disorder. (Arnold Schoenberg, that still-challenging giant of 20th-century music, is said to have declared it his mission as a teacher to stop his students from composing. Those who failed to be stopped would turn out to be the real thing.) As someone who has for some reason had the compulsion to compose music for some 40 years, I nonetheless have no overarching theory to offer about the nature of creativity. I only know that sometimes I am actively working on a piece of music (often goaded by a commission and a deadline), and sometimes I am not, or rather am "between pieces." Even during those times, I still understand myself as a composer; I hear and think about music as a composer, and I believe that musical ideas are arising and being considered, somewhere in the mind behind the scenes, to rise to consciousness at some later point. In the reminiscences that follow, I offer anecdotal moments along my own gradual route to self-discovery, followed by some thoughts about what it is I do when I'm working.

EARLY DISCOVERIES IN MUSIC

There was no active music making in my family when I grew up in mid-1950s Connecticut. In my mother's poor, old-country family in a shtetl-like enclave of St. Louis, there had been no music at all (and she claimed, with some accuracy, to be quite tone-deaf). My father's mother, from a more urban German Jewish background, had studied singing and was something of an opera buff. My father had had some instrumental lessons (violin, I believe) in childhood, but little or no technical musical knowledge or literacy remained with him. However, he did acquire and retain a lifelong love of "fine" music and had a modest record collection of the most typical pieces from the "standard repertoire," namely, those pieces so well-known that they were identifiable by their nicknames without reference to their composers: the *Jupiter*, the *Unfinished*, the *Surprise*, the *Moonlight*, the *Appassionata*, the *Italian*, the *Pathétique* (both of them), and so on. In the evening he would relax and read the paper with music playing, either one of these records or the radio tuned to WQXR, the "classical" station of the *New York Times* (whose playlist was limited pretty much to the same top-50 "classics"). Because we lived in a split-level house with an open living room, the music would waft upstairs where I could still hear it after going to bed. Those works, through frequent repeated exposure in my earliest years, including in my half-sleep, were engraved so deeply on my subconscious that when I hear them to this day I am transported back to my childhood. Whatever my parents later did both to encourage and to discourage my relationship to music, this constant presence of fine music in the house, even as background, was a great gift to me and a formative influence. They were also subscribers to the New York Philharmonic, and those few concerts I attended with them were tremendous experiences, as were Leonard Bernstein's Young People's Concerts on television.

At some early age I must have begun to listen very closely. For example, I retain a very specific and concrete memory of puzzlement at the meter of the Trio of the minuet of Mozart's *G-Minor Symphony* (K.550). When you tapped your feet to the tune, at the end of each phrase it didn't make sense somehow. I was listening closely enough, without any understanding, to notice that some kind of trick was being played with rhythm.[3]

When I was 8, my parents proposed buying a piano if I would be interested in taking lessons. To have a piano in the house and have your child take piano lessons was no more than a conventional thing to do, but I still have no idea why they waited to ask me, rather than my brother, 4 years older. I don't remember taking the initiative to ask. In any case this was a pivotal, ultimately life-changing event for me. I could hardly be torn away from the piano from then on. (That very piano, a small console described by my tuner as "not very endearing," now resides in my studio and is the one I use while composing.)

My first teacher was young and encouraging; she was the daughter of one of the most respected piano teachers in our town, and after a while she felt I was outstripping her pedagogy and (to her credit) wanted to pass me on to her mother. That fine musician, unfortunately, soon became ill and retired from teaching. This is relevant because although I excelled in enthusiasm, I lacked discipline, and my teacher knew I needed the firmer, experienced hand of her mother to instill in me the value of serious practice and the development of keyboard technique. The teacher to whom I eventually went noticed and supported my growing musical imagination (and, later, my first attempts at composition) and exposed me to a wide range of music but did not insist firmly enough on such dull matters as developing a reliable technique, and despite my love for the piano, I never acquired the skills of a real pianist.

What was I doing during all those hours at the piano, when I wasn't really learning how to play the piano better? I was more likely to be improvising, sight reading, or just fooling around than practicing scales and arpeggios. I was fairly adept at reading and learning the assigned pieces quickly and would not bother to practice them to perfection. I was more interested in trying something else, for instance attempting to play by ear the latest pop hit from the radio (my own radio was tuned to something other than WQXR). The new pop music from when I was 12 or so was dominated by the Beatles, and I can say that I owe them a great deal, because my efforts to reproduce their melodies and harmonies constituted some of my earliest exercises in ear training, an essential element in a composer's equipment. What this means is the ability to hear precisely melodic intervals, harmonic progressions, and rhythms so that one can not only play back what one hears but also write it down if needed. This cultivates the skill of hearing *internally*, in the imagination, which is the essence of what composers do. From an early age I had had the impulse to try to "figure out" music I heard; I remember trying to write down songs like "Waltzing Mathilda" after hearing them in music class in the third or fourth grade. What made the Beatles' music especially fruitful was their own rapidly growing adventurousness and sophistication, which forced my "hearing" skills to develop to keep pace with their changing music. I also made my own "transcriptions" of other music that was in the air, including movie themes like those of *Goldfinger* and *Doctor Zhivago*, sometimes including another instrument, which I would perform with pals at school "talent shows."[4]

My undisciplined approach to the keyboard did have some positive consequences. The tendency toward improvisation led toward composition, and the habit of sight reading has served me well as a means of getting acquainted with music in a direct, physical way, internalizing it through the fingers. In my post–graduate school years in Paris, I had a piano but no stereo in my studio. I acquired hundreds of cheap scores from used-music sellers along the Seine and spent countless hours reading through huge amounts of music, much of which has become part of my musical bloodstream. A physical, tactile connection to music—existing music or my own emerging ideas—has always been central to me, though I have never been a professional performer.

ADOLESCENT PREOCCUPATIONS: EXPERIMENTING WITH SOUNDS AND NOTATING COMPOSITIONS

In middle school I took up the clarinet and played in the band. I disliked marching but enjoyed concert band, which in high school became a very important part of my musical education, though I never became very proficient on the clarinet. The high school concert band was fairly good and often played high-quality music by masters like Gustav Holst and such contemporary composers as Vincent Persichetti, Vaclav Nelhybel, and William Schuman. This was an invaluable experience for me for several reasons. First, playing in a group with other people made me listen and respond to the sounds around me, and to the conductor, in a way pianists, thinking themselves self-sufficient, often don't. Then I was fascinated by the combinations of instrumental colors, which encouraged my nascent urge to think in terms of combinations of sounds. Finally, school wind ensembles often play more "modern" music than school orchestras, because the medium is a 20th-century invention. This enables young wind players to be more at home with, and more open-eared toward, a wider range of harmony, timbre, and rhythm than young string players. Some of the music we played, and the richly varied coloristic possibilities of the wind ensemble, have remained quite close to me. In my early 30s, I served for 3 years as the founding director of the Swarthmore College Wind Ensemble, and I have written two band pieces so far (both, in fact, for later incarnations of my old high school band) and look forward to more. Moreover, my whole concept of orchestral sound is conditioned by wind sonorities, and my ideal orchestra (a rather grand, Berlioz-like notion) would consist of all the resources of the modern symphonic wind ensemble—which are much bigger and more varied than the wind section of a symphony orchestra—combined with the usual 60-plus member string section and a large percussion ensemble.[5]

Two other musical preoccupations during my early teenage years clearly (in retrospect, of course) led toward composition. Somehow I acquired an intense curiosity about the latest, most "modern" contemporary music along with my lifelong habit of record collecting. Between the bargain bins at Sam Goody and the unusually interesting music section at our town library (yes, you could borrow LPs), I sought out complex "new music" like that of Karlheinz Stockhausen, Elliott Carter, and Pierre Boulez and discovered as well a great affinity for Igor Stravinsky and for Charles Ives. I couldn't possibly "understand" how most of this music was conceived, but I was fascinated by all the new sounds and the bracingly strange new notions of what music could be. It was deeply thrilling to know that, in the mid-1960s, Stravinsky, the composer of *Petrushka* and *Le Sacre du Printemps* from an antediluvian age, was still an active and evolving composer, moreover in what was a currently "cutting-edge" style. (He described himself in his 80s as a promising young composer.) And a major discovery of the mid-1960s, the single work that most powerfully made me start to think of myself as a composer, was the monumental, mystical *Fourth Symphony* of Ives, which was finally brought to life 50 years after its completion and a decade after Ives' death by the octogenarian conductor Leopold Stokowski. This model of composing as perpetual exploration still resonates very deeply for me. I may have unintentionally tested some friendships at the time with my enthusiasm over my latest musical finds; however, one who bore with my proselytizing then has been my wife for almost 30 years and my vital moral support and principal inspiration for longer than that.

The other forerunner of composition was improvisation and collage. The piano was (is) a tantalizing reservoir of sound possibilities, including not only everything possible on the keyboard and the resonance effects afforded by the pedals but also sounds produced directly on the strings and elsewhere inside the piano. I recall sitting on the floor under the keyboard, plucking and strumming the strings, knocking on the beams and the soundboard, and recording the results.[6] The tape recorder also offered possibilities for playing with sound. I figured out ways to combine, superimpose, and manipulate sounds I produced myself, mostly on and in the piano, as well as from such other sources as a toy organ and even whatever was playing on the radio. With two reel-to-reel tape recorders, I could superimpose recordings, change the speed, and even play sounds backward (by twisting the tape and playing the "back" side). In the process I listened to sounds in a very focused, detailed way, noticing fine points of attack and decay, overtones, resonances, and the like.[7] Manipulating sounds in these ways is close to composition but without the elements of forethought, working through alternatives, or planning shapes beyond the moment-to-moment level. This larger scale, "architectural" aspect of composition will be discussed later.

I took the leap into composing—on paper—in the middle of high school, at age 15 or 16. At first, not surprisingly, I wrote quite a number of piano pieces, which explored a wide range of stylistic elements, though mostly within a "modernist" vocabulary, including dissonant intervals (sometimes treated in a constructivist, organized manner; e.g., using sequences of intervals systematically, as in the 12-tone method), irregular or fluctuating rhythms (sometimes involving organized treatment of durations, and sometimes unmeasured notation), dense cluster chords, resonance effects, and an exploration of the full range of the keyboard (but not including inside-the-piano effects, interestingly). Occasionally they drew on a more "tonal," more "American" idiom; my lifelong nondoctrinaire approach to musical languages was thus established from the very beginning.[8] Eventually I collected four of these pieces under the title of *Four Introspections*, which I performed at my piano teacher's group recitals and elsewhere. (Her support and encouragement for my nascent compositional urge were very helpful at this stage.) These pieces capitalized on my musical intelligence and coloristic sensitivity but did not overtax the less advanced aspects of my keyboard technique; in other words, they were interestingly put together and sophisticated in sound but not technically virtuosic. I also began to write chamber pieces for friends who played other instruments, including an intricate 12-tone piece for flute, clarinet, violin, and piano, and even fulfilled a requirement for a history class by setting the first paragraph of Genesis for tenor and piano. Virtually all these pieces were performed by friends and classmates, usually with me at the piano—which was the most valuable experience imaginable. My first orchestral imaginings also date from this time; I sketched out in short score (with only general indications of instrumentation) attempts at two short pieces, both largely made up of massive sound blocks and ringing percussion. One of these, though not fully realized, remained an interesting conception, as it developed some elaborate polyphonic textures and dramatic contrasts. Though I did not yet possess sufficient knowledge of craft to write out an orchestral score, I did already have a characteristic tendency to "hear" orchestrally, in terms of large sound masses.

PASSION AND COMMITMENT: MOVING TOWARD MUSIC AS A CAREER PATH

As my focus on music grew more consuming, my practically minded parents grew ever more worried that I would be distracted from a "real" professional direction by what properly ought to be understood as a hobby. My girlfriend Nanine Valen, from a family of writers, offered compensating and indeed vital encouragement at a critical time of adolescent uncertainty. In fact she and her family offered a haven of support and sympathetic interest while tension was mounting at home over my deepening obsession with music. (At that time she also influenced my future development in a quite specific way via a marvelous 17th birthday gift, William Austin's magisterial book *Music in the 20th Century*, which opened whole worlds to me.) It had been a long-standing assumption, based on not very much, that I was headed for a medical career, and my decision to attend the University of Pennsylvania rested on its advantages for a premed program. During my freshman year there I began their music theory (harmony and counterpoint) sequence, which built on a rudimentary harmony class I had taken in high school.[9] I did not yet study composition per se, and did not yet become acquainted with the world-class composers on the faculty there, whose work and reputations were then completely unknown to me but who were soon to become important mentors. However, I did continue to compose chamber pieces, which were performed at a student-run concert series. One of these foreshadowed my later fondness for composing tiny, timbrally distinctive miniatures; it consisted of 12 duos for varying and very odd combinations of instruments, followed by a finale in which most of those duos were superimposed in a kind of semichaotic (but fully written-out) free-for-all. I also began submitting my music (though not that piece) to student composers' contests just to see what would happen.

Though the medical career path was still "on the books" (and my probable music major was still considered compatible with a premed program), I was beginning to face the question of how central a role music was to play in my life and made plans to explore two divergent possibilities over the following summer: With my girlfriend I would attend a music festival where I would actually take composition lessons, but before that I would spend some weeks with my brother's father-in-law, a prominent radiologist and teacher in Milwaukee, making the rounds with him and observing a doctor's life firsthand. This experience turned out to be revelatory; everything I saw was fascinating, but from the first day it was clear that this was not for me. I spent those weeks in a state of relaxed clarity and worked late into the night trying to realize that old orchestral sketch in the hope that it could be played at the music festival later that summer. The notion of combining a medical profession with a serious avocation as a composer faded rapidly, to my parents' dismay—which, however, was allayed slightly by a small prize my music was awarded in the BMI competition.

My first composition lessons thus took place at a summer institute, at which two very well-known composer-teachers shared the teaching duties. They were George Rochberg, by complete coincidence the senior composer on the Penn faculty, and Vincent Persichetti, whose band pieces had made such a strong impression on me in high school. They helped me bring that orchestral piece to completion, and it was indeed played there—as the orchestra rehearsed it in an open tent, a small boy, taken aback by the strange sounds, wandered in, walked right up to Mr. Persichetti, and demanded, "Who WROTE that?" Persichetti pointed to me and said, "That young man over there," to which the boy responded, "No, really!" At that moment I felt like a real composer.

When I returned to Penn in the fall of my sophomore year, the music department responded to demand by offering (for the first time in memory) a course in composition for undergraduates, to be shared by George Crumb and Richard Wernick. Crumb had been in the news for his Pulitzer Prize, but I did not know his music except for an incomprehensible bit of his winning piece I had heard on the radio. My very first meeting with him amounted to an epiphany; I came upon him crouching by a giant tamtam, scraping it with a coin, peering over his glasses, and musing, "It's a beautiful sound, isn't it?" This intense focus on the most refined and imaginative aspects of sound itself, Crumb's most celebrated trait, accorded well with my own developing way of hearing. During my work with him over that year, my music grew in subtlety, resulting in a fanciful, impressionistic vocal chamber work, *in wind*, set to a nature poem by my girlfriend, written the following summer while I was a nature counselor at a camp. However, despite its sophistication, this piece remains a student work because of its too obvious debt to Crumb, even in the elegance of the ink calligraphy of its manuscript.[10]

My continued work at Penn with Richard Wernick and George Rochberg confirmed what a happy accident it was that had led me there. Wernick, a tougher, more challenging, and more practical teacher than the easygoing Crumb, helped sharpen my sense of the importance of craft, organization, attention to form, self-critical awareness, and the frequent necessity of revision; in other words, the realization that composition involves a sometimes protracted *search* for the right way. George Rochberg, having passed beyond his earlier achievements as a powerful composer of what one might call romantic-modernist (i.e., 12-tone) inclinations, was deeply involved at that time in his own characteristically intense search for a more inclusive musical language that could recapture more of the essence of the great music of the past. Approaching this ideal at first obliquely, by way of quotation and collage, he was then beginning to throw off conventional inhibitions and allowing himself to write using the actual sound and syntax of composers of past centuries. He saw this both as a reaffirmation of human and expressive values in music and as a protest against the cerebral modernist aesthetic that seemed to dominate the American academic and international musical scene in the 1950s and 1960s.[11] Accordingly he urged me to put aside my own projects for a time and focus on a study of fugue, a most rigorous traditional discipline, not coincidentally related to his then-current compositional preoccupations.

During the next summer, at age 20, I was lucky enough to attend the Tanglewood Festival as a composition fellow, where the work I presented for public performance was a piano quintet, dedicated to Rochberg, whose central movement was … a big fugue in F minor, in a grandly Romantic, somewhat Brahmsian manner, framed by two ruminative movements in a tense, 20th-century manner, including an Ivesian offstage flute at the end. In 1971 such stylistic mixing was more or less unheard of; the works by which Rochberg was to attract enormous attention and controversy to this open, sincere eclecticism had not yet been heard in public. My quintet was greeted with curiosity and consternation and described as "so reactionary it's avant-garde." I was proud of the achievement but have never been tempted again to explore such explicitly "historical" stylistic allusions. Nor have I had any interest in being reactionary or avant-garde.

The following year, my last at Penn, I continued to work with Rochberg, but this time on two ambitious pieces of my own devising. One of them, *in dark*—a setting of a mystical poem of the night poem by my girlfriend and two by Robert Lax (about whom more later; these poems were written as aerograms to my girlfriend)—turned out to be my Opus 1, the earliest piece I'm still happy to have performed. It continues the "exotic" instrumental coloration of the earlier vocal piece, with its fusion of the voice with low flutes and strings, harp, piano, and percussion and a "French" coloration in the harmony. In this piece, my growing interest in the music of Olivier Messiaen can be heard. My curiosity about his music had been piqued by the Austin book on 20th-century music, and I had begun to seek it out on recordings. (George Crumb recalls that I frequently shared my enthusiasm for Messiaen and increased his acquaintance with Messiaen's music.)[12] Although the rarefied world of this piece was remote from Rochberg's sympathies, he was supportive and encouraging; he may have sensed how deeply I was committed to this project and that it would have been useless to try to push it in a different direction. It was the occasion for one of the finest composition lessons I ever had: I brought in the setting of one of the Lax poems, for voice and two low flutes, with occasional interventions by the harp, which Rochberg insisted that I sing and play for him ("You have vocal chords? You have fingers?"). After I limped through the ordeal, he waited without a word, until at last I said, "I see what you mean." I hadn't really made the connection between *thinking* about a vocal line, setting text, and the physical reality of *singing*.

DISCOVERING MY OWN COMPOSITIONAL VOICE

Originality, personality, or style can neither be encouraged or prevented. Forget the matter.

—Lou Harrison, *Lou Harrison's Music Primer*

By the time of my graduation from Penn, it had long since been clear that I was committed to a career path centered on music, specifically composition, and most likely also on teaching, which seemed an attractive way to earn a living for someone who loved to think and talk about music—and so it has proved for decades. I was already thinking about trying to study with Messiaen, whom I had by then met at a concert. I was impressed by his warmth and unpretentiousness, so at odds with his severe and otherworldly public persona, but intimidated by what he told me about the entrance requirements for the Paris Conservatory, for which I wasn't ready. So I graduated to the University of Chicago in order to study with that great, feisty iconoclast, Ralph Shapey. This was not an obvious match, given the differences between his musical world and mine, but his example and influence were nonetheless profound. His commitment to the highest standards of rigor, intensity, and challenge, and the uncompromising, elemental power of his music, set inspiring standards to live up to. He also forced his students to push hard to develop their rhythmic imaginations and their understanding of the possibilities and limitations of instruments. His motto, "That which the mind of man can conceive will be done," encouraged pursuing one's inner vision wherever it might lead, and his trademark "sculptural" metaphor of music as "graven image" resonates deeply in my music.

After 2 years in Chicago I did venture to Paris, began auditing Messiaen's class at the Conservatoire while preparing (amazingly with the help of Messiaen himself, who came to class early to help drill the foreign applicants in musical dictations and other exercises) for the many-tiered entrance exams, and was eventually accepted after several months. This entitled me to performances and broadcasts of my music at Radio France by high-level professional musicians, in addition to the cornucopia that was Messiaen's class: 12 hours per week during which he shared everything that he had ever loved and studied, with unstinting generosity. He also devoted as much attention to the work-in-progress of the students as we asked and kept us abreast of the latest in new music. Much has been written about Messiaen's class, which I will not describe in any detail, except to say that the combination of wonder and profound knowledge, resulting from relentless study, in that class fully justified its now legendary reputation. My own work developed there slowly at first, perhaps because of the richness of the environment, but later during the first year gathered momentum and resulted in an ambitious 40-minute work for chamber orchestra, which I ill advisedly conducted myself very late at night at a marathon radio concert. Though I have withdrawn the piece (it's too "hypersensitive," too unsure in its management of pacing, and sometimes too permeated by undigested Messiaen), it was a major learning experience. For one thing, it became clearer to me that even in a very spacious, meditative musical climate, music must still have a living metabolism, a sense of breath, however slow or distended. Messiaen, having steadfastly and almost alone remained to the end of the concert, reproached me for having waited until it was finished to show it to him, rather than bringing it in while in progress, and he was right. He was quite capable of giving down-to-earth, pragmatic compositional advice if asked, but too gentle to insist.

My relationship with Messiaen deepened over the next summer when I served as the designated translator, chauffeur, and general assistant for his residency at Tanglewood. When I returned for a second year in Paris, I found my compositional "voice" growing bolder and produced two pieces, both more successful than their predecessor—one of them, for large orchestra, included the first of many homages in my music to the stark, craggy landscapes of the French Alps. My music often aspires to the feeling of cosmic power or monumentality that I associate with mountains, at times with the aid of evocations of Tibetan ritual music (a mountain music *par excellence*). In fact, one of Messiaen's own signature characteristics was a profoundly catholic (small c) appreciation of ideas and musics all over the world and a creative approach to incorporating sounds and ways of thinking from "other" cultures into his own work (as well as his teaching) without pastiche. The way was being prepared for my later immersion in the musics of Bali, India, and elsewhere in Asia.

NEW WORLDS, EXPANDING SONORITIES, AND STOCKING THE COMPOSER'S TOOLBOX

After one more year back in Chicago, I began teaching at Swarthmore College, which has been my home base ever since.[13] Teaching of course entails an inevitable competition for time and mental space with creative work, but it is also stimulating in itself and constantly keeps my mind fresh—especially because at a small college we often teach a wider range of subjects than our specialties. Another happy accident in my development occurred when, as a lark, the college nominated me for a Luce Scholarship, a grant that sends young Americans in any profession to live in an Asian country for a year, working in some capacity with their peers—provided they have no direct professional reason to be interested in Asia!

So, completely serendipitously, my wife and I, just married, spent a year in Bali, absorbing the music and culture and experiencing a profound change in our worldview. I studied gamelan with a revered elder master of a rare classical tradition (continuing the lucky streak I had had all along when seeking out teachers—as John Cage said about his own experience, "always going to the president of the company"). In this case, the guru, who contained in his being the entire repertoire of an exceptionally refined, elegant court music and was also a brilliant composer, was at the same time a coarse, illiterate rice farmer who professed to disdain Westerners like me who were so dependent on notation that they couldn't *really* learn, or fully internalize, music. Some Westerners can, and do, but they have to acquire a different way of "processing" music, perhaps with greater emphasis on muscular memory. Performance and composition are not so separated in Bali as in latter-day western music; such a dichotomy of musical thought and musical reality as was revealed in that lesson with Rochberg couldn't arise in such a tradition. I was not proficient at this kind of learning for at least two reasons: Not being a practicing performer even in my "own" tradition, I had not developed much of a habit of this kind of assimilation; and the purpose of my lessons was more to understand the compositional structure of the music from the inside than to master it as a performer.[14] One of the results of my lessons was a set of written-out scores or transcriptions of a number of Balinese compositions, which I wrote out part by part as I learned them. I was fascinated equally by the beauty of this music, sometimes brilliant and virtuosic, sometimes shimmering and delicate, and by its unexpected variety. We explored all around the less well-traveled, remote mountainous regions of Bali where a number of strange and archaic ensembles survive, each with its own musical structure and instrumental color, making innumerable hours of rather low-quality recordings.

At first my mind was so flooded with all this that I could not conceive of "my own" music. My response was to attempt a sort of musical exorcism by writing my own quasi-Balinese music for that very Western ensemble, the concert band. This piece appropriates elements from a few different Balinese styles, with a touch of Javanese practice, and could almost pass for a transcription of a Balinese piece (except that the original does not exist). Thus "cleansed," I worked on a song cycle, *Black Magic/White Magic*, to my wife's poems, organized according to shamanistic Balinese ideas. Though largely written in Bali, this work shows only occasional influences from Balinese music, but it is conceptually imbued with a Balinese spirit. We returned to Bali 2 years later for half a year, followed by months of travels through Asia and Europe. During this period I wrote *For the Morning of the World*, my most ambitious homage to Bali, a large chamber orchestra work in which each of the six movements is a take-off on a specific Balinese genre or ensemble. This time I was able more adventurously to fuse specific Balinese modes, textures, rhythms, and sonorities with my own ways of hearing. From that time, Balinese music has been a presence in much of my music, but often subliminally and rarely explicitly; in all its range and variety, it has become part of my bloodstream.

During these travels I drew close to and began to internalize another Asian musical tradition, that of North India. When due to illness our visit to Nepal became an extended rest in a hotel in the heart of the old city in Kathmandu, a hotel employee invited me to a weekly ceremony at a temple by the river, consisting entirely of *bhajan* (devotional songs) sung both communally (folksong style) and solo (classical style). The vitality and beauty of the music were overwhelming; the solo songs, performed by a revered older master, were in "strange" ragas using hauntingly unfamiliar scales quite remote from Western interval patterns.[15]

Though I was already attracted by Indian music and had learned enough about its workings that I had begun to introduce it in my teaching, this encounter was profoundly affecting and led to an influx of new ways of musical thinking. At the most basic level, I found myself imagining melodic lines infused with the intervallic colorations of the actual music I had just heard, as may be heard in my first symphony, *Anahata*. Over the years since, I have continued to study those ragas and families of related ones and have found them a still-fertile source of melodic ideas. I have also taken the most un-Indian step of exploring harmonic (chordal) developments (chord types, progressions) within these ragas. All in all, this way of hearing reinforced a modal conception of melody and harmony, perhaps parallel to Messiaen's extensive explorations of his own modal system—not as a limiting, closed system, but as one important element in a composer's "toolbox."

A second, broader result was a renewed focus on melody per se; like much of the world's music but unlike the Western tradition, Indian music consists entirely of single-line melody and its evolution, hand-in-hand with rhythmic development: no harmony, no progression, no counterpoint, no "orchestration" to speak of.[16] During this time in Kathmandu, I worked on one of the movements of *For the Morning of the World*, in the form of a single, relentlessly focused, gradually accelerating melodic line, developing within evolving, partly Balinese modes, which is clearly derived from Indian templates—at the same time as it reflects the timbre and texture of an archaic form of Balinese gamelan.

Finally, this experience of music as devotional or celebratory ritual rather than as performance before an audience—similar to the role of music and art in Bali, or even to Messiaen's sense of spiritual purpose in music—reinforced my deepest conception of the ultimate raison d'être of music.

THOUGHTS ON MUSICAL CREATIVITY:
THE PROCESS OF COMPOSING

What is it an artist does?... The artist says, "I can do very little about the chaos around me, but at least I can reduce to perfect order this square of canvas, this piece of paper, this chunk of stone.".... He meditates. He connects his hand and paintbrush to the deeper, quieter, more mysterious parts of his mind—and he paints pictures of what he sees and feels down there.

—Kurt Vonnegut, *Palm Sunday* (1981, pp. 292–293; 2006, pp. 145–146)

Where do musical ideas come from? I wish I knew. As Stravinsky said, waiting is a big part of the process. Virgil Thomson pointed out that regular work habits help prepare the mind to be tuned in whenever it is fortunate enough to "receive" ideas.[17] When I am actively at work I see myself as a craft worker, *making things*, albeit in the seemingly ethereal medium of imaginary sound. The process is one of striving to make convincing shapes, "sculpted" in sound and time; the sculptural or spatial metaphor is very real to me. My work is not based on any precompositional system or theoretically generalizable method, from which two things follow: My working process is necessarily ad hoc, and it is determined by the specific materials (i.e., concrete sound ideas) at hand. In other words, I am more likely to work from the very small toward the larger than to begin from a grand plan and work toward the details.[18]

The starting point is free association: simply imagining sounds for whatever the medium is to be, with absolutely no preconditions and no critical judgment. The most conducive state of mind is akin to some kinds of meditation, a close but nondirective focus on the inner workings of the mind. This can be done both at or away from the piano; the piano is conducive to close, detailed work with harmony, whereas other, big-picture imagination may well be freer away from it, including outdoors, on walks, in nature. In my small sketchbooks I jot down anything: melodic motifs (or even less well-defined interval cells), rhythms, textures, chords. Some of these primordial notions involve specific notes; some do not. Pitch is sometimes, but not necessarily, primary. When the initial sound image is not defined by pitch, I find whatever kind of notation will suffice to "fix" the idea and recall it to my memory. This could require precise musical notation, but just as often I use verbal description, drawings, and so on instead of, or in addition to, notation.

Because one kind of stimulus to musical ideas is other music (all the music we carry around in our heads),[19] one useful kind of mnemonic "notation" for me is to name the composer or music that sparked my own "sound image." Thus I labeled a notion for a fast, buzzing, lightweight string passage in my first symphony as the "Mendelssohn scherzo," though no one hearing it would be likely to think of Mendelssohn. For me, stimuli may arise from a wide range of musics with which I identify, from the whole range of Western art music, sometimes popular music, and more recently, thanks to our son Adam's involvement, jazz. Sound images may also arise from my deep-seated relationship with gamelan, both Balinese and Javanese, and other Asian musics, especially North Indian ragas. My ear could even be caught be some fleeting moment in music to which I feel no other particular connection, leading to some creative "spinoff." Messiaen's openly acknowledged, unashamed assimilation of ideas from other composers and cultures seems a healthy model, confirming my own instinctively eclectic instincts.[20]

Musical "germ" ideas can also be stimulated by sounds not commonly classified as music, especially (in my case) natural sounds. Messiaen's lifelong love (and careful study) of birdsong is an inspiring example, and in my own work I have derived musical motifs from my transcriptions (or impressions), not only of birdsong but also of such other natural phenomena as whale songs and insect sounds.[21]

"Sound images" can also arise in response to visual or other stimuli as well. At times I have sought musical equivalents to paintings (e.g., Monet's water lilies), to landscapes (e.g., mountain and seascapes), and to poetic images, whether or not verbal texts are to be sung.

Over time I have accumulated many pages of sketches in small musical notebooks (convenient to carry on walks; I find spending time outdoors conducive to creative work). There are also long tables of chords, or variations of harmonic ideas, and of raga or raga-like scales and harmonic derivations; these constitute a reservoir of potential raw material. Sometimes an idea may sit untouched in my sketchbook for years before finding the right context to call it forth. I'm heartened by the knowledge that Prokokiev's *Third Piano Sonata*, one of his most explosively vital and concentrated works, is headed "from old notebooks." Many composers save up ideas for years and refer back to them when seeking materials or concepts for new works; most aren't as frank about it as Prokofiev.

Suspension of judgment, evaluation, and self-criticism is essential during this initial sketching phase of the process. The purpose is to accumulate a large field of possibilities, excluding nothing for the moment, and the activity is one of play rather than work. Here I want to cite remarks by the late poet Robert Lax. Lax, a cousin of my wife, was an important inspiration and influence for both of us and for my sense of musical vocation, and his poetry has been, explicitly or subliminally, the source of the text or title or concept of more than one of my works.

> An artist who's working and happy in his work … all he's doing is playing. And he's been playing well today, so he wants to tell you about it.…

This business of playing—musicians do it in jam sessions and really do it best [Lax was a devotee of jazz], do it as a regular thing—if you don't have some sort of joy in a jam session or what you're doing, you really shouldn't be there—for the kind of art I'm thinking of now.... Unless it's really a pleasure to make and a pleasure to show your friends and a pleasure for them to see, you're not sure why you're doing it. If it is all these things, then I know why I'm, I know why anyone is doing it, because that's just living, it promotes life, it sustains life, so that it's good stuff, I think—it justifies itself. All it has to be is that sort of poem or that sort of thing; it's got a place in this little world anyway, in any place. Whereas if it's trying to do anything very important, I don't know, it is a different thing. It may actually do that very important thing, just trying to.... But I don't know how to think about that kind of writing.

After a certain point, if you're playing the best thing that happens when you're playing is you become unselfconscious.

—From *Robert Lax: Word & Image*, a film by Judith Emery and Michael Lastnite

So in the first phase, for which I try to allow myself quite a lot of unstructured time, I am at play in the field of sound (and time). Eventually I find myself moving into the next phase, that of seeking the larger shape and plan for the piece. Promising ideas are extended, varied, and juxtaposed (or even, given my predilection for multilayered musics, superimposed) in a kind of larger scale play with the materials. As I work, I often become increasingly aware of relationships among ideas I had conceived separately. I am convinced that much of the real work of the imagination goes on intuitively, subconsciously, so that there are often quite sensible, logical connections among what seemed to have occurred to me as separate, isolated thoughts. As one gets more and more involved with one's materials, it is useful and important to become as aware and conscious as possible about their substance and their interrelationships; this is an important component of craftsmanship. The more one really knows about one's ideas, the more profoundly one can explore their potential.

As I begin to form longer continuities, I may use some kind of shorthand such as using letters to identify various ideas and to try out various orders and combinations. These can also be quickly sketched as rhythms on plain (nonstaff) paper, with indications of timbre (instrumentation) and dynamics—which are in today's musical world (since, say, Debussy) equally important aspects of sound to pitch and melodic line. Like the first, sketching phase, this too can be a highly intuitive process of free association, trusting the hunch. Sometimes it's obvious why two ideas might belong together; sometimes logical reasons become apparent only later, or never. I have no system or method, which is why I feel like each piece is my first work all over again. However, I would like to believe that instinct trained by decades of experience, and reflection, must count for something.

Nonprofessional listeners are often surprised to learn that the eventual, moment-to-moment continuity of a piece of music is usually not the result of an ordered process of composing in real time, or in the real order of events, one bar (or the equivalent) following another. I might work from the end back toward earlier sections, from the inside out, or in unordered fragments that only gradually find their proper order or sequence. The beginning of a piece has often been the very last part to be composed; once I started with a concluding passage I had jotted down while improvising 2 years earlier, well before the conception of the piece. In this sense, again, the musical shaping process resembles that of a sculptor, who might work now on this part of the marble, now on that part—or a painter concentrating on an area in the lower right corner of the canvas, then a spot in the middle, then the upper left. Even novelists, for whom a logical development of the plot might require a greater responsibility to "realistic" causality and narrative logic, do not necessarily work in one direction, from beginning to end.

The result of this building process is some kind of continuity draft of the whole piece or movement, which lays out the entire shape in time, though not necessarily all the details or even all the exact notes. (My original sketches usually contain a reservoir of intervallic and harmonic material so that I know what the various events are actually going to be made of.) This draft is subject to much scrutiny; the architecture has to feel convincing and right. At this point the faculty of critical judgment has long since been plugged back in, and its demands can be unrelenting. I confess to sometimes being prone to bouts of fatigue and frustration around this stage, as it may take a lot of work to feel I am approaching the *mot juste*. It can be difficult for people to be around me, preoccupied and anxious as I may be, and I'm more than grateful to my family for their tolerance and support, as this has occurred repeatedly over the years. In fact it is rarely the case that the epiphany, the moment of clarity in which the perfected form appears, ever arrives. Like many composers I know, I declare the plan finished when I come to believe that any further alterations are as likely to make matters worse as to improve them. George Crumb, a highly refined perfectionist in his work, told me, "I never finish works, I just abandon them." And

Stravinsky admitted to dissatisfaction of some kind with every one of his works but remarked that it was for that reason that he would go on to write the next one.

My own sense of form, continuity, and gesture has been shaped not only by the "logical," narrative, directed rhetoric of mainstream Western art music but also by alternative conceptions of musical time, such as the slow unfolding of Indian music; the ceremonial stasis (which sometimes conceals a deep sense of development and evolution of tension) of ancient gamelan music; the brilliant, dynamic cross-cutting of more modern Balinese gamelan; or the block-like juxtapositional discontinuities of Stravinsky ("composing with scissors," in his words). It has occurred to me that this new, antitraditional kind of "continuity through discontinuity" entered into Western music at about the same time as the early development of cinema, in which individual shots or scenes were quite literally cut with scissors and spliced together, and the narrative is constructed in the viewer's mind by connecting the events in successive but separate visual moments. Given this characteristic of my music, perhaps my work is not so different from that of our filmmaker son, Ari. In some works, such as in my *Second Symphony*, I have tried to push this "sculptural" conception of musical space rather far, building large-scale structures of juxtaposed and superimposed, more or less static "sound blocks." They actually do shift and develop as they are combined, but their *rhetoric* may be static. I believe that the mind constructs a continuity between successive recurrences of similar ideas, across the interruptions of contrasting ideas, as if they were always present and progressing, but sometimes unheard.

A complementary preoccupation has been a focus on the single, disconnected moment, resulting in works consisting of a series of tiny miniatures, self-contained moments of "stopped time," such as *Here of Amazing Most Now*, a set of 12 tiny miniatures for shifting instrumental combinations, each a depiction of a haiku or other brief poetic image. My music is also infused sometimes with a multilayered richness of texture, with multiple strata moving at different speeds, perhaps recalling the music of Charles Ives, who like Mahler (or Messiaen) strove to embrace the whole world in music.

The last phase is to realize in all its detail the plan already arrived at. For an orchestral work this would require first writing out a condensed score, which would contain all the music on as few staves as possible, with shorthand indications of orchestration, to be followed by the full score on very large paper, sometimes with 40 or more staves. In the process of working out the details, changes in the pacing, rhythm, or even sequence of events may occur. The continuity plan is not final until it has been fully realized, after much manual labor.

Unlike most of the other arts, a musical composition—a completed score—is not so much a finished product as a plan of action for others to realize, more analogous to the script of a play than to a painting.[22] Although a score may aspire to specify every detail of what happens through the time span of the work, it still depends on performers to bring it into physical (albeit fleeting) reality so that it can be experienced by others. Up until that moment of the first performance, or at least rehearsal, it has existed only as an imaginary construct in the composer's mind (or in the mind of any other musician sufficiently skilled to read the score and imagine in his or her own mind the same sound image).

For me, the experience of the first actual hearing of a new piece is very intense. If my craft has been up to the task I set myself, it will sound like my imaginings, but nevertheless there are always differences between the physical and the imaginary realities. Often these differences are gratifying and exciting; the actual impact of the sounds may be even more vivid than I had hoped for. Sometimes they are troublesome, often involving a lack of clarity; generally these problems can be worked out in rehearsal by small refinements of balancing, dynamics, and so on, but sufficient rehearsal time is not always available. Sometimes problems require some compositional or orchestrational reconsideration. But it is important to separate problems inherent in the score from inaccuracies in the performers' emerging realization of it. It is also a useful professional skill in rehearsal to distinguish between errors requiring attention and those that the performers will sort out themselves with more familiarity. With top-level orchestras and performers, it is astonishing how much can be left to the players without comment, and the best conductors know this; nervous composers have to learn it, sometimes over and over.

A final peculiarity of musical composition is that each performance of a work, even by the same performers, will be different from all others. During rehearsals I am often too preoccupied with troubleshooting, with listening for what needs attention, to actually enjoy the sheer experience of hearing my imaginary sound worlds become real. Once the rehearsals are over, I still have difficulty "joining the audience" at the concert—in other words, pretending I don't know what is to come and experiencing it as one of the listeners in the hall. But this is the ideal state of listening to which I aspire—becoming, in Stravinsky's words, the "hypothetical other" for whom one composes. It may take years, until the tensions and uncertainties of rehearsals are forgotten, before I can hear my own music with some degree of objectivity. Even so, there is a considerable thrill when I hear the sound world I imagined and worked at, for months or even years, finally become real.

I strongly believe that whatever an artist is actually thinking about while at work (the craft aspect), at the deepest level one makes art from absolutely everything in one's experience of life. Love, a rich family life, a sense of spiritual connection to the natural world, the physical and cultural dimensions of travel (outer and inner)—all contribute to the inner world from which my music springs.

> *"Why should I write?" said the pencil.*
> *"What else can you do?" said the knife.*

—**Robert Lax**[23]

NOTES

1. I was struck by this widely quoted remark of the great Mexican painter when I saw it displayed at an exhibition of her work at the Philadelphia Museum of Art in 2008.

2. This iconic remark, encapsulating the essence both of the creative process and of Stravinsky's own diminutive, wiry physique, is widely known to composers and aficionados of twentieth-century music and is commonly cited, though its provenance is uncertain (possibly from a BBC interview). I have heard a recording of it somewhere, spoken in Stravinsky's inimitable voice.

3. This remembered experience of hearing turned out to be useful decades later in graduate school, as supporting evidence for a speculation by the theorist Leonard Meyer about ways in which purely melodic shapes, in the abstract, might have specific implications for meter. His suggestion of that very same Mozart melody as a possible example was greeted with general skepticism, because "everyone" knew how the tune really goes, but my memory of my naïve puzzlement bore out Meyer's theory perfectly.

4. Twenty years later, one of my former teachers noticed a resemblance between a key motif of my first symphony, *Anahata*, and the *Goldfinger* theme. As for *Doctor Zhivago*, it too contributed in a peculiar way to my musical development, in that the tune was often requested by my parents' friends at parties. To counter my condescension toward this "corny" tune, I would sneak in inappropriate key changes in the middles of phrases so that an attentive listener would feel seasick—but at parties no one was really listening, so I was able to explore and develop my sense of harmony without alienating too many people.

5. My publisher, hearing the solemn chorale that begins the finale of my *Second Symphony*, said, "There's that band piece you've been talking about writing, right there."

6. It seems foreordained that not so many years later I would find myself, quite by chance, studying with George Crumb, renowned for his poetic and pioneering use of just such sounds.

7. Given this background it may be curious that I have never seriously pursued electronic or computer music. I still prefer sounds produced directly by human beings playing instruments (including the voice) to sounds emanating from loudspeakers.

8. I still have the music notebook containing all my earliest efforts, emblazoned with a "Eugene McCarthy for President" bumper sticker.

9. My teaching to this day incorporates pedagogical methods and ways of understanding harmony from those first courses taught by Constant Vauclain.

10. Like Crumb, and encouraged by his example. I have always placed a high value on the visual appearance of my scores.

11. Though there is some truth to this generalization, this domination was not nearly as absolute as hindsight would have it, as the three Penn composers themselves demonstrate. I count myself fortunate to have found myself in such a nondoctrinaire musical environment during such a formative period.

12. Later, *in dark* was the piece that won me admission to the Paris Conservatory to study with Messiaen. There I was able to stimulate Messiaen's admiration for Crumb, and a few years ago I lectured on Crumb's music at the Messiaen Festival in France, for which Crumb wrote a beautiful and heartfelt tribute to Messiaen.

13. I was hired at a young age, despite an absolutely perfect lack of teaching experience, because my music was found to be appealing; one of the pieces that found favor was *in dark*, from my own college years.

14. By contrast, a colleague of mine studied a few years later with the same teacher and fully engaged in a more Balinese-style learning process. He went on to found and direct Swarthmore's Balinese gamelan, in which he teaches the music in the same notation-less, hands-on style as our teacher. Interestingly, he has also extended this learning experience to young inner-city children in an after-school program.

15. It was moving to learn that he had chosen these ragas because he knew they would be especially interesting to a western musician.

16. Western music at its origins (plainchant) was such music, and it has begun to rediscover the possibilities of pure melody again in the posttonal period, from the early 20th century on.

17. Thomson proposed that the artist should show up in his studio, as a metaphorical train station, to greet the muse at the same time every day; if she doesn't arrive on the train, at least *you* were there.

18. At Tanglewood in 1971, a well-known serialist (i.e., highly systematizing) composer responded to a question of mine by supposing that whereas he would characterize himself as a "relationalist," I could probably be described as a "concretist." I thought that if he meant that he was more

interested in how such aspects of sound as pitch, interval, duration, dynamics, and so on *related* to one another, whereas I was more interested in how things *sounded*, I accepted the distinction.

19. Composers of all stylistic stripes have affirmed that it is common for musical ideas to arise in response to other people's music.

20. In his writings he was extraordinarily self-revealing about his musical sources; most composers tend to deemphasize or even conceal this aspect of creativity.

21. My second symphony includes elaborate string textures evoking the polyrhythmic repeated-note "music" of a meadow full of crickets, perhaps in the tradition of Berg's depiction of frogs in the drowning scene of *Wozzeck*.

22. This and the following do not apply to composers of electronic and computer music, whose final product is in fact a recorded performance.

23. The title quotation, repeated here, is most likely unpublished. It is excerpted from a personal letter either to me or to my wife, Nanine Valen.

REFERENCES

Harrison, L. (1971). *Music primer.* New York: C. F. Peters Corp.

Vonnegut, K. (c1981/2006). *Palm Sunday: An autobiographical collage.* Ramjac Corporation/Dial Press.

7

COMMENTARY
A View of Levinson's Development

Jeanne Bamberger

Gerald Levinson's *Anahata: Symphony No. 1* is an exuberant 30-minute work of tremendous inventions and aural seductiveness ... with its utter sincerity and clear-skied, all encompassing horizons, this symphony, quite literally, ravishes you. When the final notes faded away, it was Leonard Bernstein, seated in the audience, who started the standing ovation.

—Anthony Tommasini, *Boston Globe* (Presser.com)

Black Magic/White Magic. Levinson is particularly gifted at creating harmonies whose voicings and intervals (and extensive use of winds as coloring) take on the quality of exotic "meta-instruments." It's almost as though the whole ensemble were a single, large instrument playing in a wholly natural, yet alternative, tuning.

—Robert Carl, *Fanfare* (Presser.com)

INTRODUCTION

The reviews quoted above help to place Gerald Levinson among the composers of his generation—how he is heard and how he is valued in the world of contemporary music. A brief description will sum up the facts of his achievements:

Gerald Levinson, born in 1951 and raised in Connecticut, has been increasingly recognized as one of the major composers of his generation. In 1990, he received the Music Award (for lifetime achievement) of the American Academy of Arts and Letters, which cited his "sensitive poetic spirit, imaginative treatment of texture and color," and his "potent and very personal idiom which projects immediately to the listener."[1]

Reading the reminiscences that Levinson has given us, there emerges a path of development that is adventuresome and strongly self-directed. In reading the comments that follow, it is important to recognize that to pursue such a path in today's musical scene is a difficult challenge and one from which Levinson has not wavered.

The creative process is often thought of as a matter of "inspiration"—nonreflective, "free," "nonlinear," purely sensuous, and even mindless. In school, for instance, "creativity" is left for the afternoon free periods when the students are finished "working." I shall propose instead that inherent in Levinson's deep learning and ultimately his artistic development are recurring cycles of action and sensory experience merging and converging with intense reflection and analysis.

To frame this proposal, I argue that there is a mutual support between

- the fluidity of felt order (Hasty, 1997, p. 3), where configurations of action and sound shapes are experienced in the elusive passing present; and
- reflective abstraction ... connections "drawn out" of the sensorimotor schemas and "projected upon" the new plane of thought (Piaget, 1970, p. 64).

I will call these cycles *dialectical spirals*.[2] I use the term to point not only to recurring instances that I find critical in Levinson's development but also to an aspect that may well be implicated in musical development more generally. It is a process of circling through a spiral of modes: deeply engaging, spontaneous, sensuous experience including listening (heard internally in imagination or heard from an outside source); reflecting back on these perceptions often to seek the constituents of an initially elusive hearing and to construct internal and external representations; then circling back again to rehear, and to reshape, initial perceptions of the working material. These recurring cycles may extend over long periods of development as well as in brief moments during the course of work on an emerging composition.

What I find particularly intriguing is the notion of "dialectical" when taken as Hegel construes it: "a continuous unification of opposites." Is this again an issue of perception ⇔ conception: opposites or dialectical pairs?

COUPLED EXAMPLES OF DIALECTICAL SPIRALS

In the following examples, I have paired moments of direct sensory experience with related instances of reflective inquiry in search of explanations, sources, and the ongoing construction of inner and outer representations.

Childhood

While taking piano lessons as a child, Levinson did not aspire to become a professional pianist, spending more time improvising and exploring than practicing. However, the piano continued to play an important role in his development:

> My undisciplined approach to the keyboard did have some positive consequences. … [It was] a means of getting acquainted with music in a direct, physical way, internalizing it through the fingers.… A physical, tactile connection to music—existing music or my own emerging ideas—has always been central to me, though I have never been a professional performer.

At much the same time but now in a reflective mode, Levinson reports trying to "figure out" what precisely is going on in the music he is listening to. And a bit later, his search becomes more serious, contributing to the development of fundamental skills:

> From an early age I had had the impulse to "figure out" music I heard. I remember trying to write down songs … after hearing them in music class in the third or fourth grade.
>   When I was 12 or so … I owe [the Beatles] a great deal because my efforts to reproduce their melodies and harmonies constituted some of my earliest exercises … in the ability to hear precisely melodic intervals, harmonic progressions, and rhythms so that one can not only play back what one hears but also write it down if needed. This cultivates the skill of hearing internally, in the imagination, which is the essence of what composers do.

Listening

A most striking influence throughout Levinson's development is his persistent and concentrated *listening* to music. He tells of the formative listening to a wide range of music including music that just happens to be around at some point in time, as well as music that he has explicitly sought out. But again, listening circles—at times it is simply there, whereas at other times Levinson once more reports questioning, analyzing.

As an experienced musician, we find him listening intently to the music of Bali and India. However, as a child lying in bed at night before falling asleep, he simply absorbs the music that would "waft upstairs." He reports that "this constant presence of fine music in the house, even as background, was a great gift to me and a *formative influence*" (emphasis added).

But early absorbent listening soon develops into listening very closely:

> At some early age I must have begun to listen very closely. I retain a specific and concrete memory of puzzlement at the meter of the Trio of the minuet of Mozart's *G-Minor Symphony*. I was listening closely enough, *without any understanding*, to notice that some kind of trick was being played with rhythm. This turned out to be useful decades later as supporting evidence by the theorist Leonard Meyer about ways in which purely melodic shapes, in the abstract, might have specific implications for meter.[3] (Emphasis added)

Levinson's "close listening" to this Mozart symphony movement leaves him puzzled but "without any understanding." What, then, might constitute understanding? Many years later, Levinson is able to point to, to extract, the specific pitch–time relations of the music that had generated the surprising effect and its affect. Understanding, if taken in this way, is, as suggested above, a process much like "reflective abstraction": *connections "drawn out" of the sensorimotor schemas and "projected upon" the new plane of thought.*

TEACHERS

Levinson's development has clearly been influenced by a distinguished group of musicians—composers and performers, together with poets and painters. These teachers, consistent with his respective temperament and collectively, also contributed to furthering these dialectical spirals.

For instance, while an undergraduate student at university, Levinson reports on a composition lesson with the distinguished composer, George Rochberg. This lesson turns the spiral around—reflection circling to, and learning from, sensory experience. Levinson describes it as "one of the finest composition lessons I ever had." He brings to his lesson a song with instrumental ensemble that he has just completed. To his surprise, Rochberg insists that he play and sing the composition for him, saying, "You have vocal chords? You have fingers?" After he "limped" through the performance of his own composition, Levinson pauses and then says, " I see what you mean." And until that moment, he "hadn't made the connection between *thinking* about a vocal line, setting text, and the physical reality of *singing*" (emphasis in original).

Richard Wernick, "a tougher, more challenging, and more practical teacher," made the reflective turn of the spiral: "[Wernick] helped sharpen my sense of the importance of craft, organization, attention to form, self-critical awareness, and the frequent necessity of revision ... a sometimes protracted *search* for the right way" (emphasis in original).

MUSICAL LOGIC

In the course of Levinson's "thick description" of both his personal development and the development of a composition, the notion of "logic" takes on important meaning but meaning quite different from what we might find in Piaget or, indeed, among the great logicians— Aristotle, Russell, or early Wittgenstein. Rather than a way of reasoning that is context free and intended as a means toward "objective truth," logic for a composer is a continuously emergent, continuously generative process. That is, it is particular to the musical materials with which the composer is working and highly dependent on the immediate context as it unfolds. Thus for Levinson as for other composers, logic is not given but rather imminent—that is, responsive to *musical implication* and yet, importantly, not at all arbitrary.

With respect to musical "implication," Leonard Meyer (1973) said,

> An implicative relationship is one in which an event—be it a motive, a phrase, and so on—is patterned in such a way that reasonable inferences can be made both about its connections with preceding events and about how the event itself might continue and perhaps reach closure and stability.... Implicative inferences, then, are like hypotheses which experienced listeners entertain (perhaps unconsciously) about the connections between musical events ... in a particular movement or work. (p. 110)

And Levinson, in much the same spirit, comments on the logic in his own composition experience:

> [T]here are often quite sensible, logical connections among what seemed to have occurred to me as separate, isolated thoughts....
>
> Sometimes it's obvious why two ideas might belong together; sometimes logical reasons become apparent only later or never.

These comments suggest that the development of a composer's logic, in particular the logic of musical implication, contrasts in distinct ways with Piaget's theories of the development of formal logic. To say this opens up the possibility of a whole discussion that is not appropriate here, but one that should be pursued. To give just a single example, I will point to the importance Piaget gives to the development of reversibility, which he characterizes as follows: "The end result is independent of the route taken" (Piaget, 1976, p. 54). By contrast, in an unfolding musical structure, the potential for change in meanings as a result of the "route taken" is deeply important to the composer and also to the listener. To develop a feeling for musical implication and logic, the composer must be continuously alert to the unique "route taken" by the evolving music, for the functional meaning of the same notated pitch, configuration, or even whole phrase always has the potential to change in response to each context as it occurs.

For instance, in the first section of a classical minuet or scherzo movement in a symphony, the opening, usually a relatively brief section of the movement, is immediately repeated. And yet we often hear the repetition as something new. That "hearing" may seem strange to those who are reading the score because we just "go back to play it again." But in fact we can never go back in time, we can only go on. Listening to a live performance, then, an immediate, literal repetition of thematic material has good reason to sound quite different: With the repeat of the opening material, the context has importantly changed. The movement begins out of silence, but at the moment the repeat starts, instead of appearing out of silence, the beginning section of the movement is now attached to its own "tail."

David Soyer, the cellist in the Guarneri String Quartet, tells of changing meanings in his performance of a moment in one of the late Beethoven Quartets (despite the technical language, I think the pre-eminent importance given to context will be clear):

> When G-natural comes again, its harmonic function is altered....
> The subsequent G-sharp is no longer the tonic but acts as the leading note in a-minor and should be sharpened. This is the explanation from the harmonic standpoint, but your hearing once sensitized to such things, will often be able to put you there quite of itself without your needing to think it out. (Quoted in Blum, 1986, p. 33)

But it would be impossible even to notice the remarkable shifts in meaning that the same notated pitch may undergo, if one were not able to recognize that, indeed, it is the same pitch. And thus, the development of an emergent or imminent musical logic is again related to the continuous interaction of sensory experience and reflection. Whereas Piaget tends to keep sensorimotor intelligence apart from reflection in the course of the developing reversibility and other formal logics, the composer's developing logic, as exemplified in the above comments, is a logic critically dependent on the functional, active, mobile intercourse between sense and reflective thought.[4]

The Composition Process

Levinson's description of his composing process is quite extraordinary in the detail with which he traces the phases and the evolution of his own compositional process. As such he gives us an unusual, perhaps unique window into how a composer actual works. I trust that the reader has read this account carefully because there is much more from which to learn than I can comment on here. On that assumption, I will again follow the theme, now in more dramatic form, of the function of dialectical spirals in the moment-to-moment work of bringing to life an initial intuitive, elusive musical "idea." In his thoughts on the process of composing, Levinson provides the most telling examples of the intimate engagement of fluidity of felt order, with "reflective abstraction," and a new and different sense of close listening:

> The starting point is free association: simply imagining sounds for whatever the medium is to be, with absolutely no preconditions and no critical judgment ... promising ideas are extended, varied, juxtaposed ... in a kind of larger scale play with materials.... As one gets more and more involved with one's materials, it is useful and important to become as aware and conscious as possible about their substance and their interrelationships.... *The more one really knows about one's ideas, the more profoundly one can explore their potential* ... [T]he experience of the first actual hearing of a new piece is very intense ... but nevertheless there are always differences between the physical and the imaginary realities. (Emphasis added)

Similar cycles are found in the reports of composers throughout history: an initial vague impression, form, or sound image that may remain with them hovering in the background for extended periods of time. There follows, as each of these composers make quite clear, the work of reflection, craft, and focused attention to detail and large design. Here, the initially vague "idea" becomes the notes, the instrumentation, the contrast, and the internal coherence of a particular passage and eventually of the completed composition. This work of bringing the potential of a sounding image to life is also a kind of inspiration. And surprisingly, it is one that is fully realized only later and from a distance on listening to the first performance of the completed work.

Roger Sessions

The important thing is that I knew—and simply from following the music as I had conceived and written it up to that point—what must come next, and was able to describe it quite accurately in words. I knew it, that is, in terms of everything except the specific musical pattern, itself.... One knows exactly what one wants, but has not yet succeeded in finding its definite shape. (Sessions, 1971, pp. 29, 96)

Tchaikowsky

Only after strenuous labor, have I at last succeeded in making the form of my composition correspond, more or less, with their contents. Formerly I was careless and did not give sufficient attention to the critical overhauling of my sketches. Consequently my *seams* showed, and there was not organic union between my individual episodes. (Quoted in Sloboda, 1985, p. 120)

Ravel

[Ravel,] when asked about the progress of a work which he was then composing ... replied that he had it all finished except the themes. (Quoted in Prausnitz, 2002, p. 95)

DEVELOPING A UNIQUE "VOICE"

Finally, a word about Levinson's development of his own style or "voice." As the reviews quoted above suggest, the most unusual quality of Levinson's work is his invention and creation of unique sound worlds ("aural seductiveness"). Beginning at a very young age, he has continued to develop this unique creative force. He reports on experimenting with sound and also seeking out new sounds already in his teenage years:

I recall sitting on the floor under the keyboard, plucking and strumming the strings, knocking on the beams and the soundboard and recording the results. I sought out complex "new music".... I couldn't possibly "understand" how most of this music was conceived, but I was fascinated by all the new sounds.

Joining the band in middle school

was an invaluable experience.... I was fascinated by the combinations of instrumental colors which encouraged my nascent urge to think in terms of combinations of sound.... The richly varied coloristic possibilities of the wind ensemble have remained quite close to me.

But the dialectical spiral is also at work: "I listened to sounds in a very focused, detailed way, noticing fine points of attack and decay, overtones, resonances, and the like."

In 1972, at the age of 20 and during his last year as an undergraduate, Levinson's continuing development of unique sound worlds culminates in his Opus 1, *in dark*:

I continued working with Rochberg, but this time on two ambitious pieces of my own devising. One of them, *in dark* ... turned out to be my Opus 1, the earliest piece I'm still happy to have performed.[5] It continues the "exotic" instrumental coloration ... with its fusion of the voice with low flutes and strings, harp, piano, and percussion, and a "French" coloration in the harmony.

Probably the greatest influence on this and other aspects of his development came with Levinson's move to Paris and his studies with the great French composer, Olivier Messiaen. Messiaen's composition class, as Levinson points out, has been much proclaimed over the years: "12 hours per week during which he shared everything he had ever loved and studied ... the combination of wonder and profound knowledge, resulting from relentless study, in that class fully justified its now legendary reputation."

Levinson shared with Messiaen a profound interest in creating new sound worlds. For example,

In the time that I spent in Messiaen's class, we were all deeply involved in Messiaen's close listening to birdsong, which he often illustrated, including the ways in which he had incorporated what he had learned into his own compositions.[6] (personal communication)

But Levinson's critique of his first composition during that time once more demonstrates the importance in his development of close attention to reflecting on and learning from his own work:

I have withdrawn the piece ... it was a major learning experience. For one thing, it became clearer to me that even in a very spacious, meditative musical climate, music must still have a living metabolism, a sense of breath, however slow or distended.... When I returned for a second year in Paris, I found my compositional "voice" growing bolder and produced two pieces, both more successful than their predecessor.

And at last, there is the time Levinson spent in Bali (1979–1980), which had a seminal effect on his work. I was particularly intrigued by the description of the Balinese guru with whom he studied. As he describes the man and particularly the relationship between them, it seems a particularly poignant example of the importance I have given to the dialectical spirals. The description of the guru is itself representative of the dialectic. The guru,

> who contained in his being the entire repertoire of an exceptionally refined, elegant court music and was also a brilliant composer, was at the same time a coarse, illiterate rice farmer who professed to disdain Westerners like me who were so dependent on notation that they couldn't really learn, or fully internalize, music.

And harking back to his early lesson with Rochberg, what Levinson refers to as a *dichotomy* I prefer to think of as a potentially generative dialectic:[7]

> Performance and composition in Bali are not so separated as in latter-day Western music; such a dichotomy of musical thought and musical reality as was revealed in that lesson with Rochberg couldn't arise in such a tradition ... the purpose of my lessons was more to understand the compositional structure of the music from the inside than to master it as a performer.... One of the results of my lessons was a set of written-out scores or transcriptions of a number of Balinese compositions, which I wrote out part by part as I learned them.

There follows in Levinson's development a series of new works, each showing the strong effect of his time in Bali and each adding new character to his individual voice: *Black Magic/White* Magic (composed in 1980–1981 and reviewed in the introductory quotes), and *For the Morning of the World*. "From that time, Balinese music has been a presence in much of my music, but often subliminally and rarely explicitly; in all its range and variety, it has become part of my bloodstream."

The extended visit to Nepal also has a "profoundly affecting" influence leading "to an influx of new ways of musical thinking." This new way of thinking is incorporated particularly in *For the Morning of the World*, in which he develops a new focus on melody that he eloquently describes as "a single, relentlessly focused, gradually accelerating melodic line, developing within evolving, partly Balinese modes, which is clearly derived from Indian templates—at the same time as it reflects the timbre and texture of an archaic form of Balinese gamelan."

CONCLUSIONS

Levinson's rich description of his musical development is particularly interesting in the context of this volume in giving us an unusual window into the special characteristics of musical development and, perhaps more by its differences, into development more generally, as well. In particular, my construal of dialectical spirals as a pervasive theme in Levinson's story resonates, more in retrospect, as pointing to important aspects of what I have seen in my previous studies of musical development, including but not only musically gifted youngsters, as well as among adult musicians (Bamberger, 1982, 1991/1995, 2003). It reinforces what I have emphasized, particularly in my studies of musically gifted children, of the critical importance of helping these children and encouraging them from the outset to learn how to reflect on and to think critically about the music they are studying and on their own performance. Unfortunately the young violinists or pianists are so extraordinary in their abilities, including their abilities to imitate another's performance, that their teachers are often hesitant to ask the children just to stop and think. This comes back to haunt these children in midadolescence when they quite naturally begin asking such questions of themselves and find that they have no means for thinking about how to answer them. Those whose careers survive this "midlife crisis" are the few whom we know as the eminent artists of our day.

I find that the dialectical aspect of the developing spirals, circling back but also onward to immediate perception once more, is particularly germane to development more generally, that is, as an individual comes to actually see and/or hear some initially engaging phenomenon in new ways—reshaped, remade. This latter phase is illuminated by Levinson's comments:

> At this point the faculty of critical judgment has long since been plugged back in, and its demands can be unrelenting.... In the process of working out the details, changes in the pacing, rhythm, or even the sequence of events may occur. The continuity plan is not final until it has been fully realized.

Researchers have commented on sensory experience in various modalities under the general term *embodiment* as being implicated in the emergence of new ideas (Voneche, 2008; Núñez, 2004). Such initially spontaneous experience usually is seen to preface a move into reflection, analysis of constituent entities, and eventually formal, symbolic representations.

> The body is functioning as the metaphor of reality par excellence, both before the emergence of the semiotic function and after.... [I]nnovation occurs so much so that one seems to be entitled to consider the body as the workshop of thinking or the tool of invention. (Voneche, 2008, p. 80)

What is often ignored, and only hinted at by Voneche, is the coming back around of the spiral to meet a perception of the relevant phenomenon anew. Here the dialectic has its most powerful effect. For with this second round of the spiral, immediate perception of the phenomenon is itself transformed—the phenomenon is actually seen in a new way. This coming to see in a new way is, I believe, a clear sign of deep learning and perhaps development. Indeed, I would speculatively suggest that this brings us closer to Piaget's (1978–1979/2006) meaning of dialectical spirals: "conservations are simultaneously conditions and outcomes without thereby amounting to a vicious cycle" (p. 8).

Just briefly, we might think, for instance, of the changes in direct perception of same and different as described above in the example of the minuet movement, when before and after seeing the score, perceptions are transformed from a hearing of context-dependent changing events into constant, invariant properties; or Soyer's both same and different hearing in his performance of the Beethoven Quartet. And this dialectic is, I would propose, quite similar to what I have seen happen with college students as their actual seeing of ordinary, everyday phenomena changes as they learn the physics explanations of what's happening.

Finally, I would like to thank Gerald Levinson for all the time he has taken from his own teaching and certainly from his composing to give us such insight into his personal and musical development—a process that usually remains silent, making itself known only through the extraordinary sounds of its results.

NOTES

1. Theodore Presser, music publisher.
2. I borrow the term from Piaget but use it in a somewhat different way: "as soon as the links become clear, and therefore everything is organized, it tends to take the form of dialectical spirals ... conservations are simultaneously conditions and outcomes without thereby amounting to a vicious cycle" (Piaget, 1978–1979/2006, p. 8). I am grateful to Constance Milbrath for pointing me to this article.

3. "The patternings are, so-to-speak, 'out-of-phase.' Since pitch relationships are fixed, the discrepancy can be resolved only by a change in rhythmic/metric patterning" (Meyer, 2000, p. 75).
4. Again such inferences need to be much more carefully studied and documented. But Piaget (1960/1976) did note, "Sensori-motor-intelligence is thus an intelligence in action and in no way reflective" (p. 121).
5. *In dark* is recorded on the CRI label, CD 760, *Orchestra 2001: Night of the four moons*.
6. "Messiaen found birdsong fascinating. He notated birdsongs worldwide, and he incorporated birdsong transcriptions into a majority of his music. His innovative use of colour, his personal conception of the relationship between time and music, his use of birdsong, and his intent to express religious ideas, all combine to make Messiaen's musical style notably distinctive" (Wikipedia, n.d.).
7. For another description of the teachings of a Balinese guru, see Bamberger and Ziporyn (1991).

REFERENCES

Bamberger, J. (1982). Growing up prodigies. In D. H. Feldman (Ed.), *Developmental approaches to giftedness* (pp. 61-97). San Francisco: Jossey-Bass.

Bamberger, J. (1995). *The mind behind the musical ear*. Cambridge, MA: Harvard University Press. (Original work published in 1991)

Bamberger, J. (2003). The development of intuitive understanding. *Psychology of Music, 31*(1), 7-36.

Bamberger, J., & Ziporyn, E. (1991). Getting it wrong. *The World of Music: Ethnomusicology and Music Cognition, 34*(3), 22-56.

Blum, D. (1986). *The art of quartet playing*. New York: Knopf.

Hasty, C. (1997). *Meter as rhythm*. New York: Oxford University Press.

Meyer, L. B. (2000). *The spheres of music*. Chicago: University of Chicago Press.

Núñez, R. (2004). Do real numbers really move? Language, thought, and gesture: The embodied cognitive foundations of mathematics. In F. Iida, R. Pfeifer, L. Steels, & Y. Kuniyoshi (Eds.), *Embodied artificial intelligence* (pp. 54-73). Berlin: Springer-Verlag.

Piaget, J. (1970). *Structuralism*. New York: Basic Books.

Piaget, J. (1976). *The psychology of intelligence*. Totowa, NJ: Littlefield, Adams. (Original work published in 1960)

Piaget, J. (2006). Reason (T. Brown, Trans.). *New Ideas in Psychology, 24*. (Original work published in 1978-1979)

Prausnitz, F. (2002). *Roger Sessions: How a "difficult" composer got that way*. New York: Oxford University Press.

Presser.com from http://www.presser.com/levinson.html

Sessions, R. (1971). *Questions about music*. New York: Norton.

Sloboda, J. (1985). *The musical mind*. Oxford: Clarendon.

Voneche, J. (2008). Action as the solution to the mind-body problem in Piaget's theory. In W. F. Overton, U. Muller, & J. I. Newman (Eds), *Developmental perspectives on embodiment and consciousness* (pp 69-98). New York: Lawrence Erlbaum.

Wikipedia. (N.d.). *Olivier Messiaen.* Retrieved June 19, 2009, from http://en.wikipedia.org/wiki/Olivier_Messiaen

8

EVERY SHUT EYE AIN'T SLEEP

Modeling the Scientific From the Everyday as Cultural Process

Carol D. Lee

As preparation for the topic of this volume and the conference on which it is based, I reflected on the role of the arts in my own development. For the first 3 years of high school—longer ago than I care to remember—I wanted to study mathematics. For most of my childhood and adolescence, we lived in public housing on the south and west sides of Chicago. I wanted to study mathematics, I think, because my father loved mathematics and often said that everything in the world is mathematical. In my junior year, our trigonometry teacher sent a group of us to the Illinois Institute of Technology for an advanced Saturday class. There was no preparation for either the cognitive demands of the class or its social demands. I had never been on a college campus before. We were the only African American faces in a huge college lecture room. When the professor went to the board and began to speak, as far as I was concerned he could have been speaking Greek—indeed, some of the symbols he wrote were Greek and totally foreign to me. I had no mentors or intermediaries who could represent or help me understand what was happening and how unprepared I felt, even though I had been an honor student in mathematics and all my other classes at Crane High School in Chicago. Developmentally naïve, I then interpreted that experience as signally that I could not possibly study advanced mathematics. Then, in my senior year, I had a cathartic experience. My senior

English teacher—Reverend Roy Morrison, whom I will never forget—made literature come alive for me and somehow enchanted me with the autobiography of Albert Schweitzer, who lived during the same time as Jean Piaget . Although in theory quite distinct from my experiences growing up in public housing on the west side of Chicago, somehow Schweitzer—through the scaffolding provided by Reverend Morrison—transported me into a time and place that I had never directly experienced in my life. That hermeneutical experience opened a vision of possibility for my future life.

Around the same time that I was planning my talk at the annual meeting of the Jean Piaget Society, I was in New York initially for a meeting and then to spend time with my daughter who lives there. While she was at work, I visited the Metropolitan Museum of Art. Although I have visited the museum many times, I was struck on this visit by a persistent theme, perhaps because I was still contemplating my remarks for the conference. Whether in the exhibits of the ancient Egyptians, the ancient Greeks and Romans, the indigenous communities of the Americas, the period furniture rooms of the American wing, or the exhibits of the arts of Africa, Asia, or periods of art history in Europe, it was clear that each civilization and each generation within that civilization created public representations of the stories they told about who they were; and we call those public representations *the arts*, *architecture*, and *religion*. They are all fundamentally stories of identity. I then decided that I wanted to talk about the role of the arts in the construction of knowledge and identity. I am working from a fundamental proposition that knowledge and identity are intricately linked, and that how they are intertwined entails the most fundamental tasks of human development across the life course.

I would like to first ground our discussion in several concrete examples. I want to accomplish several goals in these illustrations. The first is influenced very much by a set of ideas that are beautifully crystallized in the book *The Cultural Nature of Human Development* by Barbara Rogoff (2003). In many ways, Rogoff synthesized what we have learned about the joint influences of human biology and engagement in the world of practice from the work of Piaget (1952). But Rogoff (Rogoff & Chavajay, 1995) also discussed the kinds of challenges to Piaget's (1952, 1966/1974) assumptions about universal courses or pathways for cognitive development raised by the cross-cultural research inspired in part by Vygotsky (1978, 1981). Rogoff asserted the following: Yes, indeed, there are likely universal patterns of cognitive and related social and emotional development across the life course. Across Mother Earth, there are without question developmental constraints on what infants and young children can do. Yet, Rogoff went on to argue, what we do not know is the range of variation within those developmental periods. Her example of the 3-year-old Ewe child from the Congo who is able to forage with a machete defies western assumptions about what children of that age are capable of doing successfully. Indeed, in most western countries, the mother who lets her 3-year-old child out in the backyard with a machete would find herself in prison for child endangerment and her child placed in foster care.

My interest here is not simply to discuss the role of the arts in human development broadly speaking, but rather to wrestle with understanding the range of cultural variation in pathways through which particular culturally rooted art forms function in the lives of youth from communities that are marginalized by racism, ethnocentrism, and poverty. Because my research is in literacy, and in particular how novices come to learn to engage in literary reasoning, my examples will focus on what I am calling the *narrative arts*; those art forms that are forms of storytelling—oral storytelling traditions and the discourses that surround them; music with lyrics, with a particular emphasis on rap and rhythm & blues (R&B) genres; and film—all with an eye toward their relationships with what we consider canonical literature. I must add that by canonical literature I mean that literature across all human civilizations which stands the test of time, with each new generation—both from within the cultural community of origin and across cultural communities—revisiting such texts, recreating shared understandings that are passed on intergenerationally, as well as creating new meanings, new dances with these same texts. In linking the everyday, even the vernacular, with the canonical, I seek to document a range in pathways to literary reasoning through a hermeneutic engagement with narrative texts. Ultimately I am interested in what such youth learn in and through their everyday practices with such narrative arts in order to leverage that knowledge—including the dispositions, habits of mind, and senses of selfhood that are embedded in these everyday practices.

I see schools as unique institutional sites for leveraging what people already know. I don't necessarily think we need schools to simply reinforce what people, in particular youth, already know, but rather to expand their repertoires—not replace old ones—of what they know and what they want to know (Gutierrez, Baquedano-Lopez, & Tejeda, 1999; Gutierrez & Rogoff, 2003). Unfortunately, the history of schooling within the United States (and in many western European countries) is replete with dire examples where the goal of schooling is seen as replacing, or getting rid of, the bad things, the deficits that youth bring from their family and neighborhood lives. We know that during the 19th and early part of the 20th century, American Indian children were taken from their biological families and placed in boarding schools where they were explicitly taught not to be Indian (Lomawaima, 2004) . We know that similar efforts took place in Australia with the Aboriginal population there (Miller, 1985). For the first 400 years that Africans were brought to the United States to be bondaged in slavery, what many of us call the African Holocaust of Enslavement, it was illegal for an African to learn to read or write (Bennett, 1964; Harding, 1981). After the Civil War and Reconstruction, but particularly when attempts were made to racially integrate U.S. schools, schools were viewed as places to eradicate Black English (Smitherman, 2000) to compensate for what youth did not get at home, and thus evolved the persistent proposition of the disadvantaged or culturally deprived child (Bereiter & Engelmann, 1966; Deutsch & Brown, 1964; Hess & Shipman, 1965). Our current debates over English only (Stotsky, 1999) and the highly political battles over bilingual education (Cummins, 1989; Valdes, 1996) are simply another version of the same metastory: Eradicate that which is culturally distinct, and replace it with what are presumed to be culturally superior ways of talking, of reasoning, of interacting, and so on.

Although I am focusing today on the narrative arts, I must also acknowledge that in school mathematics and school science, there is an equally virulent set of assumptions, namely, that science and mathematics fundamentally are the outgrowth of European intellectual history and there is no place for everyday cultural forms, certainly not from the marginalized communities I have described (see the following counterarguments: Ascher, 1991; Ballenger, 1997; Bang, Medin, & Altran, 2007; Lumpkin, 1990; Moses, 1994; Rosebery, Warren, Ballenger, & Ogonowski, 2005; Secada, Fennema, & Adajian, 1995). For example, Orr (1987) has argued that competence in African American English Vernacular interferes with students' ability to reason mathematically. Although not taking the kind of cultural deficit orientation as Orr, Dowling (1990) has argued that mathematical texts that focus on real-world applications restrict students' opportunities to examine the aesthetic and theoretical underpinnings of mathematics. Dowling further argued that practically oriented textbooks are disproportionately used in schools serving students from low-income backgrounds and as a consequence restrict their opportunities to learn higher mathematics. In canonical histories, the mathematics developed in early civilizations for the purpose of solving practical problems is typically viewed as less rigorous than what is presumed to be the purely theoretical mathematics associated with later European intellectual history (but see Lumpkin, 1990, for a critique of this position). Overall, theorizing about relationships between everyday knowledge, particularly with regard to youth from nondominant groups, and theoretical mathematical reasoning is highly contested in the field of mathematics education (Nasir, Hand, & Taylor, 2008). This is especially the case with regard to the high school mathematics curriculum. Although there is a substantive body of research documenting how knowledge constructed in everyday settings can be leveraged to support rich mathematical thinking, this work has not significantly impacted school practices, and much of this work is restricted to the elementary rather than the high school curriculum (Anderson, 1970; Carraher, Carraher, & Schliemann, 1985; Civil, 2005; Cocking & Mestre, 1988; Frankenstein, 1995; Martin, 2000; Nasir, 2000, 2002; Nunes, Schliemann, & Carraher, 1993; Tate, 1993). The Algebra Project, however, is a notable example (Moses, 1994; Moses & Cobb, 2001; Moses, Kamii, Swap, & Howard, 1989; Silva, Moses, Rivers, & Johnson, 1990). Thus, although the focus of this chapter is on the narrative arts, the fundamental argument about the ways that everyday experience can offer multiple pathways through which youth learn canonical, school-based knowledge has applications to other domains.

In order to examine this idea of multiple pathways for engagement with literary reasoning about narrative texts, I will explore the following questions:

- What kinds of knowledge do youth develop as a consequence of their attempts to make sense of narrative texts in their everyday lives outside of school?
- What are the cultural features of the nonschool contexts through which such sense making takes place?
- What do these cultural features look like when they are appropriated in school contexts?

The data for this discussion come from the Cultural Modeling Project (Lee, 1995a, 1995b, 2001, 2007). Cultural Modeling is a framework for analyzing relationships between everyday and disciplinary knowledge in order to scaffold youth's everyday experiences to support discipline-specific academic learning. The framework provides guidelines for examining what may be sources of similarity or dissonance based on concepts, heuristics and strategies, habits of mind or dispositions, and fundamental epistemologies that are employed in both the everyday and the disciplinary. Where there are sources of similarity, the goal is to scaffold; where there are sources of dissonance, the goal is to help students explicitly examine what may be misconceptions. I have employed this framework to examine relationships between reasoning embedded in vernacular language practices, film, and rap music and the demands of interpreting canonical narratives.

Several insights have emerged from using this framework, both in terms of theorizing and in terms of instructional design in historically underachieving classrooms. The first is that the range of expertise in these everyday practices spans from knowledge that is tacit to knowledge that is explicit and multidimensional. The second is that this kind of analysis often invites a reexamination of what it means to know the canonical. The third is that both engagement with the everyday practice and the process of transferring and transforming the everyday knowledge to the disciplinary context involve identity work. By *identity work*, I mean establishing goals, aligning one's self with the work entailed in accomplishing those goals, wrestling with the uncertainty that inevitably accompanies significant personal transformation, and in so doing learning how to cope, be resilient, and be persistent (Lee, 2009; Nasir, Rosebery, Warren, & Lee, 2006). It is in what I am here calling *acts of identity wrestling* that the learner is weighing how self-interests and self-construals are achieved through the work required to engage in the object of the practice.

Narrative reasoning or what in the disciplinary context might be called literary reasoning about narrative texts is particularly appropriate for this kind of identity wrestling. Many have argued that narrative is one of the primary mediums through which we as humans impose meaning on disparate experiences in the world, make sense of them, by telling ourselves how experiences cohere, what experiences signify (Bruner, 1990; McAdams, 1993; Turner, 1996). Our experiences in the world typically involve other human beings, either directly or indirectly, who have goals that are driven by emotional inner states that impel them to carry out actions; and it is our imputation of the causal links among these actions that leads us to hypothesize a coda, a response to the question, "So what does all this mean?" (Trabasso, Secco, & van den Broek 1984; Trabasso & Sperry, 1985; Trabasso & van den Broek, 1985). These are the elements of all narratives, be they oral, print, or visual; be they stories or stories as poems, as plays; be they consciously constructed ahead of time as in literature or music or plays or film, or unconsciously constructed in situ as in oral storytelling inside everyday discourse. And because the goal of narrative is to understand human experience, narrative reasoning, when deeply engaged, invites wrestling with the question of, "Who am I and what does this narrativized sequence of events mean to me?"

LITERARY REASONING IN EVERYDAY AND CANONICAL NARRATIVE TEXTS

In the arts as in other disciplines, particularly in K–12 education, we have created artificial boundaries between the everyday and the canonical. This distinction is probably most notable in the teaching of literature (Fish, 1980). It is rare to find the inclusion of any kinds of popular texts in literature anthologies used in K–12 schools, particularly at the high school level. And yet, the vast majority of high school and even college graduates do not read canonical literature on a regular basis (Kaestle, Damon-Moore, Stedman, Tinsley, & Trollinger, 1991; U.S. Department of Education, National Center for Educational Statistics, 2006). In addition, the young people we are trying to reach engage with a wide range of narrative texts in popular culture, from music to film to television. It is interesting that departments of English in universities and colleges find a place for the literary examination of popular texts and narrative media, albeit a minor designation. Thus, we have a situation where young people are involved in everyday practices that share important properties with their academic tasks, but neither the students nor the teachers see the bridge between the two worlds.

There are two other dilemmas. In the teaching of literature (and reading comprehension more broadly; Durkin, 1981), teachers typically ask students to produce interpretations but rarely make explicit how a novice goes about constructing such interpretations (Lee, 2007). There is attention to strategies for reading comprehension in the research literature on reading comprehension (Fielding & Pearson, 1994; Kintsch, 1998; RAND Reading Study Group, 2002; Snow, 2002). However, much less attention is paid to the circumstances under which such strategies should be employed. We know that the demands of texts in relation to one's goals for reading will influence what strategies are appropriate when. Both the demands of texts and a reader's goals, particularly in the contexts of schooling, will be influenced by the cultures of specific disciplines. The kinds of questions, for example, that a historian will raise about a primary source document differ from the kinds of questions a scientist asks about a report published in the *New England Journal of Medicine* or that a student of science would ask about a journal article in *Nature* (Leinhardt, Stainton, Virgi, & Odoroff, 1994; Lemke, 1998). In terms of K–12 education, the discipline that has received the least amount of explicit attention to strategy use in acts of comprehension is response to literature. The work I will describe in this chapter represents an attempt to address the issues of making processes of comprehension and interpretation explicit with regard to literary narratives. There is also a significant body of research in an area referred to as *empirical studies of literature* as well as literary criticism that helps us understand what is entailed in comprehending and interpreting literary texts (Graves & Frederiksen, 1996; Halasz, 1987). However, little of this work has filtered down to K–12 education. Thus, because insufficient attention is paid both to the processes of reading comprehension broadly speaking and to the specialized processes involved in comprehending discipline-specific texts, our K–12 students are doubly constrained in terms of opportunity to learn to read deeply and widely. This problem is greatly compounded in schools serving populations that are majority ethnic minority and/or low income. This is because in these schools, one is most likely to find the greatest lack of school resources (e.g., a lack of certified teachers, low per pupil funding, little or no technology support, lack of a rigorous curriculum, and a culture of low expectations toward students; Darling-Hammond, 1999; Education Trust, 1999). Overall, students are asked to solve problems of reading without having opportunities to learn the tools for addressing such problems.

A second major dilemma is that insufficient attention is paid to the social and emotional demands of complex problem solving for novices. Much of our efforts at curriculum reform are based on the assumption that if we design rigorous learning, students will somehow automatically be drawn in and engaged. As discussed earlier, learning difficult tasks involves what I have called identity wrestling. That is, it requires an investment of ego, self-appraisal, and sustained effort (Dweck & Legget, 1988; Eccles, O'Neil, & Wigfield, 2005; Graham & Hudley, 2005). Particularly when new learning is challenging, learners are positioned to be potentially vulnerable (e.g., have the possibility of experiencing failure). Learners weigh the costs versus the benefits of investing psychological energy (and sometimes physical energy as well) into efforts that require persistence in the face of challenge. In addition, there may be social costs attached to challenging learning involving relationships with peers as well as competing obligations (e.g., family responsibilities, work, etc.). Thus, it is important to take into account both the cognitive and the social and emotional demands of complex learning. It is equally important to understand these social and emotional demands from a cultural and ecological perspective. Cultural beliefs and practices situated in the complex ecologies of peoples' lives are important sources of how people view themselves, the tasks in which they are engaged, and the settings where such learning occurs (Nasir, Rosebery, Warren, & Lee, 2006; Nasir & Saxe, 2003; Rogoff, 2003; Spencer, 1999, 2001). It is precisely this cultural and ecological orientation that informs the work in Cultural Modeling that I describe here.

Because we know that so many young people do reason in complex ways about everyday narrative texts, the demands of these everyday practices—both cognitive and social—may offer insights into the possibilities of linkages with the canonical. The everyday literary texts that I reference (e.g., rap lyrics and videos, television and film, and advertisements) are complicated in ways that are not sufficiently recognized, certainly not by schools. And yet, young people engage in social networks and recruit tools and technologies (e.g., popular rap magazines such as *The Source* and *Vibe*, Internet sites, MP3 players, etc.) to support their opportunities to experience and make sense of these popular texts. Understanding what motivates such rich involvement with literary narratives and what supports a critical examination of these texts can offer useful insights that I believe can be recruited to improve youths' engagement with canonical narratives in schools. To illustrate, I offer a critical analysis of the rap song "The Mask" by the Fugees (1996) and the novel *Beloved* by Toni Morrison (1987). From the analysis, I infer heuristics and strategies that can be used in both contexts. I have employed these strategies in high schools with great success (Lee, 1995a, 1995b, 2007).

"The Mask," written and performed by the Fugees, is a metastatement about hypocrisy. Each stanza takes place in a different setting with an example of people who are wearing a mask of hypocrisy. *Beloved*, by Toni Morrison, is the story of a woman named Sethe, enslaved during what many call the African Holocaust. Sethe, her husband, and her children lived on a plantation ironically called "Sweet Home." At the time she is trying to escape from enslavement, she is pregnant and is brutally raped by a group of White men who work on the plantation as overseers. When she is finally able to escape, the same men who brutally beat and raped her locate her to try to take her and her children back into bondage. In a moment of sheer terror, she slits the throat of her baby girl to keep her from being taken back into the inferno of American slavery. The novel is about the consequences of that act, and ultimately of the meaning of America's brutal enslavement of Africans, on the lives of the people, in this case on Sethe, her children (including the baby who was killed), and her circle of friends.

From a technical standpoint, each text poses similar interpretive problems. In each text there is a central image that is *symbolic*. *Beloved* as a novel actually has many symbols. Both have *multiple narrators*, which involve a shift in point of view that is unmarked. In "The Mask," for example, the narrator of the stanza in Table 8.1 is not the same as the female narrator in the stanza that begins,

> I thought he was the wonder, I was stunned by his lips,
> Takin' sips of an Amaretto Sour with a twist,
> Shook my hips to the base line, this joker grabbed my
>   waistline …

In *Beloved*, the storyline about the protagonist Sethe's escape from enslavement shifts from Sethe's, Amy's, and Denver's points of view. Amy is the young White woman who was escaping from indentured servitude and helped Sethe give birth to her daughter Denver, the daughter she was carrying when she was brutally raped. Denver's sister was the child killed by Sethe. Both texts have *time shifts* that are also not directly marked. In the stanza from "The Mask" in Table 8.1, the action moves from one point in the past to a more recent point when the narrator says, "hired now I'm fired, sober now I'm wired," to a contemporary time point where he or she has been kidnapped by the feds, who "took me to DC, had me workin' underground, loadin' missiles for World War III." Similarly in *Beloved*, there are paragraphs in which the time frame seamlessly moves from the present to the past. There is also a common use of a chorus in which testimony to the coda, the so-what, the theme, is communicated. In "The Mask," the chorus is a straightforward stanza that is repeated with minor variations across the song/poem. In *Beloved*, the chorus is situated in two powerful scenes, one in which Sethe recalls the powerful impact of Baby Suggs in the community. Baby Suggs is Sethe's mother-in-law, who is dead during the contemporary timeline of the novel. Sethe recalls how Baby Suggs, a preacher, called together the community. A choral scene appears again near the end of the novel, when the embodied ghost of Beloved disembodies to return to the world of spirit. The community of women surround to protect Sethe, but also to make sense of the lessons to be learned from the experience. A third common feature is that both texts pose *complex problems of imposing coherence*. Both have a series of disparate actions that are not straightforwardly connected. These interpretive problems common to the everyday and the canonical texts are neither straightforward nor simple in either text. However, many youth have the requisite background knowledge, available sense-making strategies, as well as the inclination and disposition to attend to these interpretive problems in such popular texts but are not helped to conceptualize how these meaning-making resources can be leveraged to support the interpretation of canonical literary narratives.

In order to illustrate strategies for making such literary meaning making explicit, I will focus my analysis on the demands of interpreting the symbolism in each text: the image of the mask in "The Mask" and

Table 8.1 Excerpts Illustrating "Rules of Notice" in Two Texts

From "The Mask" by the Fugees	From Beloved by Toni Morrison

I used to work at Burger King,
A king takin' orders
Punching my clock now I'm wanted by
  the manager
Soupin' me up sayin' "You're a good
  worker,
How would you like a quarter raise, move
  up to the register."
Large in charge, but you gotta be a spy
Come back and tell me who's baggin' my
  fries, gettin' high on company time
No siree, wrong MC,
Why should I be a spy when you're spyin'
  me
	"I had milk," she said. "I was pregnant with Denver but I had milk for my baby girl. I hadn't stopped nursing her when I sent her on ahead with Howard and Buglar."…
	"After I left you, those boys came in there and took my milk. That's what they came in there for. Held me down and took it…."
	"They used cowhide on you?"
	"And they took my milk."
	"They beat you and you was pregnant?"
	"And they took my milk!"
	The fat white circles of dough lined the pan in rows. Once more Sethe touched a wet forefinger to the stove. She opened the oven door and slid the pan of biscuits in. As she raised up from the heat she felt Paul D behind her and his hands under her breasts. She straightened up and knew, but could not feel that his cheek was pressing into the branches of her chokecherry….
	Would there be a little space, she wondered, a little time, some way to hold off eventfulness, to push busyness into the corners of the room and just stand there a minute or two, naked from shoulder blade to waist, relieved of the weight of her breasts, smelling the stolen milk again and the pleasure of baking bread? Maybe this one time she could stop dead still in the middle of a cooking meal—not even leave the stove—and feel the hurt her back ought to. Trust things and remember things because the last of the Sweet Home men was there to catch her if she sank?

Source: Fugees (1996) and Morrison (1987, pp. 16–18).

images of the tree and the dough in *Beloved*. I use this analysis to make two points. First, the strategies and habits of mind demanded are similar. Second, the problems can be identified and tackled strategically in ways that are teachable. This latter point is important because it opens up a world of narrative texts to students who are often turned off by the canonical. This distancing, among poor as well as more competent readers, is largely because they do not perceive they have tools to unravel the problems these texts pose and as a consequence the mysteries of the human experience they unveil. And these mysteries can be unveiled in both the canonical and the everyday. One advantage the canonical narrative texts offer, particularly the short story, the play, longer poetic genres, and the novel, are what length emboldened with the tools of metaphor, satire, and the nuanced manipulation of point of view makes possible. It is an imaginary world into which schools are uniquely positioned to invite young people, particularly young people from families living in poverty.

I focus here on the analysis of symbolism not only because it is central to the interpretation of both of these texts but also because symbolism is a kind of interpretive problem that readers will meet across genres, across the canonical and the everyday, and across national literatures and literary movements (Smith & Hillocks, 1988). Thus, learning to identify when problems of symbolism are posed and having analytic resources for tackling such problems constitute generative knowledge in terms of literary reasoning (Lee, 2004).

In the Table 8.1 excerpts from "The Mask" and *Beloved*, I anchor my illustrations around the symbols in each of these passages. The stanza from "The Mask" is about a kind of class hypocrisy where a manager tries to use one of his workers. The selection from *Beloved* is a scene where Paul D, a man who had been enslaved at the plantation "Sweet Home" along with Sethe, hears Sethe tell the story of how she had been beaten and raped. While Sethe is telling Paul D her story, she is also baking biscuits.

Peter Rabinowitz (1987) said that as readers we come to narrative texts with knowledge, strategies, and assumptions before we ever begin to read. He described what he called rules of notice. These involve recognizing the strategies that authors use to draw our attention. Such rules of notice include when text is in a prominent position—such as in a title, opening, closing, or critical juncture—or when a stretch of text is repeated. Both of these rules of notice apply to the image of the mask in "The Mask" and the images of the tree and the dough in *Beloved*. The mask is the title of the song, and the image is repeated in each stanza. In the scene where Sethe is kneading the dough, there is a very detailed description of what on the surface would appear to be a relatively insignificant act, the action of baking bread. The line "the branches of her chokecherry" refers literally to the fact that the scars on her back look like the branches of a chokecherry tree, as she was told by Amy, who helped her give birth to Denver while she was trying to escape to the Ohio River. The image of the tree is repeated throughout the novel— the tree at Sweet Home, the tree on Sethe's back, the tree stump on which the ghost returned to life, Beloved, sits when she first comes out of the water. These are images of a tree that the reader meets in different chapters of the novel. So in both texts, rules of notice with regard to privileged positioning and repetition draw the reader's attention as something that may be important.

Once the reader determines that these details deserve her attention, the question is then whether to interpret these details (an image, an action) literally or figuratively. Typically, if a literal interpretation seems insufficient or doesn't make sense in terms of what we know of the real world, a figurative interpretation is called for. For example, in the description of the worker at Burger King who wears a mask, we know that in the real world workers at Burger King do not wear masks. Although this might seem trivial, it is actually a powerful observation. No young person listening to this song by the Fugees imagines people behind the fast-food counter wearing masks. They intuitively realize that the mask stands for something, even if they do not have the language to describe it as such, nor even consciously have such a discussion with themselves. In the case of the tree image in *Beloved*, when we are told that Amy tells Sethe she has a tree on her back, that literally is not possible. This leads us to impute a figurative meaning to the image.

The act of interpreting such details as figurative rather than literal leads us to a kind of decision tree (Ortony, 1979; Winner, 1988). This is because figuration can work in the direction of adding what are essentially metaphoric meanings to the literal; that is, the image of the dough is really dough, but it's also more than dough. But figuration can also work in the opposite direction; that is, we can impute meanings or significances that act in contradiction to or in tension with the literal. This is the case with satire and problems of unreliable narration. In satire, we recognize some points of similarity with the target, but the exaggerations stand to critique the target. Others have tested pedagogical strategies for detecting irony and unreliable narration (Smith, 1989, 1991).

I have hypothesized and tested in Cultural Modeling interventions the following strategies for imputing figurative meanings to stretches of text that as readers we determine are potentially symbolic, not to be read as solely literal (see Lee, 2007, for a full discussion). These strategies include the following:

- Identify the stretches of text we believe are symbolic, based on the rules of notice articulated by Rabinowitz (1987).
- Analyze points of similarity across these stretches of text (in "The Mask," all those lines referring to people wearing masks; in *Beloved*, all the lines describing the act of Sethe working with the dough, or all the places across the text where the image of a tree is invoked).
- Brainstorm about real-world associations with the target image or actions.
- Construct an explanation that links your real-world associations and the patterns you have inferred about the textual details you have noticed; also consider associations with the author and similar texts.

Here I apply this line of logic to the image of the mask. We find that the image is repeated across stanzas. In each stanza and in the chorus, some character is wearing a mask to hide his or her identity. Each example involves a different strata of people, from public officials to gangbangers. In terms of real-world associations, we know many examples where people try to hide their intentions. What is salient across the text examples is how this deception can be found from the highest to the lowest strands of society. We can also extend our thinking to what we know about Wyclef Jean and Lauren Hill, major players in the Fugees. Both routinely write and sing about issues of power and political domination. Thus, both our real-world associations and our associations with the authors and their other texts lead us to infer that the mask symbolizes a societal hypocrisy.

In terms of the tree on Sethe's back, we pay attention to the detailed description of the intricate scars on her back that Amy says look like a chokecherry tree. We know the scars came from a monstrous beating from the men who raped her after her first attempt to escape from slavery. We can make many real-world and textual associations with the image of the tree as well as the scars. In the Bible, we have the tree of life. In Africa, we have the baobob tree with huge roots that grow above the surface of the ground. We also know that in traditional African societies, ritual scarification is a practice that signals group membership and identity and is often associated with rites of passage. When we ask ourselves what these textual patterns, real-world associations, and associations with other texts have in common, a number of possible inferences arise: the tree as symbolic of both life and death, Sethe's resilience in the face of unbelievable horror, Sethe's spiritual death after killing her baby, and Sethe's loss of ethnic identity and family as a consequence of enslavement. It is important to note that these strategies I describe do not necessarily lead to a single, and certainly not an indisputable, interpretation. I have argued that literary reasoning is a form of ill-structured problem solving. What we ultimately value are the debates of evidence and warrants among competing claims about what these tropes imply.

In addition to these strategies, both texts invite certain habits of mind. These include a disposition to pay attention to the aesthetic dimensions of language, a proclivity to impose coherence on disparate details, and a willingness to be imaginative in making associations. These also include what Samuel Taylor Coleridge (2005) called a willing suspension of disbelief. It is through this suspension of disbelief that we are able to enter and construe ourselves inside imaginary worlds. We do this when we view a science fiction film like *Star Wars*. Whether it be rap, R&B, the blues, popular films, or television programming, we find people, including students who are struggling in school literature classes, engaging in these dispositions, in deep appreciation of the aesthetic dimensions of language use, and intuitively using the strategies I have described (Lee, 1997, 2005a, 2005b). Because of this, I argue that narrative reasoning in everyday texts—be they print or digital media—provides a generative bridge to the kinds of wrestling that canonical works of literature invite. These are resources that we typically do not acknowledge in K–12 schools. Our work in Cultural Modeling has demonstrated the power of this kind of scaffolding.

STUDENT ENGAGEMENT IN LITERARY REASONING: PEDAGOGICAL IMPLICATIONS

It is not difficult to make the case that narrative texts—be they stories in films, television, music, or written texts from the popular to the canonical—invite reflection on the self: How do I align myself with the motives, internal states, and actions of characters I meet in these stories? What do their stories mean to me? It is equally clear that popular texts may present trivial as well as compelling explanations about the dilemmas of the human experience. I would like to think that canonical narratives—which I would extend to include classic films, television programs, music lyrics, as well as classic short stories, plays, poems, and novels—offer compelling explanations and illustrations, and that these texts last over time precisely because of the human insights they offer up. They wrestle with questions for which there are not simple right and wrong answers and make visible the identity wrestling that is always deeply embedded in dealing with such questions, both in theory and in life. This has at least two implications.

First, our curriculum in K–12 schools would be deeply enriched by expanding to include classic narratives across these various genres and media. Our young people, especially those who face persistent intergenerational challenges due to race, ethnic, and class biases, face many life challenges. These include both normative developmental challenges (e.g., transitions from late childhood into adolescence) and the challenges of learning to make sense of and respond to these persistent structural barriers and stereotypes (Boykin, 1986; Nasir & Saxe, 2003; Spencer, 1999, 2001). As a field, we typically approach the problems of the achievement gap based on race, ethnicity, and class from either a purely cognitive perspective (that is, the problem is acquiring academic knowledge) or a purely socioemotional perspective (that is, the problem is social supports for families and young people). We are shortsighted in not recognizing that there are social and emotional demands to engaging new academic problems that are difficult. As learners, how we view our own abilities, the relevance of the task to our short- and long-term goals, the internal states and motives of those with whom we are engaged (be they teachers, peers, school administrators, or others) influence whether we wish to pursue the goal and our willingness to exert effort to overcome the difficulties the new work presents us (Dweck, 1999; Eccles, Wigfield, & Schiefele, 1998; Graham & Hudley, 2005).

It is in the context of this integrated view of human learning—integrating cognition and human development—that I believe the study of the range of narrative texts I have described can play a central role in helping young people to engage in productive ways with the kind of identity wrestling that deep learning always demands. The kinds of academic effort that we want to inspire requires that young people are willing to deal with uncertainty, to impute enough significance to academic work to be willing to prioritize it even when they face an array of life challenges that can easily draw them away from the academic endeavor (Burton, Allison, & Obeidallah, 1995).

With regard to the teaching of literature at the high school level, we approach this challenge in Cultural Modeling through a two-pronged approach. First, we design instruction in ways that make the *relevance of the task visible and salient*. We do this in two ways. By starting instruction using what I call *cultural data sets*, students begin to apply strategies for literary reasoning to texts with which they are already familiar. This shows them not only that they are capable of this work but also that in fact they typically enjoy it. Young people elect to listen to rap and place great value on making sense of the lyrics. Young people who are speakers of African American English grow up engaging in signifying and thus place great value on the aesthetic dimensions of language play and figuration in particular (Smitherman, 1977). Second, we sequence the transition from everyday to canonical literature by first examining literary works for which we feel the students already bring significant prior knowledge of the social worlds of the texts. For the African American students with whom we have worked, this means starting with African American literary works where the experiences of the characters and themes of the work have direct relevance to the life experiences of the students. This sequencing means that students enter the canonical texts with a sense that literary reasoning is a game that they can and like to play; and that students begin this work with explicit strategies and heuristics that they are consciously aware of and have been using, including beginning to develop a disposition to pay attention to subtle features of the text, and with significant prior knowledge to draw on in interpreting the canonical text, particularly the internal states and motivations of characters. From there, we begin to introduce canonical texts that pose similar rhetorical and structural problems as well as themes from other national and ethnic traditions. From a cognitive perspective, one can think about this as carefully sequencing of the degrees of freedom for a series of transfer tasks. Another way we think about making the relevance of the task salient has to do with the themes selected. We are careful to select texts, especially in the first phases of a unit, that invite students to reflect in complex ways with life challenges they face. For adolescents, particularly students of color living in low-income communities, these life challenges may include managing family and school responsibilities (for example, being a parent and student; having to work to supplement the family income and be a student at the same time); wrestling with stereotypes about skin color and body type, especially for females, at a developmental period when relationships with peers are especially important; managing conflicting values posed by affiliations with peers; and making sense of violence in one's communities, such as the death of more than one dear friend or family members. We have used texts such as Richard Wright's *Black Boy* and *Native Son*, Alice Walker's *The Color Purple*, Toni Morrison's *The Bluest Eye* and *Beloved*, and Amy Tan's *The Joy Luck Club*, among others. We have found that with proper preparation—in this case, building up knowledge of strategies and heuristics as well as repeated experience with playing this literary game with cultural data sets from their everyday experience—students who have previously been disengaged and low achievers identify with the texts and value the problem solving these texts invite.

The second prong in the Cultural Modeling toolkit has to do with how we go about making problem identification and strategies explicit and public. The process I have described in the prior section illustrates strategies for detecting and interpreting symbolism as these apply to both the everyday and the canonical narrative texts. Here I want to illustrate what literary reasoning looks like with the cultural data sets and then with the canonical texts. In each of these brief examples, I argue there is evidence that students are deeply engaged with making sense of these texts in ways that are complex and compelling. This kind of engagement is an indicator of identification with the practice.

The first example is Jonetha, who is putting forth a hypothesis about the significance of the mask in the stanza from "The Mask" in the last section. In this stanza, a worker at Burger King, whom we are told is a "king takin' orders," is being told by the manager to go and spy on other workers.

Jonetha: I'm saying I think he had a mask on when he was fighting, when he beat him up, because in order for him to have the mask on, he was spying on that person. He was spying on somebody. I don't know who he was spying on. But in order for him to realize that the man was spying on him, he had to take off his mask. In order to realize that the man was saying.... I don't know, shoot.

Teacher: Let me try to break this out a little bit. Jonetha, give me the words. You're saying ...

Jonetha: I'm saying that the man, in order for him to realize that the other man was spying on him, that he had to take off his mask.

This kind of reasoning about rap lyrics and other cultural data sets was typical (see Lee, 2007). There are several important observations about Jonetha's response. First, the kinds of explicit analysis that we support students in making about cultural data sets is work that is typically done tacitly in everyday practice. In addition, for many young people, this kind of reasoning is within what Vygotsky (1978; 1981) called their zone of proximal development. It is not precisely what they do when they play a CD with "The Mask" or when they hear it on the radio or their iPods. They do intuitively recognize that the image of the mask is symbolic, but they do not typically deconstruct the symbol using the kind of hermeneutics that Jonetha employs. There are communities of young people, those who see themselves doing what has come to be called *wordsmithing*, who do explicity talk about both what and how a text means (Fisher, 2003, 2004). Thus, I argue that cultural data sets pose problems that share sufficient attributes with the targeted new task, but that the ways of making explicit the processes of problem solving (talking about not only what you know but also how you know it) do not directly map on to the everyday practice but represent a sufficient stretch to be achievable with guided support.

Here we see that Jonetha is hypothesizing. She is not certain about her proposition, but she is willing to stretch herself to make this uncertainty public. This is a process of creating a classroom culture that values attacking complex problems with the recognition that there are no simple, straightforward answers, in which supporting one's claims with evidence is valued, and where not being sure is actually a good thing.

My gloss of her response is as follows. In order for a king to work at Burger King, he must hide the fact that he is a king (i.e., wear a mask). The manager does not intend to make explicit that he wishes to use the worker for his own ends, that is, to spy on the others; the manager also must put on a mask. Thus, in order for the king to recognize that he is being used, he must remove his mask of servility. This logic focuses on a set of parallel propositions. It attends to small linguistic details, such as a king working at Burger King. It is precisely the kind of reasoning that we want Jonetha to employ when she meets the canonical text that follows, in this case Toni Morrison's *Beloved*. In the background, other students are very loud, having side bar discussions about what they think is going on in the stanza. It is clear that Jonetha and her fellow students value this kind of problem solving. The role of the teacher in these episodes is to revoice the logic and to elicit from students why they pay attention to particular features of the text, why they hypothesize that the words have a figurative intent, and what evidence they use to make claims.

About a month later, this same class is now reading Toni Morrison's *Beloved*. *Beloved* is an extraordinarily complex novel. It poses problems of symbolism, unreliable narration, and inverted chronology, and represents the genre of magical realism. If the reader does not comprehend the symbolism, he or she will not understand why we are told that the scars on the protagonist Sethe's back look like a chokecherry tree, nor why the image of the tree is repeated throughout the novel, nor why Sethe is kneading dough in her kitchen when she recounts the story of her rape to Paul D. If the reader does not comprehend the unreliable narration, as well as the implications of magical realism as a genre, he or she will not understand the self-presentations of the character Beloved and may go on to interpret this as a ghost story.

This second example of how students engage in literary reasoning with the supports of Cultural Modeling comes from discussions of *Beloved*. As discussed earlier, *Beloved* is the story of Sethe, an enslaved

African woman, who in trying to escape from slavery is brutally raped. She escapes to Ohio to live initially with her children and her mother-in-law, Baby Suggs. When the same men who raped her while she was pregnant with her youngest child locate her to try to take her back, in a moment of desperation, she slits the throat of her second youngest child. The story is fundamentally about the consequences of that act for the entire family, including the baby who was killed. Students have read the chapter that begins as follows:

> A fully dressed woman walked out of the water. She barely gained the dry bank of the stream before she sat down and leaned against a mulberry tree. All day and all night she sat there, her head resting on the trunk in a position abandoned enough to crack the brim in her straw hat. Everything hurt but her lungs most of all. Sopping wet and breathing shallow she spent those hours trying to negotiate the weight of her eyelids. The day breeze blew her dress dry; the night wind wrinkled it. Nobody saw her emerge or came accidentally by. If they had, chances are they would have hesitated before approaching her. Not because she was wet, or dozing or had what sounded like asthma, but because amid all that she was smiling. It took her the whole of the next morning to lift herself from the ground, make her way through the woods past a giant temple of boxwood to the field and then the yard of the slate-gray house. Exhausted again, she sat down on the first handy place—a stump not far from the steps of 124. By then keeping her eyes open was less of an effort. She could manage it for a full two minutes or more. Her neck, its circumference no wider than a parlor-service saucer, kept bending and her chin brushed the bit of lace edging her dress. (p. 50)
>
> The woman gulped water from a speckled tin cup and held it out for more. Four times Denver filled it, and four times the woman drank as though she had crossed a desert. When she was finished a little water was on her chin, but she did not wipe it away. Instead she gazed at Sethe with sleepy eyes. Poorly fed, thought Sethe, and younger than her clothes suggested—good lace at the throat, and a rich woman's hat. Her skin was flawless except for three vertical scratches on her forehead so fine and thin they seemed at first like hair, baby hair before it bloomed and roped into the masses of black yarn under her hat. (p. 51)

The important question is, "Who is this woman?" Taquisha, along with most of the other students, believes this woman is the ghost of Sethe's baby, returned as a woman. Taquisha then heatedly acclaims,

Now wouldn't you want to know? You know! The questions—
hair all straight like a baby, you know and stuff, drinking all this
water? Okay! You know she said she ran away and stuff. You got
some brand new shoes on yo' feet. You too clean to run away. Yo
feet ain't swole. You ain't gonna expect nothing? You ain't gonna
ask her no questions? (Lee, 2007, p. 97)

I have tried here to capture some of the features that signal Taquisha
is a speaker of African American English. There are many other features, such as phonetics and prosody, that signal not only that she is an
African American English speaker but also the intensity with which
she communicates her ideas. It is precisely her intensity, her logic, and
her alignment with the text that represent the kind of literary reasoning
that ideally we want to see in high school literature classrooms.

Taquisha sees this new character as an unreliable narrator. She does
not trust what Beloved says. She pays attention to small details as evidence to support her claims. These include both details from within
the text and details on which she draws from her prior knowledge.
There was explicit attention to learning about the African Holocaust
of Enslavement prior to reading the novel. The details such as having
"hair all straight like a baby" and "drinking all this water" signal to
Taquisha that this woman is indeed the baby. She draws on her prior
knowledge about the fact that it was not unusual for people escaping
from enslavement to show up unannounced at someone's door, but it
would be clear that these people had been running through the woods,
mud, and water. Taquisha asserts that this woman looks too good to
have just escaped from enslavement. Taquisha also is attending to past
events before this chapter where the ghost of the baby comes back to
Sethe's house in great anger, knocks over furniture, and shows a fright-
ening red light across the house. So Taquisha reasons that if this is the
baby ghost returned, she is dangerous and angry.

Besides the logic of her assertion, based on careful attention to small
but highly salient details in the text and her ability to draw on historical
knowledge outside but relevant to the text, Taquisha embodies another
important disposition. As mentioned earlier, Samuel Taylor Coleridge
(2005) discussed what he called the suspension of disbelief as readers
enter the imaginary world of a narrative text. Here Taquisha talks as
though she and the other students are actually there inside the world
of the text, watching this woman come out of the water and approach
Sethe's house. When Taquisha says, "You ain't gonna expect nothing?
You ain't gonna ask her no questions?" it is as though she and the other
students are actually right there outside of Sethe's house. The willingness

and ability to put one's self inside the narrative are what open up our abilities as readers to step inside the shoes of a character, to feel what we imagine the characters feel, to imagine some alignment between ourselves and the story. This is not a disposition that is measured on our inadequate measures of literary reasoning used for accountability in K–12 schools (Lee, 2008; Lee & Spratley, 2009), but it is a disposition that people who love to read fiction, or to see fiction in movies and films, or to hear fiction in the lyrics of music all share. It is because she cares about what happens that she is willing and able to enter the subjunctive world of this text, including recognizing that the author is also a character, the person who is ultimately telling us this story, and that she also here implicitly questions the author's choices in this scene.

CONCLUSION

I have tried to make a case for the centrality of the arts, specifically narrative reasoning, to identity development and the ways that narrative reasoning is fertile ground for making generative connections between the everyday and the canonical. The academy, particularly K–12, has reified the canonical in ways that lead more young people than not away from the very disciplinary world into which schools seek to apprentice them. This disconnect is very evident in schools serving Black and Brown youth living in low-income communities. This differential impact is also devastating because the consequences of not becoming a lifelong reader can have more egregious effects on life course outcomes (i.e., high school graduation, college and postsecondary training, and preparation for the world of 21st-century work) for these young people. The Cultural Modeling framework and intervention studies have demonstrated the powerful impact of scaffolding the range of intellective resources for narrative reasoning that youth develop from their experiences in everyday contexts, including culturally specific contexts.

REFERENCES

Anderson, S. E. (1970, September). Mathematics and the struggle for Black liberation. *The Black Scholar*, 20–30.

Ascher, M. (1991). *Ethnomathematics: A multicultural view of mathematical ideas*. Pacific Grove, CA: Brooks/Cole.

Ballenger, C. (1997). Social identities, moral narratives, scientific argumentation: Science talk in a bilingual classroom. *Language and Education*, *11*(1), 1–14.

Bang, M., Medin, D. L., & Altran, S. (2007). Cultural mosaics and mental models of nature. *Proceedings of the National Academy of Sciences, 104*, 13868–13874.

Bennett, L. (1964). *Before the Mayflower: A history of the Negro in America, 1619–1964*. Chicago: Johnson.

Bereiter, C., & Engelmann, S. (1966). *Teaching disadvantaged children in preschool*. Englewood Cliffs, NJ: Prentice Hall.

Boykin, A. W. (1986). The triple quandary and the schooling of Afro-American children. In U. Neisser (Ed.), *The school achievement of minority children* (pp. 57–92). Hillsdale, NJ: Lawrence Erlbaum.

Bruner, J. (1990). *Acts of meaning*. Cambridge, MA: Harvard University Press.

Burton, L., Allison, K., & Obeidallah, D. (1995). Social context and adolescents: Perspectives on development among inner-city African-American teens. In L. Crockett & A. Crouter (Eds.), *Pathways through adolescence: Individual development in social contexts* (pp. 119–138). Mahwah, NJ: Erlbaum.

Carraher, T. N., Carraher, D. W., & Schliemann, A. D. (1985). Mathematics in the street and in school. *British Journal of Developmental Psychology, 3*, 21–29.

Civil, M. (2005). *Building on community knowledge: An avenue to equity in mathematics education*. Tuscon: University of Arizona, Department of Mathematics. Retrieved June 21, 2009, from http://math.arizona.edu/~cemela/english/content/workingpapers/MCivil-CommunKnow-Equity-long.pdf

Cocking, R. R., & Mestre, J. P. (1988). *Linguistic and cultural influences on learning mathematics*. Hillsdale, NJ: Erlbaum.

Coleridge, S. T. (2005). *Biographia literaria*. Whitefish, MT: Kessinger.

Cummins, J. (1989). *Empowering minority students: Education for empowerment in a diverse society*. Ontario: California Association for Bilingual Education.

Darling-Hammond, L. (1999). *Teacher quality and student achievement: A review of state policy evidence*. Seattle, WA: Center for the Study of Teaching and Policy.

Deutsch, M., & Brown, B. (1964). Social influences in Negro-White intelligence differences. *Journal of Social Issues, 20*, 24–35.

Dowling, P. (Ed.). (1990). *Mathematics versus the national curriculum*. Bristol, PA: Falmer.

Durkin, D. (1981). Schools don't teach comprehension. *Educational Leadership, 38*, 453–454.

Dweck, C. S. (1999). *Self-theories: Their role in motivation, personality and development*. Philadelphia: Psychology Press.

Dweck, C. S., & Legget, E. (1988). A socio-cognitive approach to motivation and personality. *Psychological Review, 95*, 256–273.

Eccles, J., O'Neil, S., & Wigfield, A. (2005). Ability self-perceptions and subjective task values in adolescents and children. In K. Moore & L. Lippman (Eds.), *What do children need to flourish: Conceptualizing and measuring indicators of positive development* (pp. 237–270). New York: Springer Science.

Eccles, J. S., Wigfield, A., & Schiefele, U. (1998). Motivation to succeed. In W. Damon & N. Eisenberg (Eds.), *Handbook of child psychology* (5th ed., Vol. 3, pp. 1017–1096). New York: Wiley.

Education Trust. (1999). *Ticket to nowhere* (2nd ed., Vol. 3). Washington, DC: Author.

Fielding, L., & Pearson, P. D. (1994). Synthesis of research on reading comprehension: What works. *Educational Leadership, 51*(5), 62–68.

Fish, S. (1980). *Is there a text in this class? The authority of interpretive communities.* Cambridge, MA: Harvard University Press.

Fisher, M. T. (2003). Open mics and open minds: Spoken word poetry in African Diaspora participatory literacy communities. *Harvard Education Review, 73*(3), 362–389.

Fisher, M. T. (2004). "The song is unfinished": The new literate and the literary and their institutions. *Written Communication, 21,* 3.

Frankenstein, M. (1995). Equity in mathematics education: Class in the world outside the class. In E. F. W. Secada & L. Adajian (Eds.), *New directions for equity in mathematics education* (pp. 165–190). New York: Cambridge University Press.

Fugees. (1996). The mask. *On the score* [Record]. Holland: Ruffhouse.

Graham, S., & Hudley, C. (2005). Race and ethnicity in the study of motivation and competence. In A. J. Elliot & C. S. Dweck (Eds.), *Handbook of competence and motivation* (pp. 392–413). New York: Guilford.

Graves, B., & Frederiksen, C. H. (1996). A cognitive study of literary expertise. In R. J. Kruez & M. S. MacNealy (Eds.), *Empirical approaches to literature and aesthetics* (pp. 397–418). Norwood, NJ: Ablex.

Gutierrez, K., Baquedano-Lopez, P., & Tejeda, C. (1999). Rethinking diversity: Hybridity and hybrid language practices in the Third Space. *Mind, Culture, and Activity, 6*(4), 286–303.

Gutierrez, K., & Rogoff, B. (2003). Cultural ways of learning: Individual traits or repertoires of practice. *Educational Researcher, 32*(5), 19–25.

Halasz, L. (1987). Cognitive and social psychological approaches to literary discourse. In L. Halasz (Ed.), *Literary discourse: Aspects of cognitive and social psychological approaches* (pp. 1–37). New York: Walter de Gruyter.

Harding, V. (1981). *There is a river: The Black struggle for freedom in America.* New York: Harcourt Brace Jovanovich.

Hess, R., & Shipman, V. (1965). Early experience and the socialization of cognitive modes in children. *Child Development, 36,* 869–886.

Kaestle, C., Damon-Moore, H., Stedman, L., Tinsley, K., & Trollinger, W. V. (1991). *Literacy in the United States: Readers and reading since 1880.* New Haven, CT: Yale University Press.

Kintsch, W. (1998). *Comprehension: A paradigm for cognition.* New York: Cambridge University Press.

Lee, C. D. (1995a). A culturally based cognitive apprenticeship: Teaching African American high school students skills in literary interpretation. *Reading Research Quarterly, 30*(4), 608–631.

Lee, C. D. (1995b). Signifying as a scaffold for literary interpretation. *Journal of Black Psychology, 21*(4), 357–381.

Lee, C. D. (1997). Bridging home and school literacies: A model of culturally responsive teaching. In J. Flood, S. B. Heath, & D. Lapp (Eds.), *A handbook for literacy educators: Research on teaching the communicative and visual arts* (pp. 330–341). New York: Macmillan.

Lee, C. D. (2001). Is October Brown Chinese: A cultural modeling activity system for underachieving students. *American Educational Research Journal, 38*(1), 97–142.

Lee, C. D. (2004). Literacy in the academic disciplines and the needs of adolescent struggling readers. *Voices in Urban Education, 3*, 14–25.

Lee, C. D. (2005a). Culture and language: Bi-dialectical issues in literacy. In P. L. Anders & J. Flood (Eds.), *Culture and language: Bi-dialectical issues in literacy*. Newark, DE: International Reading Association.

Lee, C. D. (2005b). Double voiced discourse: African American Vernacular English as resource in cultural modeling classrooms. In A. F. Ball & S. W. Freedman (Eds.), *New literacies for new times: Bakhtinian perspectives on language, literacy, and learning for the 21st century*. New York: Cambridge University Press.

Lee, C. D. (2007). *Culture, literacy and learning: Taking bloom in the midst of the whirlwind*. New York: Teachers College Press.

Lee, C. D. (2008). Cultural modeling as opportunity to learn: Making problem solving explicit in culturally robust classrooms and implications for assessment. In P. Moss, D. Pullin, J. P. Gee, E. Haertel, & L. J. Young (Eds.), *Assessment, equity, and opportunity to learn* (pp. 136–169). New York: Cambridge University Press.

Lee, C. D. (2009). Historical evolution of risk and equity: Interdisciplinary issues and critiques. *Review of Research in Education 33*(1), 63–100.

Lee, C. D., & Spratley, A. (2009). *Reading in the disciplines and the challenges of adolescent literacy*. New York: Carnegie Foundation of New York.

Leinhardt, G., Stainton, C., Virgi, S., & Odoroff, E. (1994). Learning to reason in history: Mindlessness to mindfulness. In M. Carretero & J. F. Voss (Eds.), *Cognitive and instructional processes in history and the social sciences* (pp. 131–158). Hillsdale, NJ: Erlbaum.

Lemke, J. (1998). Multiplying meaning: Visual and verbal semiotics in scientific text. In J. R. Martin & R. Veel (Eds.), *Reading science: Critical and functional perspectives on discourse of science* (pp. 87–113). New York: Routledge.

Lomawaima, K. T. (2004). Educating Native Americans. In J. Banks & C. Banks (Eds.), *Handbook of research on multicultural education* (2nd ed., pp. 441–461). San Francisco: Jossey-Bass.

Lumpkin, B. (1990). Mathematics. In A. G. Hilliard & C. Leonard (Eds.), *African American baseline essays*. Portland, OR: Portland Public Schools.

Martin, D. (2000). *Mathematics success and failure among African-American youth: The roles of sociohistorical context, community forces, school influence, and individual agency*. Mahwah, NJ: Erlbaum.

McAdams, D. P. (1993). *Stories we live by: Personal myths and the making of the self.* New York: Morrow.

Miller, J. (1985). *Koori: A will to win.* Sydney, Australia: Angus and Roberston.

Morrison, T. (1987). *Beloved.* New York: Knopf.

Moses, R. P. (1994). The struggle for citizenship and math/sciences literacy. *Journal of Mathematical Behavior, 13,* 107–111.

Moses, R. P., & Cobb, C. E. (2001). *Radical equations: Math literacy and civil rights.* Boston: Beacon

Moses, R. P., Kamii, M., Swap, S. M., & Howard, J. (1989). The Algebra Project: Organizing in the spirit of Ella. *Harvard Educational Review, 59*(4), 423–443.

Nasir, N. (2000). "Points ain't everything": Emergent goals and average and percent understandings in the play of basketball among African American students. *Anthropology and Education, 31*(1), 283–305.

Nasir, N. (2002). Identity, goals, and learning: Mathematics in cultural practice. In N. Nasir & P. Cobb (Eds.), *Mathematical Thinking and Learning: Special issue on Diversity, Equity and Mathematics Learning, 4*(2/3), 211–247.

Nasir, N., Hand, V., & Taylor, E. (2008). Culture and mathematics in school: Boundaries between "cultural" and "domain" knowledge in the mathematics classroom and beyond. *Review of Research in Education, 32,* 187–240.

Nasir, N., Rosebery, A. S., Warren, B., & Lee, C. D. (2006). Learning as a cultural process: Achieving equity through diversity. In K. Sawyer (Ed.), *Handbook of the learning sciences* (pp. 489–504). New York: Cambridge University Press.

Nasir, N., & Saxe, G. (2003). Emerging tensions and their management in the lives of minority students. *Educational Researcher, 32*(5), 14–18.

Nunes, T., Schliemann, A. D., & Carraher, D. W. (1993). *Street mathematics and school mathematics.* New York: Cambridge University Press.

Orr, E. W. (1987). *Twice as less: Black English and the performance of Black students in mathematics and science.* New York: Norton.

Ortony, A. (1979). *Metaphor and thought* (2nd ed.). New York: Cambridge University Press.

Piaget, J. (1952). *The origins of intelligence in children* (M. Cook, Trans.). New York: International Universities Press.

Piaget, J. (1974). Need and significance of cross-cultural studies in genetic psychology. In J. W. Berry & P. R. Dasen (Eds.), *Culture and cognition: Readings in cross-cultural psychology* (pp. 299–309). London: Methuen. (Original work published in 1966)

Rabinowitz, P. (1987). *Before reading: Narrative conventions and the politics of interpretation.* Ithaca, NY: Cornell University Press.

RAND Reading Study Group. (2002). *Reading for understanding: Toward an R&D program in reading comprehension.* Santa Monica, CA: RAND.

Rogoff, B. (2003). *The cultural nature of human development.* New York: Oxford University Press.

Rogoff, B., & Chavajay, P. (1995). What's become of research on the cultural basis of cognitive development. *American Psychologist, 50*(10), 859–877.

Rosebery, A. S., Warren, B., Ballenger, C., & Ogonowski, M. (2005). The generative potential of students' everyday knowledge in learning science. In T. Romberg, T. Carpenter, & D. Fae (Eds.), *Understanding mathematics and science matters* (pp. 55–80). Mahwah, NJ: Erlbaum.

Secada, W., Fennema, E., & Adajian, L. B. (1995). *New directions for equity in mathematics education.* New York: Cambridge University Press.

Silva, C. M., Moses, R. P., Rivers, J., & Johnson, P. (1990). The algebra project: Making middle school mathematics count. *Journal of Negro Education, 59*(3), 375–392.

Smith, M. (1989). Teaching the interpretation of irony in poetry. *Research in the Teaching of English, 23,* 254–272.

Smith, M. (1991). *Understanding unreliable narrators: Reading between the lines in the literature classroom.* Urbana, IL: National Council of Teachers of English.

Smith, M., & Hillocks, G. (1988, October). Sensible sequencing: Developing knowledge about literature text by text. *English Journal,* 44–49.

Smitherman, G. (1977). *Talkin and testifyin: The language of Black America.* Boston: Houghton Mifflin.

Smitherman, G. (2000). Ebonics, King, and Oakland: Some folks don't believe fat meat is greasy. In G. Smitherman (Ed.), *Talkin that talk: Language, culture and education in African America* (pp. 150–162). New York: Routledge.

Snow, C. (2002). *Reading for understanding: Toward an R&D program in reading comprehension.* Santa Monica, CA: Rand Reading Study Group.

Spencer, M. B. (1999). Social and cultural influences on school adjustment: The application of an identity-focused cultural ecological perspective. *Educational Psychologist, 34*(1), 43–57.

Spencer, M. B. (2001). Identity, achievement orientation and race: "Lessons learned" about the normative, developmental experience of African American males. In W. H. Watkins, J. H. Lewis, & V. Chou (Eds.), *Race and education: The role of history and society in educating African American students* (pp. 100–127). Needham Heights, MA: Allyn & Bacon.

Stotsky, S. (1999). *Losing our language: How multicultural classroom instruction is undermining our children's ability to read, write, and reason.* New York: Free Press.

Tate, W. (1993, April). *Can America have a colorblind national assessment in mathematics?* Paper presented at the annual meeting of the American Educational Research Association, Atlanta, GA.

Trabasso, T., Secco, T., & van den Broek, P. (1984). Causal cohesion and story coherence. In H. Mandl, N. L. Stein, & T. Trabasso (Eds.), *Learning and comprehension of text* (pp. 83–111). Hillsdale, NJ: Erlbaum.

Trabasso, T., & Sperry, L. L. (1985). Causal relatedness and importance of story events. *Journal of Memory and Language, 24,* 595–611.

Trabasso, T., & van den Broek, P. (1985). Causal thinking and the representation of narrative events. *Journal of Memory and Language, 24,* 612–630.

Turner, M. (1996). *The literary mind.* New York: Oxford University Press.

U.S. Department of Education, National Center for Educational Statistics. (2006). *The condition of education 2005: Indicator 15, trends in adult literary reading habits* (NCES 2005-094). Washington, DC: Author.

Valdes, G. (1996). *Con respeto: Bridging the distances between culturally diverse families and schools*. New York: Teachers College Press.

Vygotsky, L. (1978). *Mind in society: The development of higher psychological processes* (M. Cole, V. John-Steiner, S. Scribner, & E. Souberman, Eds.). Cambridge, MA: Harvard University Press.

Vygotsky, L. (1981). The genesis of higher mental functions. In J. Wertsch (Ed.), *The concept of activity in Soviet psychology* (pp. 3–36). Armonk, NY: Sharp

Winner, E. (1988). *The point of words: Children's understanding of metaphor and irony*. Cambridge, MA: Harvard University Press.

9

COMMENTARY
Adolescents' Purposeful Uses of Culture

Colette Daiute

In "Every Shut Eye Ain't Sleep: Modeling the 'Scientific' From the Everyday as Cultural Processes," Carol Lee offers a lucid analysis of "cultural modeling" to bridge high school students' out-of-school arts and in-school literary reasoning. Moreover, Lee emphasizes educators' responsibility to build a bridge for students, especially in schools "serving Black and Brown youth living in low-income communities." With a comparison of "the everyday" and "the scientific," Lee focuses on the higher order skills inherent in artistic media used by young people in their daily lives and crafted in literary reasoning in standard high school English curricula. Lee argues, furthermore, that a major catalyst for bridging across everyday and scientific cultures is "identity work." In order to master the values and tools of mainstream culture, according to Lee and others (Fisher, 2004; Mahiri, 2006), young people from minority backgrounds must shift the identities they have developed with everyday arts to those embedded in the disciplinary sciences of mainstream schooling. Because mainstream identities are, by extension, required for graduation from high school, progress to college, and successful participation in professional employment, we can consider the contribution of multicultural flexibility as a catalyst for development.

In this commentary, I discuss Lee's argument in terms of questions about culture, cultural processes, and identity in human development, as these apply in particular to youth growing up in especially challenging

167

circumstances. Given the increasing disparity in economic and social capital across low-, middle-, and higher income neighborhoods in the United States, the circumstances of young people growing up in the poorest neighborhoods, the ones Lee is discussing, can be characterized as extreme, perhaps in similar ways to those of youth in other extreme environments such as those involved in armed conflict, major political transitions, and long-term poverty. Considering issues of culture and identity across challenging contexts may offer insights about the inter-dependent nature of individual and societal development.

I read Carol Lee's important chapter when working on a project on development among the generation growing up in the aftermath of the violent breakup of Yugoslavia during the 1990s. Given the centrality of ethnic identity in inquiry by Lee and others in the United States, I have been intrigued that personal identity is *not* emerging as particularly salient to adolescents and young adults across the former Yugoslavian contexts of Bosnia and Herzegovina, Croatia, Serbia, and a refugee community in the United States. In their completion of surveys, narratives, group dis-cussions, letters to public officials, and writing of surveys for other youth from the region, the 12- through 27-year-olds who participated in this study focused on the development of their societies and their own roles in that development rather than on personal ethnic and religious identi-ties (Daiute, in press; Daiute & Lucic, 2008). This may not be surprising given the human and environmental destruction that occurred in the name of ethnicity just a decade ago. If ethnic identity work is central to adolescent development, why wouldn't it emerge consistently across contexts? Bringing cultural identity in relief to address such issues, we ask "What is culture?" and "What is its role in development?" In relation to Lee's argument, we also consider: "Does distinguishing everyday and scientific knowledge in terms of ethnic culture and school culture offer a productive foundation for developmental analyses?"

To address these questions, I build on theory and research defining culture in terms of adolescents' uses of symbolic tools, such as narra-tives, songs, values, and ideological scripts, to mediate actual and ideal circumstances in which they live and, thus, their development. I focus on the sociohistorical concepts of *mediation* and *goal-directed activity* for insights to expand theory and practice related to development in culturally heterogeneous contexts. I argue for research supporting ado-lescents' identification of salient goal-directed activities, presumably those circumstances presenting threats and opportunities toward their ongoing development, and adolescents' use of cultural tools to mediate actual and ideal environments. Mediation may involve identity work in cases where it is threatened, as among certain groups of U.S. minority youth, but the mediation process itself may be more pivotal to adolescents than identity work per se.

WHAT IS CULTURE?

Consistent with much contemporary research in cultural psychology and education, Carol Lee considers context with the concepts of the "everyday" and "scientific," as shown in Table 9.1. Acknowledging that K–12 education has created "artificial boundaries between the everyday and the canonical," Lee contrasts these two domains of human behavior for youth of color in low-income communities and considers educators' responsibility to guide their motivation for and achievement in school. Lee builds on the sociohistorical comparison of spontaneous and scientific concepts (Vygotsky, 1978) as a foundation for positing that students' preferred cultural media should be the foundation for disciplinary knowledge.

The "everyday" includes familiar stories, popular discourses such as rap music, identity statements, emotional orientations, spontaneous preferred habits of mind, and behaviors that educational contexts consider deficient. In contrast, the "scientific" includes universals, discipline-based ways of knowing, canonical stories, abstract discourse, scaffolded practices, and cognitive orientations. This review of differences between

Table 9.1 Lee's Definitions and Representations of "Everyday" and "Scientific" Thought

The Everyday	The Scientific
Spontaneous knowledge, processes, and discourses	General knowledge, processes, and discourses
Specific cultural features	Universal knowledge; disciplinary (school subjects) processes
Familiar stories; popular discourses in music lyrics, like rap	Canonical stories
Identity-based knowledge	Identity-suppressing, discriminating knowledge
Non-school-based knowledge (tacit)	School-based knowledge (explicit, multiple)
Habits of mind	Scaffolded strategies
What students know from their cultures	Cultural features to be "appropriated" in school
What students like	What students need to learn to like
Motivational, emotional	Cognitive
Human development	Cognitive development
Students come to school with it	School must foster it

Source: Lee (this volume).

everyday and scientific modes suggests that "everyday" is akin to ethnic culture, whereas "scientific" is akin to mainstream culture and by implication is the universal standard. It would, furthermore, be possible from this comparison to equate "everyday" with natural and "scientific" with artificial. It has also become increasingly common to define school as a culture modeled on mainstream values, discourses, and modes of thought, thereby requiring the unequal burden on minority youth to translate between their everyday and scholastic lives (Mahiri, 2005). These issues revolve around the role of culture in development, a vexing issue under scrutiny at this time in developmental psychology (Chandler, Lalonde, & Teucheer, 2004; Turiel, 2002).

Although consistent with details of Lee's discussion and examples, it would be a mistake to distinguish everyday and scientific knowledge on the basis of culture, given the theory from which she is deriving central principles. For Vygotsky, the major developmental achievement during the "transitional age" of adolescence is the ability to use elements in the environment as tools for social relations, that is, to change self-perspective in relation to the environment. Identity discourse could, thus, serve development as a mediator or "conductor of human influence on the object of activity … externally oriented … aimed at mastering and triumphing over nature … and … a means of internal activity aimed at mastering oneself" (Vygotsky, 1978, p. 55). Building on such interaction with the environment, scholars have offered the notion of "leading activity" defined as "the leading relation of the child to reality" (Veresov, 2006, p. 14), which is further refined in connecting "intention and realization" (Polivanova, 2006, p. 83). These theoretical concepts of *mastery, leading, intentions,* and *realization* imply goal-directed activity, suggesting that the developmental foci of mediation during adolescence are context dependent. Identity work may or may not be as salient in all contexts.

Diverse theorists explain that normally developing adolescents have the higher order cognitive, social, and emotional capacities for analysis and hypothetical thinking (Erikson, 1994; Piaget, 1968; Vygotsky, 1978). They would also, by extension, be able to perceive obstacles in their environments, to create relevant goals, and to use symbol systems or "cultural tools" to achieve those goals. Instead of focusing on this integration of emotion, cognition, and culture in the meditational uses of tools to control environment and self, many researchers have focused more literally on identity in the context of peer relationships via mechanisms of perspective taking (Selman, Watts, & Schults, 1997). Developmentally leading activities across contexts may occur within a self-in-society relation, which is tested, salient, and enacted very differently across circumstances. Identity work is thus not central everywhere. Relationships are certainly important during adolescence, as they are in other phases of life, but psychosocial dynamics other than identity confirmation are central to relationship processes.

When participation in society is threatened explicitly or implicitly, identity may become a pivotal mechanism for adolescents beginning to make decisions that have lifelong implications. For example, a comparison of the strategies used by Bosnian youth, of the same ethnic, religious, and historical backgrounds, showed that those whose families remained in the war zone and those whose families migrated to safer ground focused on different kinds of features in their environments and crafted different psychosocial orientations to those salient features (Daiute & Lucic, 2008). Moreover, a notable difference was that Bosnian Muslim youth who remained in their homelands in extremely challenging political-economic circumstances demonstrated a penchant for identity work, whereas youth of the same ethic, religious, and historical origins who had migrated to the United States did not mediate their experiences in terms of identity (Daiute & Lucic, 2008). Instead, they focused on the activities and orientations of others, whom they perceived as alien and unfair, yet important to get along with. The relative self-centeredness and other-centeredness of young people's orientations to conflicts is less the issue than the fact that they used narrating as a cultural tool to mediate broader challenges they perceived in their societies. Identity work is thus not central everywhere. This is not to say there's no discrimination in other contexts but that we must not assume that identity is central to adolescents even where discrimination occurs. Young people who perceive other obstacles, like threats to their ability to make a living, as paramount may gravitate to relevant cultural tools for protection, connection, or explanation, such as the apparent cultural obsession for political analysis, as a catalyst for development (Daiute, in press).

The distinction between "natural" and "artificial" is especially relevant to deconstruct. If we equate everyday with natural or authentic and scientific with unnatural or crafted, we have to note that some of the practices and language associated with the scientific occur spontaneously in child-rearing because parents apprentice their children to habits of mind (Heath, 1983; Nelson, 1986). Heath found, for example, that white parents in a low-income community in North Carolina socialized their children to speak in the decontextualized vocabulary and subjects of school, whereas parents in the economically equivalent African American community nearby socialized their children in the cadences and values of their home. Each of these ways of knowing is modeled on scripts consistent with values and ideologies that organize events, perception, and meanings in a context (Nelson, 1986). As noted by other scholars, socialization among African American and other marginalized groups also includes the ability to identify discrimination, practice strategies for dealing with it in daily life, and distinguishing interpersonal from institutional manifestations of racist views that lead to it (Cross & Fhagen-Smith, 2001). Emphasis on ethnic discourses, also referred to "essentializing," can be used as an "ideological tool to create social categories and representations of marginalized groups that are racist, discriminatory, and demeaning" (Bhatia, 2007) within as well as outside these groups to mediate broader power relations (Bhatia). Ways of knowing may be defined by ethnic culture, socioeconomic class, gender, educational background, and myriad other factors. Interestingly, qualities that Lee identifies as everyday versus scientific have also been associated with gendered discourses (Gilligan, 1993). We can point to previous research to suggest loosening the connection between culture and ethnic identity, while continuing to recognize the need to support flexibility of participation across modes of thinking, like the everyday and the scientific, as Lee does with the Cultural Modeling process.

CULTURAL MODELING TO ADDRESS INEQUALITY

Lee proposes "Cultural Modeling" to bridge everyday (out-of-school) and scientific (in-school) ways of knowing, and she offers an extended example from her research to illustrate such a bridging process. Central in this analysis is the concept of "scaffolding" (Vygotsky, 1978), the basis with "cultural data sets" of texts in African American vernacular and canonical texts, such as the European literature typically predominating in literature curricula. Educators have successfully guided students "to apply strategies for literary reasoning to texts with which they are already familiar" and then to "enter the canonical texts with a sense that literary reasoning is a game that they can and like to play" (Lee, this volume). By engaging students to work with these carefully matched familiar and unfamiliar literary texts, savvy teachers are supporting higher order (Vygotsky, 1978), formal operational (Piaget, 1968) thinking among students in schools where relatively few graduate.

Lee explains how with cultural modeling, young people from nonprivileged backgrounds draw on familiar texts as foundations for interpreting unfamiliar texts privileged in school to identify "the stretches of text we believe are symbolic," "analyze points of similarity," "brainstorm about real-world associations with the target image or action," and "construct an explanation that links your real-world associations and the patterns you have inferred about the textual details you have noticed." Cultural modeling assumes, with evidence from Lee's empirical research, that students identify with their cultural media in ways that provide strong and positive foundations for understanding and eventually for identifying with the less familiar cultural media of school. Given the symbolic realm in which this must occur, however, we ask whether it is the identity element of the media that holds the power for change or the application of symbolic tools for challenging power relations that put one at a disadvantage.

The issue of inequality is, moreover, one that involves interaction, especially as adolescents, like adults, have cognitive capacities and experiences for identifying problems and focus their energies on them (Turiel, 2002). Also related are findings that conformity to conventional thinking over certain more universal moral thinking increases in adolescence in part because of adolescents' ability to deal with complexity and because they are aligning functionally with their sociopolitical environments (Turiel, 2002). In this regard, it is worth noting that the argument for society's responsibility to model cultural processes is crafted and, thus, scientific. It is not necessarily natural or spontaneous when educational practices ignore, discriminate against, or exclude students' knowledge, but is a concerted effort to maintain majority political, economic, or social power in the United States (Bhatia, 2007; Mahiri, 2005). Albeit not the intent of the comparison, to equate the everyday with the ethnic language and practices of one's home community while equating the scientific with the academic practices of strange communities embeds "culture" in identity politics rather than in uniquely human meaning-making processes via purposeful uses of symbol systems. Reducing these diverse contexts to cultural identities minimizes the power dynamic in development. When we separate everyday from scientific art, we are then also implying a distinction between lower and higher art. Another problem with equating everyday practices with home culture is that this could render school culture unproblematic. Lee checks this by noting that ethnic discriminatory practices in schools define minority cultural practices as deficient, but this stops short of defining school culture as problematic.

By not figuring in adolescents' goals, as they perceive them in relation to challenges and opportunities, we may be underutilizing the academic context and adolescents' abilities, including their motivations, by focusing on the familiar, such as ethnic practices, rather than on identifying interesting unfamiliar problems to solve.

WHAT IS DEVELOPMENT?

Along with others exploring alternatives to fixed developmental stages, Lee defines human development as a right for high school students

Table 9.2 Lee's Distinctions Between Human Development and Cognitive Development

Human Development	Cognitive Development
Everyday	Scientific
Identity work	Not identity
Intuitive	Scaffolded
Single repertoire	Expanded repertoires
Particular	Universal, enduring
Coherent and overarching	Isolated disciplines
In life contexts	Decontextualized
Project for life course	School-based project

Source: Lee (this volume).

who are alienated in high schools that marginalize the artistic forms familiar and dear to them. These students have the right to establish "goals, aligning one's self with the work entailed in accomplishing those goals ... and in so doing learning how to cope, be resilient, and be persistent" (Lee, this volume). Toward these psychosocial ends typically ignored in public institutions, Lee distinguishes human development from cognitive development (see Table 9.2).

On this view, human development is broader than cognitive development, a premise that many contemporary researchers, educators, and students would find compelling. It may be easier for individuals from diverse perspectives to agree on the nature of cognitive development, that it involves generalized scientific processes requiring instruction abstracted from spontaneous practices and the province of school, the disciplines there, and discriminatory orientations toward the noncognitive. With this background of agreement about the nature, inclusions, and exclusions of cognitive development, Lee challenges us to think about whether that set of important albeit relatively limited orientations count as human development. Questioning that it does, Lee equates real human development with goals and processes of everyday life. Ideally, moreover, Lee argues that cultural modeling supports a process of "intergenerality" fostered via identity work, rooted in the broader everyday developmental processes and transferred to those more limited cognitive processes. This comparison of cognitive and human development in Lee's discussion opens a range of interesting issues, including that school must fit into the broader scope of life rather than life fitting into school, a point consistent with research by scholars who focus on out-of-school practices (Heath, 1983; Rogoff, 2003).

In studies of apprenticeship into trades like tailoring or weaving in rural communities, for example, scholars have illustrated how experts, parents, and older children use guided participation to involve children in the culture (Rogoff, 2003). Scholars have applied such ethnographic notions to suggest processes of "cognitive apprenticeship" as a revolutionary way of organizing school learning in disciplines including literacy (Fisher, 2004), science (Lemke, 2001), and mathematics (Newman, Griffin, & Cole, 1989). This line of analysis posits that school is but one place for enculturation, whereas scientific processes and thinking such as problem solving, counting, and other analytic skills needed for weaving and other activities in everyday plazas, shops, streets, churches, and youth gathering places involve authentic motivation and learning. Although belonging to and identifying with communities of practice emerge as relevant to such research, the focus has been on the nature of scaffolding with processes like guided participation (Rogoff) and the nature of symbolic mediators that evolve in those contexts (Newman et al., 1989). Given the wealth of theory and research indicating the interaction of development with environments, we can usefully question whether, when, and how identity becomes a social-developmental tool, rather than assuming that it is universally central to resolve the adolescent development crisis (Erikson, 1994). Although myriad diverse theories agree that adolescents have the physical, cognitive, social, and emotional capacities for self-reflection, there is evidence of the need to focus on self-identity as a goal that varies across contexts (Brown, Larson, & Saraswathi, 2002).

In what circumstances and how do we decouple the everyday from an implicit connection with identity through specific goal making and allowing youth to focus on the salient affordances in their environments (expressions, problems, appealing rituals, costumes, and other media) they can use to mediate transitions to their goals? By shifting from ethnic identity and practices to goals-in-context, we encourage curiosity and goal setting to which students can select and apply meditational tools and processes. When focusing on context as melded with identity, we may, in contrast, miss the importance of goal setting and mediation. Future research can address such issues by examining how environmental media are useful because of their familiarity, their uniqueness, or some other quality. The appropriation of unfamiliar cultural tools, like a strange word used in curiosity or in jest, could, for example, function in transformative ways. Students already know their favorite songs, sayings, and jargon, but they may also use affordances of unfamiliar canons, such as seemingly odd phrases in mainstream literature, like the "fie" in Shakespeare, that are intriguing and available in contexts where adolescents' goals set the scene.

An alternative example to the goal of "identity work" for "aligning one's self with the work entailed in accomplishing those goals, wrestling with the uncertainty that inevitably accompanies significant personal transformation, and in so doing learning how to cope, be resilient, and be persistent" (Lee, this volume) could be the development of generationally relevant social change, which is, after all, a solution to mediating the actual and the ideal.

Identity and/or Mediation as a Developmental Catalyst

"Identity work" may apply especially for young people of color growing up in low-income neighborhoods and being educated in schools that do not tend to assume and ensure the success of all students. Identity work may also, however, be one among other developmental strategies, depending on the goals, challenges, and opportunities in the context of transition. Although identity work may be catalytic at some points in development of higher order thinking and psychosocial skills, whether we can take it for granted as being transformational during adolescence and/or constituting a developmental telos remains open to question. Carol Lee helps us identify the need for such a question and for some analytic means of addressing it.

"Identity work" presumably creates the goals for making these connections and, in turn, addressing injustices inherent in the devaluing of students' everyday knowledge in school. Building on the motivation of identity work and educators' cultural modeling, students can then, according to Lee, achieve "multigenerality," or flexible bicultural knowing. If discourse serves to maintain power, how might contrasting the everyday and the scientific obscure those power relations? Teachers and researchers could instead work with students to elicit meaningful learning goals and to identify cultural tools for mediating the distance between their actual and ideal situations. Foregrounding goals in this way may lead to surprising uses of the strange mainstream symbols on the periphery of consciousness in the classrooms.

An increasing number of scholars is defining cultural processes as the uses of salient and/or contentious affordances in society (enacted in songs, sayings, actions, dress, rituals, etc.) to mediate issues larger than individual identity, that is, to mediate the self–society relations that are contentious and salient in the context. On this view, although social-relational work may be universal, the specific domains where they matter are defined by specific threats to youth development. Circumstances in culturally heterogeneous contexts like the United States may elicit identity concerns around ethnicity, race, class, gender, and sexuality, whereas circumstances in other geopolitical contexts such as those involved in armed conflicts or postwar and postcolonial transitions may elicit goals beyond personal identity to which adolescents apply their higher order thinking. Broad distinctions of individualist and collectivist cultures fail to explain the real-life dilemmas that adolescents face (Turiel, 2002) to explain the emergence of political understanding, so the need for analyses of such diverse contexts is great. Rather than analyzing minority youth culture and identity as dualities like everyday/scientific and human development/cognitive development, which reduces these categories to internalized states or stages, the theoretical concept of mediation is useful for more dynamic notions of culture and identity. Among youth in the former Yugoslavia, ethnic identity is dysfunctional, in part because of recent wars fought in the name of ethnicity and in part because future goals to enter the international market economy require moving identity conflicts. This lack of focus on identity also results from pressures to conform, so we must question silencing as well as the voicing of identity work. The use of complex methods engaging young people in multiple-positioning activities opens the discourse not only for researchers but also for adolescent participants themselves (Daiute, in press).

Scholars in the United States have tended to apply sociohistorical principles to ethnic diversity because those have been prominent issues for us. This has led to an unintended reduction of culture to ethnicity, which may not leave sufficient room in research and practice for students to raise other goals and injustices in the way of those goals. Although Vygotsky focused on the interdependence of individual and social thought and development, the process driving this interaction is "mediation," which is not natural, comfortable, organic, or familiar but is "artificial" and thus can serve for externalizing and expanding thought and behavior. "The use of artificial means, the transition to mediated activity, fundamentally changes all psychological operations just as the use of tools limitlessly broadens the range of activities within which the new psychological functions may operate" (Vygotsky, 1978, p. 55). This does not mean that catalytic developmental activities are alienating but that they are related to garnering common means for achieving uncommon goals, which would be those relevant to the challenges people face living in communities organized by ethnicity, income, or other goals, such as the goal of education, which may bring unlikely neighbors together. If goals and circumstances differ, issues at the center of meditational activity may as well. We must, therefore, learn more about the situational features and the kind of identity work or other kinds of work they require.

Assuming that culture is embodied in cultural data sets and that analysis of these cultural data sets is guided by teachers through the process of identity transfer involves a very different set of research and practice methods. If scientific knowledge is mediation, then those processes of creating, using, and transforming cultural tools must be in the hands of the students themselves. To foster these as developmental processes, we need to shift from identity projects that might reduce "culture" to individuals, contents, rituals, and static symbols. Why must identity be the object or the goal rather than learning, future employment, or understanding historical facts, as occurs in some situations of war? Why would identity always be the major adolescent focus, rather than context-sensitive problem finding or problem solving? The premise that object-oriented meaning making via mediation with cultural tools is the leading activity of development rather any specific domain per se takes the project away from identity toward action.

On this view, familiar narratives from home, ethnic, or religious cultures, for example, and those of the new capitalist democratic society are not defined as cultures, everyday or scientific, but as contexts (Bruner, 1986; Nelson, 1986). When students, working with others of identities who were their parents' enemies, work together in groups, they evaluate the society as they find it and identify challenges to their own future development, learning, and well-being (Daiute, in press). With such goals, their curriculum proposes using a range of narrative genres, not to reify or to transfer identity but to mediate living history (lived experience), that is, as tools to help them consider self–society relations in the service of having a future as adults, which is the primary challenge they face. This example suggests how we might shift from identity goals to youth-defined life goals, thus setting contexts where they do the scientific activity of mediating the various contested contexts they perceive. In this case, it was often something referred to as "last-century mentality" and "prospects for a future to be an adult with a job, a home, and a family." What shifts here are two notions, the goal and the mediator. This process of object-oriented mediation thus allows individuals and groups to exert some control over their destinies and, thus, as much as possible their physical and social environments. As presented above, for example, are individuals who had lived as Yugoslavs from 1945 to the 1990s, when outside pressures (manipulations) became persuasive enough for them to re-create, live, and die by different identities (Gagnon, 2006). Another example offered insights about how socioeconomic class qualifies ethnicity (Ball, 1992). Given these examples, we can continue to explore the strategies situated across diverse contexts for whether and how they suggest defining *culture* in terms of identity groups or psychosocial practices, like mediating gaps between challenges and opportunities. Such a context-dependent analysis explores "the higher functions that are the product of the historical development of behavior [which] arise and are shaped during the transitional age in direct dependence on the environment that develops during the process of sociocultural development of the adolescent" (Vygotsky, 1998, p. 84). These concepts of object oriented activity and mediation are consistent with Lee's overarching argument but require more discussion and, I argue, questions about the primary identity of work.

The Arts of Symbolic Thought and Development

Returning to development and the arts, we must reconsider issues of symbolic thought in context. Separating everyday and scientific media, as Lee has astutely guided us to do based on her research, we learn how relatively spontaneous uses of popular arts, like contemporary music, can provide African American youth growing up in low-income neighborhoods the basis for scientific analysis of canonical arts, like the literature taught in schools. If these youth can, moreover, identify with the scientific material of school, they can expand their ways of knowing. To support these ideas, we have noted contributions of this analysis and raised questions about it, in particular those related to applying this argument to other groups of young people who know that identity work is dangerous not only because of their personal positions but also because of the positions of their nations regarding the interdependent development of young people, the future adults in those nations. Although revealing how young people can apply their everyday arts to the scientific arts deemed worthy of study in school, this argument leaves aside the basic concept of symbolic thought, which is generating goals and appropriating cultural tools to achieve goals. Research and practice can, with Lee's lead, continue efforts to figure out how to help students identify goals and strategies themselves, because it is this mediation process that counts as culture, not the rituals on both sides of the bridge. "In this context, we can use the term *higher* psychological function, or *higher behavior* as referring to the combination of tool and sign in psychological activity" (Vygotsky, 1978, p. 55).

When differences between everyday and scientific thinking are defined in terms of identity, an important point that Lee is making could be missed. This point is that culture is the mediation of experience, the shared meanings crafted with affordances in the material and symbolic environments to control the environment. As stated 100 years ago yet not fully realized in research,

> Just as the first use of tools refutes the notion that development represents the mere unfolding of the child's organically predetermined system of activity, so the first use of signs demonstrates

that there cannot be a single organically predetermined internal system of activity that exists for each psychological function. (Vygotsky, 1978, p. 55)

The gradual transfer of logical thinking from the familiar to the unfamiliar has been an emphasis in recent scholarship, especially given concerns about injustice for minorities in heterogeneous societies. Such analysis is important and consistent with theory and research on focusing on developmental progressions from egocentric thought to decontextualized thought characterized by multiple perspective taking. Adolescents can reproduce such perspective-taking skills, yet is continued examination of those skills the best way to direct their intellectual abilities? Focusing on injustice may not be practical for adolescents already left behind in high school education, but establishing challenging educational contexts that rely from the beginning on motivation, curiosity, and analytic skills would place the definition and creation of goals and application of cultural tools ito meet those goals in the students' hands. This inquiry could explore the still unconventional idea that adolescence is not the birth of conceptual thought or obsessively focused on peer relations but the more deliberate use of media to control the environment and one's self. Although identity may be one meditational strategy in some contexts, we must explore the idea outside the realm of culture as identity. "If in the child, intellect is a function of memory (perception, will, etc.), then in the adolescent, memory is a function of the intellect" (Vygotsky, 1998, p. 96). These troubled times in a shrinking bellicose world suffering from identity conflicts implore us to foster intellectual skills toward collective ends. Lee is promoting cultural bridging, multiplicity, and, by extension, mutual understanding, but would maintaining identity as the object pulling us toward development open or shut our eyes?

REFERENCES

Ball, A. F. (1992). Cultural preference and the expository writing of African-American adolescents. *Written Communication, 9*(4), 501–532.

Bhatia, S. (2007). Opening up cultural psychology: Analyzing race, caste, and migrant identities. *Human Development, 50*, 320–327.

Brown, B. B., Larson, R. W., & Saraswathi, T. S. (Eds.). (2002). *The world's youth: Adolescence in eight regions of the globe.* New York: Cambridge University Press.

Bruner, J. (1986). *Actual minds, possible worlds.* Cambridge, MA: Harvard University Press.

Chandler, M. J., Lalonde, C. E., & Teucheer, U. (2004). Culture, continuity, and the limits of narrativity: A comparison of the self-narratives of native and non-native youth. In C. Daiute & C. Lightfoot (Eds.), *Narrative analysis: Studying the development of individuals in society* (pp. 245–266). Thousand Oaks, CA: Sage.

Cross, W. E., Jr., & Fhagen-Smith, P. (2001). Patterns of African-American identity development: A life space perspective. In C. L. Wijeyesinghe & B. W. Jackson (Eds.), *New perspectives on racial identity development: A theoretical and practical anthology* (pp. 243–270). New York: New York University Press.

Daiute, C. (In press). *Human development in political violence.* New York: Cambridge University Press.

Daiute, C., & Lucic, L. (2008, September 11). A cultural-historical analysis of migration out of war. Paper presented at the Convention of the International Society of Cultural Historical Activity Research, San Diego, CA.

Erikson, E. H. (1994). *Identity in the life cycle.* New York: Norton.

Fisher, M. T. (2004). "The song is unfinished": The new literate and literacy and their institutions. *Written Communication, 21,* 290–309.

Gagnon, V. P., Jr. (2006). *The myth of ethnic war: Serbia and Croatia in the 1990s.* Ithaca, NY: Cornell University Press.

Gilligan, C. (1993). *In a different voice: Psychological theory and women's development.* Cambridge, MA: Harvard University Press.

Heath, S. B. (1983). *Ways with words: Language, life, and work in communities and classrooms.* New York: Cambridge University Press.

Lemke, J. L. (2001). Articulating communities: Sociocultural perspectives on science education. *Journal of Research in Science Teaching, 38,* 296–316.

Mahiri, J. (2005). From 3 R's to 3 C's: Corporate curriculum and culture in public schools. *Social Justice, 32,* 72–88.

Mahiri, J. (2006). Digital DJ-ing: Rhythms of learning in an urban school. *Language Arts, 84,* 55–62.

Nelson, K. N. (1986). *Event knowledge: Structure and function in development.* Hillsdale, NJ: Lawrence Erlbaum.

Newman, D., Griffin, P., & Cole, M. (1989). *The construction zone: Working for cognitive change in school.* New York: Cambridge University Press.

Piaget, J. (1968). *Six psychological studies.* New York: Norton.

Polivanova, K. N. (2006). On the problem of the leading activity in adolescence. *Journal of Russian and East European Psychology, 44,* 78–84.

Rogoff, B. (2003). *The cultural nature of human development.* New York: Oxford University Press.

Selman, R. L., Watts, C. L., & Schults, L. H. (1997). *Fostering friendship: Pair therapy for treatment and prevention.* New York: Aldine de Gruyter.

Turiel, E. (2002). *The culture of morality: Social development, context, and conflict.* New York: Cambridge University Press.

Veresov, N. (2006). Leading activity in developmental psychology. *Journal of Russian and East European Psychology, 44,* 7–25.

Vygotsky, L. S. (1978). *Mind in society: The development of higher ordering thinking*. Cambridge, MA: Harvard University Press.

Vygotsky, L. S. (1998). Psychology of the adolescent. In R. W. Rieber (Ed. English translation), *The collected works of L. S. Vygotksy: Vol. 5. Child psychology* (pp. 3–186; M. J. Hall, Trans.). New York: Plenum.

III
Artistic Development

10

CHILDREN AS INTUITIVE ART CRITICS

Norman H. Freeman

Many children leave behind them a trail of pictures over the years. The preservation of some of those pictures makes possible a sort of archaeology of childhood whence experimental psychologists can generate testable hypotheses (Freeman, 1980). Those same children will also have left a stream of opinions about pictures. Those opinions are ephemera. So they are difficult and frustrating to study. Therefore, let us study them.

Studies in psychology often start with a functional analysis. One would ask, "What can children do with pictures?" Let us, though, immediately reverse it to, "What can pictures do for children?" One can expect children gradually to develop conceptions about what pictures are good for. Pictures, it is universally agreed, excel in the display of appearances that can be "emotionally engaging, eye-catching, and memorable" (Willats, 1997, p. 25). Those three aspects of pictorial vividness are usually discussed under the broad headings of expressivity, attractiveness, and recognizability. Any account of what people think about pictures has to find a way of formulating the three in a common framework (Freeman, 2004, 2008; Freeman & Adi-Japha, 2008). My suggestion is that a reasonable way to understand children's conceptualizations of those core pictorial functions is to investigate the proposition that all children inexorably start off on a path as though they were going to become art critics. In the course of the investigation, we shall encounter a range of questions, such as the following:

Is an art critic a clear role model for anyone?

Why an art critic, rather than another role such as an art historian or art educator?

Why use an adult role category when considering the mentality of young children?

What cognitive-developmental account can explain art-critical development?

PLAN OF THE NEXT FIVE SECTIONS OF INVESTIGATION

In the next section we informally take note of what is involved in moving from (a) viewers looking at pictures, to (b) what the viewers say about pictures. Second, we discuss at some length why it is so difficult to define the field of enquiry. Third, four standard sources of ideas for a developmental account are then considered. The last of those, the work of Parsons on interview, is then updated, with the emphasis on the rise of diversity in children's art-critical thinking. Fifth, as something of a corrective, the final section contains a simplifying assumption: The suggestion, for future research, is that the diversity is organized around two polar-opposite sources of evidence for a judgment.

A VERY BRIEF LOOK AT PICTURES

Starting with the pictures themselves, it is clear that people often hold some pictures in great affection and esteem. Under some circumstances, some people often want to be helped in making their pictorial judgments. Under other circumstances, a little better understood, people want to express themselves, often wanting to let off steam about the degeneracy of modern art. There are both hotly affective and coolly cognitive aspects to pictorial art criticism. One important consequence of viewing pictures is the affront people often experience. It has been noted, "Contemporary art is often judged aversive to the extent that people complain of headaches" (Wilkins & Fernandez, 2006). It is surprising (at least, it is surprising to me) that, in that same report of Wilkins and Fernandez from the University of Essex, scanning the picture surface into a Fourier power spectrum analysis explained some of the viewers' discomfort: A massive 40% of the variance in "visual discomfort" judgments of examples of contemporary art was accounted for by the deviation of the power spectrum readings from those established by natural scenes. Maybe our visual systems, even today, are roughly calibrated to rural and urban scenes, such that some artists' types of deviations from the baseline can give some of us a headache. Viewers' reflections on their emotionally charged pictorial experiences might form part of what impels them into the emergence of art criticism. Reflections on experience may on occasion be exogenously aided socially, or on other occasions may be individual achievements of the solitary viewer locked in contemplation of a masterwork.

Let us for the moment continue that emphasis on viewing the picture, for it is certainly the case that vision scientists have long sought the secrets of art in the analysis of markings on the picture plane and the viewer's perceptual processing and uptake (e.g., Little & Perrett, 2002; Vartanian, Martindale, Podsiadlo, Overbay, & Borkum, 2005). That endeavor is in full swing. It is worth noting what the lead article on the topic in a special issue on art and perception of *Spatial Vision* (2008) has to say. Although the placement of markings on the picture plane involves much control over perceptual-motor skills, some degree of severing of the relation between art and skillfulness is located to the early part of the 20th century. From 1913, with the *Black Square* of Malevich, "art is freed from both skillfulness and realistic objectivity," and, after Duchamp's *Mona Lisa With a Moustache* (1917), "artistic skill was no longer considered a condition necessary and sufficient to create art" (Pinna, 2008, p. 497). Considered by whom? Not by much of the viewing public, who thereby may act as somewhat unforgiving spontaneous art critics (Freeman, 2004). Is *art critic* a useful term here? It seems to be: Pinna remarked that Duchamp's interventions had the effect of "revolutionizing contemporary art that has become a mixture of creation and criticism" (p. 497). Art critics are not often talked about as members of a collective endeavor, or, indeed, often talked about at all, as we shall soon note.

One would not, perhaps, at this stage care to lay down a general ruling on how the benefits of experience accrue and may take off into critical and self-critical thinking. Whatever the causal process, it is straightforward to gather initial raw observational data on untutored art criticism, because people readily pass judgments on artworks. There is a simple reason for extending interest into studying how children intuitively develop into art critics; the reason being that young children do develop art judgments (Hart & Goldin-Meadow, 1984; Rosensteil, Morison, Silverman, & Gardner, 1978), naturally and often with emotional sensitivity (Callaghan, 1997), and on a sufficiently widespread scale to have long interested educators (see Karpati, 1991, 1992). If it happens, developmentally we want to know how and why. That is the traditional default-value answer: If it's there, study it. And for art educators, if it is there, try to foster discovery of how to do criticism (Ecker,

1973). In what follows, we shall examine some examples of what children say, not in order to perpetuate rich interpretation of the manifest content of their judgments and evaluations but to discern some profound issues behind the children's concerns. That is an approach that is familiar from some writings on the child's theory of mind, where the foci of interest are the underlying profound issues of representation and communication.

For a first acquaintanceship with art-critical topics, it can be particularly useful to spend time in a gallery and just listen to the unsolicited opinions given by all manner and age of people. Adolescence seems to be a particularly useful time to make diagnoses of what can be claimed to be the incompetence of artists (evidently unaccountably unnoticed by the curators). One might have thought that the National Gallery, London, is not a place particularly noted for displays of incompetence on its walls. But as reported in a neat article by Turner (1983) on adolescents' interpretation and criticism made on a visit, the adolescents acted as though it were their job to sniff out error. It happened to be variation in coloring that exercised those viewers, which in itself is interesting because the victim of the adolescents' disdain, the Fauvist artist Derain, had taken the problematic relations between outline and color as one of the targets of his pictorial investigation!

To step back from that particular example and to view matters rather more generally, viewers' judgments are often forcefully expressed as though particular viewers had been personally affronted on purpose. That is interesting: The viewing public often needs no coercion or inveigling to engage closely with art. And people do not necessarily switch off their engagement or their judgmental mode when entering someone's home. In one study, Maridaki-Kassotaki and Freeman (2000) set out to interview people on what they thought an exhibition piece was. The adolescents in the sample were clear that you could infer something of the taste and judgment of the householders from their choices of picture to exhibit on the wall or tabletop at home. Those same adolescents who can be so spontaneously judgmental are often very open to discussion of artworks. There has historically been a great deal of pessimism about the emergence of art-critical functions before adolescence (Gaines, 1983). Rosensteil et al. (1978) reported that whereas 15-year-olds were able to distinguish between three types of judgment—their own pictorial preference, others' pictorial preference, and which is the better picture—11-year-olds and younger gave meager evidence of that sort of analytic thinking. But of course a balance sheet of what they can and cannot readily do is needed: One does not have to wait until adolescence for other sorts of judgments and reflections on artworks.

As in any other domain of judgment, young children come to develop something of a theory of how the domain works.

IT IS NOT EASY TO DEFINE THE FIELD

Thus far, we have implied that furtherance of the public understanding of art, perhaps even of art education, forms a sufficient reason for studying the work of art criticism. That is an extrinsic reason, some benefit one hopes might accrue, eventually. Closer to home, developmental psychology is often presented as though the aim of research were to help us in the scientific understanding of children, working with a domain of competence as a means to that end. Yet developmental psychology is scarcely a homogeneous enterprise with but a single overriding strategic aim. One of the lines of developmental research making up the enterprise certainly does have understanding children as its main aim; but no single aim can be complete in and of itself as though there were a single key to each behavioral enigma. For two other lines of work, the enhancement of our understanding of children is a sort of bonus more than a specific target. One of those other lines has long aimed to make developmental analyses serve the understanding of cognitive science in general by elucidating principles governing how the mind is organized. A third line aims to provide one of the answers to the question "Why do we adults do things the way we do?" Here, an avowed aim is to further our understanding of adults. That necessarily involves taking a life span perspective. When we do so, a question will later arise: Precisely how do we specify the causal connections between (a) being a child and (b) subsequently being an art critic? To approach that, we have to find out something of what art criticism encompasses.

The elements of art criticism are contained in the work of art critics. And it is here that a problem arises in acute form: Where do we look for information on how to characterize the adult steady state of expertise in art criticism? We here mean *picture critic* (although it is odd that some such term does not actually seem to exist). We shall have to settle for asking what a pictorial art critic is. When in doubt, one could do worse than to turn briefly to the classic *The Oxford Companion to Art* (Osborne, 1970). Running one's search backward from the entries for *art history*, *art education*, and *art dealing*, one finds *art critic* to be entirely absent. Not in over 1,000 packed double-column pages covering the art world is there an entry. Yet critics' writings range from newspaper advisory puffs to the equivalent of a professor for the public understanding of science. There is, of course, real gravitas behind the latter. So it is rather unlikely that one's first obvious hypothesis about the omission of the term is right, namely, that there might be something disreputable about an art critic, something irretrievably intellectually downmarket. To look on the bright side, as psychologists we might even benefit from the lack of a humanities establishment line: The elusiveness of a definition of the steady-state role does give us a free hand in research.

There is certainly an alternative hypothesis about the lack of official thanks and recognition: It might be the case that the particular work of art criticism is dispersed over work that goes into many roles in the artworld, under the general cover of aspects of aesthetics. Thus, in 1998, "[T]he Encyclopedia of Aesthetics was created using a definition of aesthetics as 'critical reflection' on art, culture, and nature" (Kelly, 1998, p. ix). Even setting aside that encyclopedic encroachment onto the terrain of "nature," perhaps the official invisibility of art criticism is because everyone in the artworld does it, in some measure? Let us test that idea against nonpictorial aesthetics. Perhaps by focusing initially on other sorts of critic, we can gain a perspective on exactly what it is that is interestingly peculiar to making judgments about pictorial art.

Major cities tend to have seasons where there is often more performing art on offer than one can possibly attend: drama, dance, and music, staged in their appropriate venues. Even if there is not a seasonal surplus, the cost of entry is often high enough to give people pause. So the public writings in outlets such as newspapers and magazines become an essential public resource. As a member of the public, one needs accounts that are well balanced in format, with some evidence and reasons for judgment being given (members of the audience have a right to have evidence spelled out; Gross, 1973). In addition, critical notices are a sort of genre, in which the pieces should not be too lengthy to serve the purpose of being a guide to alternatives, current, past, and future. A critic who brings off that act of service is a rare and valuable asset. The accomplishment needs someone who understands what we need to find out, is skilled in crafting the format that allows us to do so, and understands his or her strengths and limitations as a witness on our behalf. One needs to find out if a new production is worth going to see, if the actual performance is good, if the direction is firm of purpose, and so on. And above all, the notices should communicate well, so liberal use of imagery and metaphor is understandably common.

From the above, there is something that is rather easy to discover just by scanning the newspapers, magazines, and journals. There is a sufficient coherence of focus to writings on performance arts to enable good critics to make an approach to satisfying the objectives listed above. In one sense that is obvious, yet in another sense there is a real puzzle. The puzzle is that writings on the performance arts tend to get into a muddle when deploying powerful explanatory concepts like *authenticity* and *authority*. Who has the right to decide what a dance means? What is an authentic re-presentation of what Schubert might have been aiming at? Should "period instruments" be used? And so forth. The obvious aspect is that given that massive indeterminacy, no critical notice that failed to take root in the gap between score and performance, or in the gap between script and performance, would carry much conviction with readers. By comparison, pictorial art criticism peculiarly gives the appearance of lacking a focused concern. What is the central issue for pictorial art critics? Or, to take up an equally useful way of formulating things, what is the equivalent of the script–performance or score–performance gap that provides such a hospitable niche for other types of critic? I propose that there is no central issue, no founding niche. Pictorial art criticism is a peculiarly dispersed endeavor by comparison with narrative and performance arts.

But that dispersal of effort may be considered in a positive light: Consider the following from Adrian Searle (2006), who is much respected. He offered a critique of an exhibition at the Whitechapel Gallery, London. With a corpus of some 15,000 pages and of thousands of pictures to work with, the critic urged, on the basis of evidence presented in compressed form (the work was repetitive, and there was a sugary disquieting presentation of extreme violence), "What's lacking in [the artist's work] is much sense of development or of self-reflection." Now let us compare that with Richard Dorment (2006) on the same exhibition, here choosing another of the artists as his stalking horse: "[I]nitially impressive, her work soon reveals a limited and repetitive visual vocabulary." That masterly compression of exposition is characteristic, more or less advising the prospective viewer to use those as cues to go on his or her own search, as is the terse verdict telling the prospective viewer to fill it out for herself. Those essential compressions perhaps mislead readers into thinking that critics are both superficial and cavalier about evidence. One verdict specifies the limited and repetitive visual vocabulary, which is in fact the evidence one needs to make a judgment. The other comment uses the evidence but infers something grave about the mentality of the artist. The issue is not whether one or other or both critiques were right, wrong, or half-right. The point is that the above are the sort of easily recognizable art reasoning toward which we are all impelled when children, with vast individual differences in how far along the path of art critic we each travel, as we shall soon see when noting the material that Parsons (1987) presented as a start to his developmental analysis in what is still the most advanced monograph on the way children express opinions about pictures.

Parsons (1987) opened his pioneering work, *How We Understand Art*, with a brief account of an extract from a conversation. Two people, one an 8-year-old and one a 15-year-old, were discussing Picasso's (1936) *Head of a Weeping Woman With Hands*. That painting was something of a historical milestone, yet Parsons' book serves economically to establish the case that it is unrewarding to approach children's pictorial analyses as though the children were impelled by any art-historical considerations. Indeed, an understanding of the historical determinants of pictures and of assumptions about pictures is a developmentally very late achievement. Briefly, Parsons' discussants diverged in their evaluation, they pointed to pictorial evidence that each evidently hoped might sway the other, and, above all, they gave reasons for their propositions. To me, that part of Parsons' work looks a bit like a preliminary negotiation between two art critics deciding on whether they can establish a meeting of minds. One discussant pithily explained either what the artist could (or should) have done to improve the picture in her eyes, whereas her interlocutor explained what the artist actually had already done to achieve pictorial success in his eyes. In sum, the young girl was not too impressed, and she wanted more care and more realism; the older boy praised the artist's technique as something akin to caricature, which can self-consciously exaggerate expressivity. The positions remind one a bit of the genre into which Searle (2006) and Dorment (2006) fitted their comments noted earlier. An art critic is mandated to represent considerations of expressivity, attractiveness, and recognizability. What critics say about such issues in what is often the compressed and conventionalized format of their trade involves indeed the kind of things that children are interested in. That is not a putdown of critics, of course: It is a tribute to their involvement with issues that continue to be of basic, engaging importance.

Again, Parsons' (1987) expositions make it clear that few children seem consistently to adopt an art educator's role by asking what they themselves can learn about pictures from acting as a viewer in order to enhance their own productions. In Parsons' interviews, an art-critical stance seems more evident than an art educator's stance.

It is important to note here that from an art-educationist perspective, a perspective that is unarguably dedicated to children's development in all manner of visual-artworks production, art critics are indeed needed (it may not always have been so, but in the modern world it is so). Boughton (1989) long ago presented a view of art education that involved a meeting of role models drawn from the trio of roles: artist, historian, and art critic. There are precedents for psychologists taking seriously the concept of critical activity. Golomb (1992), in her monograph *The Child's Creation of a Pictorial World*, devoted an entire chapter (mainly on visual preferences) to "the child as art critic." Winner (1982) strongly urged that there are four participants in the artistic process: artist, performer, perceiver, and critic. The above writers cited strong evidence linking art practice and art-conceptual development (and especially see Milbrath, 1998). But the jury is out on whether and how art practice and art criticism tessellate in development. Because art criticism has remained elusive as a role, the art critic has remained elusive as a role model; so it seems safe to assert that young children do not develop into amateur art critics by attempting to emulate exogenous role model achievement. That is, whereas art-critical conceptualization evidently needs exogenous cultural support, it may be safe to regard major aspects of early art-critical development as being endogenously driven in their pacing.

Finally, how do we uncover anyone's critical thinking if they have not had the consideration of writing it out for public consumption? Exposing what anyone, adult or child, means or is thinking can well start by asking blunt questions, but then might require quite varied techniques. Technical variation is not something that is in short supply in experimental psychology, nor is conceptual variation: "By the end of the '70's, developmental psychology had evolved into a field marked by not one but several explanatory theories" (Dixon & Lerner, 1992, p. 9). Which developmental theory, along with its preferred techniques, will be appropriate to the present enquiry? Let us take a bearing on standard research resources.

A LOOK AT DEVELOPMENTAL ISSUES

First, one cannot get well started by making the standard move of turning to the Piagetian corpus. That in itself is a bit odd. One usually can get a start there. It is not as though anyone could claim that Piaget was uninterested in the thought and judgment of the child. And for someone as deeply concerned as he was with the processes of discovery in the child, the absence is both noticeable and regrettable. There are different ways of formulating why that gap should be there. But for the moment, the point is simply that the genetic epistemologist Piaget was not exactly enamored of any of the arts as a terrain for investigating epistemological issues and following the track of logically coherent thought-structures. It is the key issue of "logical necessity that was the heart of the matter for Piaget" (Kuhn, 1992, p. 246). One cannot trace the child's conception of necessity to the arts domains. That is something that is easy for a biological scientist to sympathize with: Even the very basic notion of "evidence" is quite often rather hard to come by in the arts as soon as one strays much into the analysis of judgment or diagnosis of qualities of experience. Piaget himself (1956) concluded that it was more difficult to establish the core progression of normal development in what he termed "artistic tendencies" than for other "mental functions." In sum, we have to start afresh. Or almost afresh. Let us consider what became of some of the Piagetian work, taking our bearings from the nonarts domains.

Some 30 years ago now, a landmark piece, "The Origins of Scientific Reasoning," opened with the remark, "Children and scientists have many traits in common" (Siegler, 1978, p. 109). Historically, the "child as scientist" metaphor (from the analysis of adolescence in Inhelder & Piaget, 1958) proved to be an inordinately useful research guide, with a longer than expected inspirational half-life, for although it justifiably suffered from decay under an accumulating weight of analytic distinctions, the notion then revived with formulations of domain specificity in knowledge processing. That phase of development of the metaphor involved dividing science itself into branches. Thus, mastery over biology yields a biologist, mastery over chemistry yields a chemist, and mastery over their intersection yields a biochemist. Consider a book by an heiress to the firmly rooted Piagetian tradition, one who studied with Piaget and who works in self-avowed neo-neo-Piagetian mode. Karmiloff-Smith (1992) presented a program of research that united two of the developmental lines: illuminating cognitive principles and explaining adulthood. In her formulation, the establishment of behavioral mastery over a problem type engenders an increasing representational explicitness, with the child eventually able to report on the representation and reflect on it. We may add that art is no exception: "[T]he act of drawing propels the child's conceptual understanding" (Milbrath, 1998, p. 371). Karmiloff-Smith's basic case was that whenever children immerse themselves in domains of knowledge, something inside the children impels them to develop a theory of each domain. Preadolescent children have been found to make spontaneous judgments both positive and negative, with "a very strong relationship between the level of knowledge about art and the *quality* of art criticism" (Karpati, 1992, p. 116; emphasis in original). The accumulation of a knowledge-based theory in any domain is a product of a certain type of learning, and it facilitates further learning. Each theory has its own peculiar features, necessarily so because each deals with different inputs and outputs. Pictorial theory exploits the function of pictures as input devices for extending normal vision and imagery into areas that might otherwise remain inaccessible or unregarded (Freeman, 2006, 2008). So, to sustain those propositions, it would be necessary to investigate art as constituting a domain of knowledge and to see whether the children's emerging theory ended up as something that is recognizably art criticism. Karmiloff-Smith set up the opportunity for such an analysis. But her own formulation faltered by comparison with her formulations for other domains of knowledge, as she stopped short of tracing development into the critical conceptual levels. So one would have to add something to her account. Be that as it may, Karmiloff-Smith's work tells us to look for the child's conceptual discoveries in artwork becoming endogenously channeled toward some mature state. If the above propositions are along the right lines, it follows that there is, in principle, a way of studying how children become art critics that is as direct and simple as for any domain. That way is to detect early signs of young children's engagement with an art-critical stance and to map out growing conceptual depth and flexibility.

As was noted above, Karmiloff-Smith (1992) organized her developmental account according to titles of expertise: "The child as a physicist; The child as a psychologist; The child as a mathematician," and so forth. The titles of expertise do not indicate that the roles are those of paid professionals. The study of the child's theory of mind under the title *The child as psychologist* need not be extended beyond the child's development of what used to be called *folk psychology*. Whatever one's particular stance on the child-as-scientist idea, there is every reason to ask (a) whether there is any respect in which any adult amateur or professional specialism is traceable into early childhood, (b) whether much in common between that adult and that child has survived the individual's transition from childhood, and (c) whether a glance at the adult's pattern of life and work helps us better understand those of the child. It is not easy or straightforward to use ourselves in our adult state to gain ideas on what to search out about childhood, but it can sometimes be done.

Second, when turning to classical sources, many researchers canvass alternatives to neo-Piagetian constructivism, such as sociocultural accounts of art (see Braswell & Rosengren, 2005). A classic resource is in the tradition impelled by Vygotsky, who is so often held up as a sort of classical complementary twin to Piaget (Carpendale & Lewis, 2004). Vygotsky was the outstanding champion of the line that tools of thought are administered exogenously. Interestingly, from a guided participation viewpoint (as promulgated by Rogoff, 1990), there does not seem to be a sound set of experimental studies on art-critical joint activity. Just as lowering to the spirits, the conclusion of Szechter and Liben (2004) was that it may be that state-sponsored encouragement may need to be given to adults before they will spontaneously extend guided participation with children to the aesthetics of picture production (though see Boyatzis & Watson, 2000; Callaghan, 2000). Self-evidently, art is a cultural product, and aesthetics has been noted as a domain "where the cognitive and the cultural sciences might prove ever more mutually relevant" (Sperber & Hirschfeld, 2004, p. 45). Viewers become pictorially acculturated. Yet although Vygotsky undeniably gave us a good picture of how children might internalize their culture, he told us little of how children might come to challenge or criticize their culture (Crain, 2000, p. 240). Crain went on immediately to include 2-year-olds and adolescents in that "critical stance."

A third option is to turn to writings in cognate areas that one knows provide ingredients for critical reflection. Generations of students have been told to scan primers on philosophical aesthetics for what they can get out of them. One might start with a text advertising itself as on "the philosophy of criticism"—Beardsley's (1981) 500-plus pages of exposition. It is immediately evident on glancing at Beardsley's index that the term *criticism* is repeatedly invoked from the start to near the end of the book. One might be able to follow some sort of a thread, if not of argument, then at least of consideration. Accordingly, let us pick up a thread, and give it just one tug.

On page 20, Beardsley (1981) appealed to what might be direct evidence on intention: An artist gives you a few words about what he or she meant a work to present. Do you cross your fingers and just hope that the words capture anything of the artist's prior intention, that is, of what might have been causally effective in the making? Again, what happens if your eyes tell you differently from that which the artist has said? All is not lost. Maybe, as Beardsley proposed, it might happen that if for some reason people are disposed to regard that particular artist as an authority, they pay attention to the words, defer to the artist's opinion, and thereby "the intention, or the announcement of it, actually brings something to pass" (p. 20). But the very power of the artist here poses a problem for the critic: "[I]t presents a strong reason for not making intention the final court of appeal" (Beardsley, p. 21). In order to interpret an artwork, you want to be able to distinguish the artwork from real and imagined causal psychological processes. One can see problematic aspects of appealing to intention:

> What do you do when an articulate artist such as Juan Munoz, at his Tate Turbine Hall installation interview (2001), tells you that reliance on his intention will speedily run out of steam because he himself doesn't really understand what it is he makes?
> What if you get an artist who produces something superb but assures you that it is just a potboiler he dashed off? You need to be free to disagree.

What if you get a ferociously inarticulate artist who cannot tell you anything? You need to be free from being disarmed by that artist's silence over the question of intention.

What if the artist has a poor command of the language such that it leads to him or her just saying the wrong thing? You need to be free to override the import of the utterance.

All that can be agreed, and yet that makes it even more interesting that young children often do apparently regard a statement of intent as a potentially decisive factor in pinning a caption to a picture (Bloom & Markson, 1998; Browne & Woolley, 2001; Callaghan, 2005; Gelman & Ebeling, 1998). An interesting corpus of developmental research is gathering around the topic (Freeman & Adi-Japha, 2008). In sum, there is good reason occasionally to turn to classical philosophical aesthetics, extract formulations that are of great concern in art criticism and devise simple developmental tests. The set of so-called aesthetic fallacies to be avoided makes particularly interesting reading for the purpose of hypothesizing when and why children might affirm the fallacies. For what it is worth, I suspect that the classical intentional, affective, and genetic fallacies are merely good ideas planted in the wrong place.

Yet it is apposite here to remind ourselves again that useful material is by no means confined to heavyweight texts. The reviews in newspapers and journals often conform to a sort of moral code whereby the reviewer has a responsibility to answer questions concerning an artwork, such as what can be learned from it, how good it is, how pleasing it is, and how it might have been better (see Ricks, 2002, on the art of reviewing with narrative and other art forms). One of the attractions of studying the child's metamorphosis into amateur art critic is that the judgments and evaluations by both children and the critics with which we are concerned are often alike in being ephemeral. Children are worked with in experimental forays, or on visits to galleries, where their thinking is on the spot and may be forgotten the next day. Art critics too are most common where ephemeral judgment is made, for example in newspaper and magazine pages. They are not usually heavyweight analyses designed to be studied by ensuing generations of students. One advantage of consulting magazines and newspapers for what critics say is that one gathers a phenomenal set of what are often unofficial ideas to turn into empirical psychological questions without trouble. One has to be somewhat careful, though, for there is a whole spectrum of writing from art theory to the lightweight sort of art journalism that is no better than fashion writing (see Burgin, 1986). The level of art criticism of interest for present purposes is where judgment and evaluation are made with some degree of moral integrity:

> It would be "bad faith" for me to pretend I have no stake in what I am saying; but equally, I am not doing my job as a critic if I simply assert my views without explaining how and why I think they have … a validity which is independent of the personal history of he or she who utters them. (Burgin, p. 89)

Finally, there is a fourth resource available for launching a developmental study, a custom-made account of art thinking that is sufficiently developed to be already set up for further consideration. The work of Parsons (1987) has already been noted, and we here pick up the account promulgated by Freeman and Parsons (2001) in which Parsons' earlier stage formulation of linear development had been dethroned as a central explanatory concept.

BACK TO INTERVIEW DATA

We may now view the work of Parsons as a so-far unique documentation of outcomes of children's development of a folk theory of depiction. In that light, it is now time to consider a verbal judgment, captured as spoken off the cuff in interview, on an Albright picture, *Into the World Came a Soul Called Ida*. That portrayal is of a woman well past any hope of thinking of herself as being merely middle aged. The full interview can be found in Parsons (1987), and Parsons singled it out for succinct commentary in Freeman and Parsons (2001, pp. 83–84) as being fairly representative of its type. Instead of quoting the interview, let me list a bare summary of the assertions, in order of mention, with a bare minimum of the visual evidence and background reasoning employed:

1. The sitter looks as though she is in mourning for her lost beauty.
2. You can tell that when she was younger, she was probably fairly pretty.
3. It is like a moment when harsh reality dawns.
4. The pretty-ugly contrast is present in a contrast between clothes of hers that are pretty and clothes that look as old as she is.
5. The figural surrounds are old, worn-down, and dead.
6. There is a message from the artist to the viewer here, a powerfully presented specific message about concern with appearance.

As may have been surmised, I have listed the above propositions stripped of the utterances because the words would have betrayed that it was not an adult critic speaking. Wendy, aged 16 years old, did well. *Amateur art critic* is an appropriate term to apply to her. Parson's commentary is concerned with the quality of Wendy's thinking: Given the powerful impact of the picture on her as viewer, given the provoking presentation of someone ugly with a lot of incongruity in the clothing and unambiguous lack of contrast in the background, Wendy focuses on inferring what might have been the artist's intention, identifying how the intention is realized, and explaining why her own (Wendy's) interpretation makes sense in terms of real life (see the full transcript in Parsons, 1987, for details).

One might say that Parsons was concerned with aesthetic epistemology: How critics know things, evidence they appeal to, rules of plausibility, and so forth. In particular, Parsons exposes the prevalence of mentalistic argument and consideration. That is fine work, but it does need a complementary approach to the development of art critics, which was compared and contrasted with the above by Freeman and Parsons (2001). The complementary approach is to focus on the ontology of Wendy's account, the entities that she invokes. She evidently refers to the picture and to the artist and to a person in the outside real world who was the sitter, and she makes plentiful mention of her own responses as viewer. It is straightforward to show how those four entities are the irreducible minimum for any art criticism to develop (see Freeman 2000, 2004, 2006, 2008). Four entities can contract six direct relations between themselves. So we can profitably view children's development as increasing efforts to coordinate considerations over that net of six relations. Therefore, we must expect diversity and lack of consensus to arise amongst children as they take on such a large, dispersed task. Thus, when Kindler and Darras (1998) asked children what made a drawing good, there was such diversity within each group of the 369 children aged 7 to 14 years, encompassing skill of the artist in the execution, realism in relation to the referent, conformity to viewers' expectations, and so on, that modal consensus per category was very low indeed (often around 10% or 15%).

Parsons (1987), working in a long tradition of trying to organize aesthetic responses (see Lin & Thomas, 2002), presented a scheme of what we think of as vertical development through distinct phases (he called them *stages*, though stage theory is not actually essential to his analyses). The phases start with preschoolers, and what Parsons acutely described as preoccupations of the children are recognizably what people discuss as "matters of taste" (vibrancy of color is a fine example). The next phase involves grappling with a representational problem and also involves a concern with beauty. Thereafter, judgments and evaluations head for real sophistication, tackling problems of expressiveness and viewers' possibilities of emotional uptake. Then there is commonly a phase involving looking for causal processes started by what is on the picture plane itself (making inferences from qualities of the medium to how the composition works). Finally, the viewer comes to understand the contextual relativity of much of judgment (perhaps one could say that the young adults discover that art history has something to offer and that they have to show some self-awareness as viewers). How easy is it to apply the scheme? Parsons found that he had to use quite extensive interviewing. There have been attempts to identify incisive single-question probes that might expose the core of the child's thinking. Such work has been published by Freeman and Sanger (1995), Lin and Thomas (2002), and Maridaki-Kassotaki and Freeman (2000). Let us consider those, not so much for the quality of the evidence but more in the interests of diagnosing how research could well be organized.

Lin and Thomas (2002) devised a procedure that involved asking people, from preschool to student age, to choose five pictures that they liked out of a set of 25 pictures. So the approach is immediately recognizable as a picture-rich method, a mockup of an organized visit to a gallery or exhibition. Congruent with that focus, the experimenters took great care to ensure that their 5-picture set was very variegated (abstracts, cartoon, fine art, etc.). The experimenter wanted the participants (a) to describe each of their chosen pictures and (b) to say why they liked each. Note the contrast with Parsons (1987), who also worked with some five pictures, but these were the experimenter's choice of pictures designed so that not all would be likeable. With such different conditions of viewing, and such restricted interviewing, it may perhaps be understandable that the results both did and did not match those of Parsons. The similarity was that on the whole, the concerns identified by Parsons (color, subject matter, expression, medium, and historical context) were mostly what came up. It is impressive that that was the case, given Lin and Thomas' abbreviated interview. The difference from Parsons' findings was that no real evidence appeared of much that looked like a phase progression. It was obvious, for instance, that subject matter cropped up as a top-of-the-stack concern at all ages (except for art students, and that may have been for more than one type of reason). The conclusions were that it is best not to look for a linear progression and that instead "aesthetic development is branching and multi-directional" (Lin & Thomas, p. 278).

So, are we impelled to decide between linear and branching accounts of development in this domain as though one decisively ruled out the other (Freeman & Parsons, 2001)? Although, as was noted above, the ontology of art criticism almost certainly impels us to a nonlinear account, there is no principled reason why concerns that happen to dominate early phases have necessarily to be discarded or greatly submerged in later phases. To return to Parsons (1987), his first inarticulate phase of understanding pictures centers on delight in colors and fascination with subject matter: We each have to decide whether these are irredeemably childish concerns to be surpassed resolutely, or whether the concerns are there because they are fundamental and continuously potentially generative of new insights. To take an analogy, whereas a concern with a transitional object such as a comfort blanket is something that might be left behind before middle childhood, having fulfilled its function and having been symbolically exhausted, in contrast, some "one-word" utterances such as the social regulators *hello* and *shan't* do not need to be abandoned; indeed, they continue as vital social glue. No one would pounce on a speechmaker for having included one-word utterances to dilute a mean length of utterance of 5.7 in his peroration. In the same way, vertical development might well be viewed as not transcending previous phases but as reworking them in repeated cycles. In sum, this foray into deciding whether amateur art critics (a) pop out of the top of an escalator-type development or (b) tumble in a variety of postures from a variety of branch ends, need not yet make one legislate on how the interests of future research will best be served.

Let us look at another study involving simple questioning. One of the things we do know with some degree of assurance is that people are ready (a) to fire off heuristically guided snap judgments at the drop of a hat, and also (b) to give more considered complex judgments on reflection. Different sorts of knowledge suitable for different expediencies seem comfortably to coexist ("knowledge partitioning"). Even a post-Einsteinian theoretical astrophysicist acts in a Newtonian world, even at his desk when he picks up his coffee cup. Our species is primed for both rapid-response modes and slow-response modes. From such a viewpoint, it may be inadequate to divide people's knowledge into superficial and deep in order to denigrate first impressions. We need to know about first impressions, first reactions, what people have all primed up and ready to go. This next study that we shall consider was mentioned earlier on as a means of introducing the common critical stance in adolescence. The method dispenses with pictures altogether in favor of asking the child to do armchair contemplation of the domain. Even more anti-aesthetic, as it were, the interview is presented to the participants as an exercise in explaining a technical term that happens to be embedded in the nontechnical vocabulary of children. The Greek word *kadro* literally means *frame* but is universally used metonymically to mean "something that has been framed as an exhibition piece or a display piece," usually understood by our children participants as "something to embellish your home." Now that is indeed a useful function of the Greek word (which, from what we want, namely a vernacular point of view, seems to be fully cognate with the Spanish *cuadro* and pretty cognate with the Italian *quadro*). The usefulness is in two respects. First, the word provides a way of bypassing clumsy circumlocutions that would be necessary in English if one wanted to get at the top-of-the-stack conception of "what is worthy of being exhibited." Second, by presenting the task as one of asking for word meaning, as opposed to anything specifically to do with art, we can be sure that anything that comes up that is art related has indeed come up unsolicited via a preexisting association. Note therefore the bias in the procedure: If something does not get mentioned, one does not assume its absence in the child's mind. But if something does get mentioned, whether "superficial" or "deep," it counts as heavyweight evidence on the child as spontaneous art critic.

One hundred and twenty informants were asked to explain to a visiting alien what a *kadro* is. Children aged 4 and 8 years held that these important artefacts were held to be furnishings, useful for hanging on walls. We suspect that the children were operating with a concept of "decorativeness." For the moment, we note that adults and adolescents spontaneously referred to the use of display to commemorate artists' achievements (for inferring artists' competence, see Gross, 1973). Further, these adolescent and adult participants saw the pictorial choice as a literal display of householders' judgment. You can tell someone's artistic tastes and judgments from the pictures they put on exhibition. A communicative theory of art and a critical stance are certainly primed to be in operation after middle childhood. Whether or not such a stance is available before that age is a separate question; the data attest to the spontaneously unprimed accessibility of the critical stance.

The next study to be given brief mention was also done in the absence of pictures, so the apparatus is, as it were, just an armchair. We invite the child to ruminate so that she has to rely on her own unaided internal resources. Let us take brief note of examples of children puzzling through conceptual problems about art. Melanie King and I interviewed 15 seven-year-olds. That is a nice age group to work with over intellectual issues. Consider just three puzzles that we set that showed that most of the children were at least starting reflectively to engage with questions of beauty and of viewers' diversity.

First, when the children were told that one viewer (Jane) sees a picture that she thinks is beautiful, and asked whether another viewer (John) could find the same picture ugly, 12 said that viewers' evaluations could differ in that way, two were adamant that they couldn't, and one was unsure.

Second, another question shifted initial focus from Jane as viewer to an artist. The premise was that the artist had produced a picture that she thought was beautiful, and the question was whether a viewer (Sarah) could think that the same picture was ugly. Nine children said that an artist's evaluation and a viewer's evaluation could differ in that way, five said that they couldn't, and one child found the puzzle "too hard."

Finally, we posed the children a really abstract question to which there is a very simple answer that gives one a 100% baseline. The question is how you can tell if a picture is beautiful or ugly. All the children we have ever interviewed have told us, in varying forms of words, that all you have to do is to look at the picture. The replies often contained added evidence, considerations, and justifications; for example, if it's well done, if it reminds you of something beautiful, or if it represents a beautiful object. But for the present sample of children, we amended the question to "How can you tell whether a picture of a unicorn is beautiful or ugly if you've never seen a real unicorn?" Instead of now saying that all one has to do is to look at the picture, great diversity ensued. It will not take long to look briefly at answers. The question provoked some of the children to argue through the case. And that is what we want: to expose something of the children's range of argument.

1. Tajo (age 7; 3): *I'm not sure.*
2. Katie (age 7; 8): *I don't know.*
3. Ross (age 7; 8): *I don't know.*
4. Daniel (age 7; 6) would not expand on, *if everything was in the right places. It would be good,* thus depriving us of the opportunity to understand quite what he was getting at, although one can reasonably surmise that he meant to tell us the importance of pictorial composition in relation to the referent.
5. Terry (age 7; 6) was clear about the following: *You wouldn't be able to tell,* but he came up with no reason.
6. Gemma (age 7; 6) took a firm realist stand: *You can't tell because there's no such things as unicorns. I've never seen one.*
7. Julie (age 7; 9) spoke firmly, taking the functional stance that the job of a depiction is to depict recognizably (in accord with the philosophical aesthetics launched by Schier, 1986): *If it was a proper picture of one, then you would see what they look like.*

204 • Norman H. Freeman

Experimenter: *What would make the picture beautiful or ugly, though? Because you know it has a unicorn in it.*
Julie: *I don't think you'd be able to tell.*

8. Naomi (age 7; 7) also saw no problem: *It would be beautiful. Because it's got a nice white color.*

   That is a firm position as described by Parsons (1987): The picture transparently takes up its depicted referents' aesthetic quality.

9. Chris (age 7; 4) took a similar stance: *The horn would make it beautiful.*
   Experimenter: *Would it be possible to have an ugly picture of a unicorn?*
   Chris: *No.*

10. Tina (age 7; 3) also took that sort of stance, but instead of arguing from referent to picture she did the reverse: specifying what she wanted in the picture and demanding that the referent come up to that standard: *If it was white, I do like white a lot, so I would like a unicorn if it was white.*
    Experimenter: *But if it wasn't white?*
    Tina: *Then I wouldn't like it.*

11. Hugh (age 7; 11) was hesitant: *Well, it depends on what you're thinking about really.* He expanded that to make it clear that the *what* he meant was that the way you think about the unicorn itself is what matters: *It depends on whether you're thinking a unicorn could be like a horse with a horn, or a unicorn could be a little thing on two legs that scampers about anywhere, but they're really rare.*
    Experimenter: *They aren't real, are they?*
    Hugh: *No. So you could say it* [the picture] *would be good because you wouldn't really know what a unicorn would look like, it would just be coming out of someone's mind.*

12. Maxine (age 7; 1) was uneasy in a similar way to Hugh: *It's pretending you've seen one but you haven't.* When the experimenter posed the question again, Maxine came up with a mentalistic solution as Hugh had done, replacing the absent referent by some mental work by the viewer rather than along the lines of photography: *You would take a picture in your mind, and if it looks the same then it would be good.*

13. Max (age 7; 3) was not uneasy and straightaway came up a similar referent-centered and mentalistic solution, more succinct than Hugh's or Maxine's: *You can tell if the picture is beautiful by imagining it* [the unicorn].

Experimenter: *Once you have imagined it in your head, how do you tell if the picture is beautiful or ugly?*

Max: *See if it's similar to the one you've imagined about.*

14. Toni (age 7; 9) found a way of getting the absent unicorn into the frame: *Look it up in a dictionary, or go and see it.*

Experimenter: *But there aren't any real unicorns.*

Toni: *There are. They're in America.*

Experimenter: *What about fairies then?*

Toni: *Fairies, they're not true.*

Experimenter: *So how could you tell whether a picture of a fairy was beautiful or ugly?*

Toni: *Well, you wouldn't actually. You wouldn't be able to tell. You'd just say that's ugly and it's beautiful at the same time.*

15. Molly (age 7; 6) made the most determined effort of all to maintain a stern realist position on the world of real and fictional ranges of possibilities: *By the way I usually sort of think like you could say a princess is beautiful or like if you want you could say a tramp is ugly. Then you could say a unicorn is sort of more beautiful than a tramp and it's an animal so it's sort of as beautiful as a princess.* That is star quality reasoning by any standards. The experimenter was unsentimentally unimpressed and repeated the question, whereupon Molly immediately fell back on the qualities of the picture plane: *You can tell if the picture is beautiful by if it's dull or light colors*, explaining that light colors would be quite beautiful, whereas dull colors would make it a bit gloomy.

What can be concluded from the excerpts? Are they any sort of evidence for anything?

First, I suggest that we do not dismiss the children's efforts. Although it is true that care must be taken to avoid stimulating nonsensical answers, the open questions above (questions avoiding boxing children into a yes-no dilemma) seem to be just the sort of question to elicit considered replies (see Waterman, Blades, & Spencer, 2000, for a searching review of the general problem).

Second, I suggest that we accept the diversity of answers as being inherent in the area of art criticism. The diversity is forced on children as they attempt to coordinate considerations about the six relations between artist, viewer, picture, and referent (Freeman, 2004, 2008; Freeman & Parsons, 2001). Six relations is a lot for a child to survey. Aesthetics is irreducibly complex as a domain. It was noted earlier that Kindler and Darras (1998) found such diversity over the basic evaluative issue of what makes a drawing a good drawing, and that those authors found themselves suggesting at the end of their work that the development branches out within a multidimensional space.

Finally, given diversity and complexity in the contents of children's reflective awareness, can we find any sort of major dimension around which we might gather at least some of the diversity? To that we now turn.

A SIMPLIFICATION FOR THE FUTURE: A GENERAL POLARITY

Once we become able to identify real correspondences between (a) some of the judgments and evaluations made by children at various phases, and (b) the more sophisticated versions that are traded in by some adults on some occasions, then we shall have at our disposal a resource for refreshing our research ideas. We could trawl the adult corpus for what are held to be important ideas, useful applications, cogent criteria of evidence, and so forth, and work backward to identify their origins in childhood. Even the most banal formulations can operate in our favor here: Let us briefly note two banal instances because they serve to exemplify aspects of the process of discovery.

First, to the general public there is a timeworn way of stopping debate by legislating that there is no use arguing over matters of taste. It transpires that that position indeed characterizes numbers of children of 11 to 13 years of age, as they accord weight to the diversity of subjectivity. But below those ages, children are more likely to maintain that such matters can indeed be resolved because there is a univocal objective truth of the matter to be discovered and appealed to (Rowley & Robinson, 2007). Congruent findings were reported by Colombo, Gatti, and Galli (2003) in a follow-up of Freeman and Parsons (2001) using brief structured interviewing. Thus, when asked whether the child expected someone else to see whatever emotion the child herself saw in each of a small set of classical portraits (by Fragonard, Murillo, Parmigianino, and Pontormo), some 85% of the children ages 6 to 9 years said that another would feel as they did but that fell significantly to 57% in 10-year-olds as respect grew for diversity in subjectivity. It was noted earlier that there is indeed a relation between some aspects of the child's theory of mind and his or her theory of pictures (Browne & Woolley, 2001; Freeman, 2000, 2008; Richert & Lillard, 2002), though most probably not at the causal level of the mediating brain mechanisms (see Perner & Leekam, 2008, on beliefs, signs, and photos).

Secondly, to art critics, the banal adage "Beauty is in the eye of the beholder" is useful as a journalistic trope, a figure of speech merely to direct attention to the fact that many art critics have staked out a special claim to represent the interests of the picture-viewing public. To developmental psychologists, the adage is immediately recognizable, from our overexposure to theory of mind research, as a mentalistic formulation in opposition to something purportedly objectivist like "Beauty is an intrinsic property of some artworks; they just are beautiful, and that is all there is to it." So we can immediately ask if young children move to a mentalistic stance on evaluations of beauty some time in late childhood (Freeman, 2000; Freeman & Parsons, 2001). That polarity between mentalistic and objectivist formulations runs through psychological studies of attractiveness. Thus, Hoss, Ramsey, Griffin, and Langlois (2005) asked whether preschoolers and adults tend to categorize faces according to sex as a function of their attractiveness. Here, attractiveness is treated as a stimulus attribute. In art criticism, attractiveness has been construed not just in terms of beauty but also in terms of attracting attentiveness too (see Connors, 2001, for a succinct account of some of the history of the matter). In sum, there is a distinction between two sources of evidence for a judgment, one that starts from an appeal to external stimulus characteristics and one that starts with an appeal to characteristics of mind. The coordination of the two aspects may constitute the capacity productively to enter an ill-defined problem (Kuhn, 2000).

When do children come to consider and coordinate both sources of evidence for judgment in an art-critical stance (for an excellent angle on that for the subdomain of photographic art, see Liben, 2008)? An artist can judge her emerging picture according to external standards, such as conformity to those laid down by Alberti, whose writings gave birth to academic art theory by providing rules of composition and thoroughness in the creation of verisimilitude, "the tropes known to every student of Renaissance art" (Connors, 2001, p. 74). Or the artist can judge the correctness of what he makes not by any external criteria but solely from the reaction it produces in him. "This method of painting, now a commonplace, was largely Matisse's invention" (said the chief curator of painting at the New York Museum of Modern Art: Elderfield, 2005, p. 9). The question of when children come to consider and to coordinate both sorts of standard remains little understood in developmental psychology. Let us speculate. A sweeping statement of where research has got to on that front is that (a) the habit of coordinating the twin aspects of the evidential basis for judgment is a domain-general competence, which is (b) modulated so as to progress at different speeds in different domains (e.g., Kuhn, Cheney, & Weinstock, 2000). A causal account is discernibly on the agenda for the arts domains.

The conclusions are as follows. It is useful to take a perspective that labels children with an adult professional role. Yet Karmiloff-Smith herself (1992), in her writings, got one no further forward into understanding the child as an art critic than do the other classical sources, Piagetian or Vygotskyan in origin. I suggested how the writings of adults in criticism and in aesthetics form a largely untapped resource for ideas on how to identify what children's opinion formation might be engaged with. A bit is known about child art-critical development as revealed in interviews, and that has to be allied to a documentation of diversity in each phase of thinking that is inherent in the topic. It is perhaps a good idea to stop now and reorganize evidence according to a polarity between reliance on what is objectively on the picture plane as a basis for judgment and reliance on the subjectivity of the people involved, artist and viewer. It is bound to be the case that some researchers will put the properties of pictures at the center of their analysis, whereas other researchers will put minds centrally. Those two things are both necessarily complementary: "Without artists' minds there would be no pictures; and without pictures it would not be specifically pictorial competence that we were looking at" (Freeman, 2008, p. 33). To investigate the child as intuitive art critic is to engage with one strand of the child's journey toward a grasp of subjectivity, a journey that the typical child needs no coercion or cajoling to undertake, even though the end role is no role model for her.

REFERENCES

Beardsley, M. C. (1981). *Aesthetics: Problems in the philosophy of criticism* (2nd ed.). Indianapolis, IN: Hackett.

Bloom, P., & Markson, L. (1998). Intention and analogy in children's naming of pictorial representations. *Psychological Science, 9,* 200–204.

Boughton, D. (1989). The changing face of Australian art education: New horizons or sub-colonial policies? *Studies in Art Education, 30,* 197–211.

Boyatzis, C. J., & Watson, M. W. (2000). *Symbolic and social constraints on the development of children's artistic style.* San Francisco: Jossey-Bass.

Braswell, G. S., & Rosengren, K. S. (2005). Children and mothers drawing together: Encountering graphic conventions during social interactions. *British Journal of Developmental Psychology, 23,* 299–315.

Browne, C. A., & Woolley, J. D. (2001). Theory of mind in children's naming of drawings. *Journal of Cognition and Development, 2,* 389–412.

Burgin, V. (1986). *The end of art theory: Criticism and postmodernity.* Basingstoke, UK: Macmillan.

Callaghan, T. C. (1997). Children's judgments of emotions portrayed in museum art. *British Journal of Developmental Psychology, 15,* 515–530.

Callaghan, T. C. (2000). The role of context in preschoolers' judgments of emotion in art. *British Journal of Developmental Psychology, 18*, 465–474.

Callaghan, T. C. (2005). Developing an intention to communicate through drawing. *Enfance, 57*, 45–56.

Carpendale, J. I. M., & Lewis, C. (2004). Constructing an understanding of mind: The development of children's social understanding within social interaction. *Behavioral and Brain Sciences, 27*, 79–96.

Colombo, L., Gatti, M., & Galli, A. (2003, August 27–31). Children's understanding of works of art. Poster at the Eleventh European Conference on Developmental Psychology, Milan.

Connors, J. (2001, September 20). The lion of Florence. *New York Review of Books, 48*, 73–78.

Crain, W. (2000). *Theories of development: Concepts and applications.* Upper Saddle River, NJ: Prentice Hall.

Dixon, R. A., & Lerner, R. M. (1992). A history of systems in developmental psychology. In M. H. Bornstein & M. H. Lamb (Eds.), *Developmental psychology: An advanced textbook* (3rd ed., pp. 3–58). London: Erlbaum.

Dorment, R. (2006, May 9). Why it's mad to show art this way. *Daily Telegraph,* p. 24.

Ecker, D. W. (1973). Analyzing children's talk about art. *Journal of Aesthetic Education, 7*, 58–73.

Elderfield, J. (2005, March 19). Art before heart. *The Guardian,* p. 9.

Freeman, N. H. (1980). *Strategies of representation in young children: Analysis of drawing skills and spatial processes.* London: Academic Press.

Freeman, N. H. (2000). Communication and representation: Why mentalistic reasoning is a lifelong endeavour. In P. Mitchell & K. J. Riggs (Eds.), *Children's reasoning and the mind* (pp. 349–366). Hove, UK: Psychology Press.

Freeman, N. H. (2004). Aesthetic judgment and reasoning. In E. W. Eisner & D. M. Day (Eds.), *Handbook of research and policy in art education* (pp. 359–378). Mahwah, NJ: Erlbaum.

Freeman, N. H. (2006). Psychological analysis of deciding if something is presented in a picture. In R. Maniura & R. Shepherd (Eds.), *Presence: The inherence of the prototype within images and other objects* (pp. 135–144). Aldershot, UK: Ashgate.

Freeman, N. H. (2008). Pictorial competence generated from crosstalk between core domains. In C. Milbrath & H. M. Trauttner (Eds.), *Children's understanding and production of pictures, drawings and art* (pp. 33–52). Cambridge, MA: Hogrefe & Huber.

Freeman, N. H., & Adi-Japha, E. (2008). Pictorial intention, action and interpretation. In A. Vinter & C. Lange-Kuttner (Eds.), *The development of drawing and non-verbal intelligence.* Cambridge: Cambridge University Press.

Freeman, N. H., & Parsons, M. J. (2001). Children's intuitive understandings of pictures. In B. Torff & R. J. Sternberg (Eds.), *Understanding and teaching the intuitive mind: Student and teacher learning* (pp. 73–82). Mahwah, NJ: Erlbaum.

Freeman, N. H., & Sanger, D. (1995). Commonsense aesthetics of rural children. *Visual Arts Research, 21*, 1–10.

Gaines, R. (1983). Children's artistic abilities: Fact or fancy? *Journal of Genetic Psychology, 143*, 57–68.

Gelman, S. A., & Ebeling, K. S. (1998). Shape and representational status in children's early naming. *Cognition, 66*, B35–B47.

Golomb, C. (1992). *The child's creation of a pictorial world.* Berkeley: University of California Press.

Gross, L. (1973). Art as the communication of competence. *Social Science Information, 12*, 115–141.

Hart, L. M., & Goldin-Meadow, S. (1984). The child as a non-egocentric art critic. *Child Development, 55*, 2122–2129.

Hoss, R. A., Ramsey, J. L., Griffin, A. M., & Langlois, J. H. (2005). The role of facial attractiveness and facial masculinity/femininity in sex classification of faces. *Perception, 34*, 1459–1474.

Inhelder, B., & Piaget, J. (1958). *The growth of logical thinking from childhood to adolescence.* New York: Basic Books.

Karmiloff-Smith, A. (1992). *Beyond modularity: A developmental perspective on cognitive science.* Cambridge, MA: MIT Press.

Karpati, A. (1991). Hungarian national assessment of critical skills of 6- to 14-year-olds in art. *Visual Arts Research, 17*, 11–27.

Karpati, A. (1992). Skills in art criticism of Hungarian elementary school leavers in the 1980's. *Studies in Educational Evaluation, 18*, 111–122.

Kelly, M. (1998). *Encyclopaedia of aesthetics.* Oxford: Oxford University Press.

Kindler, A. M., & Darras, B. (1998). Culture and development of pictorial repertoires. *Studies in Art Education, 39*, 147–163.

Kuhn, D. (1992). Cognitive development. In M. H. Bornstein & M. H. Lamb (Eds.), *Developmental psychology: An advanced textbook* (pp. 211–272). London: Erlbaum.

Kuhn, D. (2000). Theory of mind, metacognition and reasoning: A life-span perspective. In P. Mitchell & K. J. Riggs (Eds.), *Children's reasoning and the mind* (pp. 301–326). Hove, UK: Psychology Press.

Kuhn, D., Cheney, R., & Weinstock, M. (2000). The development of epistemological understanding. *Cognitive Development, 15*, 309–328.

Liben, L. S. (2008). Developing children's appreciation of photographs as informative and aesthetic artefacts. In C. Milbrath & H. M. Trauttner (Eds.), *Children's understanding and production of pictures, drawings and art* (pp. 155–184). Cambridge, MA: Hogrefe & Huber.

Lin, S. F., & Thomas, G. V. (2002). Development of understanding of popular graphic art: A study of everyday aesthetics in children, adolescents, and young adults. *International Journal of Behavioral Development, 26*, 278–287.

Little, A. C., & Perrett, D. I. (2002). Putting beauty back into the eye of the beholder. *The Psychologist, 15*, 28–32.

Maridaki-Kassotaki, K., & Freeman, N. H. (2000). Concepts of pictures on display. *Empirical Studies of the Arts, 18,* 151–158.

Milbrath, C. (1998). *Patterns of artistic development in children: Comparative studies of talent.* Cambridge: Cambridge University Press.

Osborne, H. (1970). *The Oxford companion to art.* Oxford: Clarendon.

Parsons, M. J. (1987). *How we understand art.* Cambridge: Cambridge University Press.

Perner, J., & Leekam, S. (2008). The curious incident of the photo that was accused of being false: Issues of domain specificity in development, autism, and brain imaging. *Quarterly Journal of Experimental Psychology, 61,* 76–89.

Piaget, J. (1956). Art education and child psychology. In Z. Zeigfield (Ed.), *Education and art.* Geneva: UNESCO.

Pinna, B. (2008). Art as a scientific object: Toward a visual science of art. *Spatial Vision, 20,* 493–508.

Richert, R. A., & Lillard, A. S. (2002). Children's understanding of the knowledge prerequisites of drawing and pretending. *Developmental Psychology, 38,* 1004–1015.

Ricks, C. (2002). *Reviewery.* New York: Handsel Books.

Rogoff, B. (1990). *Apprenticeship in thinking.* Oxford: Oxford University Press.

Rosensteil, A., Morison, P., Silverman, J., & Gardner, H. (1978). Critical judgment: A developmental study. *Journal of Aesthetic Education, 12,* 95–107.

Rowley, M., & Robinson, E. J. (2007). Understanding the truth about subjectivity. *Social Development, 16,* 741–759.

Schier, F. (1986). *Deeper into pictures: An essay on pictorial representation.* Cambridge: Cambridge University Press.

Searle, A. (2006, April 5). Meet the misfits. *The Guardian, g2,* pp. 18–20.

Siegler, R. S. (1978). The origins of scientific reasoning. In R. S. Siegler (Ed.), *Children's thinking: What develops?* (pp. 109–150). Hillsdale, NJ: Erlbaum.

Sperber, D., & Hirschfeld, L. A. (2004). The cognitive foundations of cultural stability and diversity. *Trends in Cognitive Sciences, 8,* 40–46.

Szechter, L. E., & Liben, L. S. (2004). Parental guidance in preschoolers' understanding of spatial-graphical representations. *Child Development, 75,* 869–885.

Turner, P. (1983). Children's responses to art: Interpretation and criticism. *Journal of Art and Design Education, 2,* 185–198.

Vartanian, O., Martindale, C., Podsiadlo, J., Overbay, S., & Borkum, J. (2005). The link between composition and balance in masterworks vs. paintings of lower artistic quality. *British Journal of Psychology, 96,* 493–504.

Waterman, A. H., Blades, M., & Spencer, C. (2000). Do children try to answer nonsensical questions? *British Journal of Developmental Psychology, 18,* 211–225.

Wilkins, A., & Fernandez, D. (2006, April 10–12). Aversion to natural and artistic images. Paper presented to 60th anniversary meeting of the Experimental Psychology Society, Birmingham, UK.

Willats, J. (1997). *Art and representation: New principles in the analysis of pictures.* Princeton, NJ: Princeton University Press.

Winner, E. (1982). *Invented worlds: The psychology of the arts.* Cambridge, MA: Harvard University Press.

11

COMMENTARY
But Is It Art?

Alan Costall

Over the last 30 years or so, we have become used to developmental theorists identifying the child with certain adult experts, or "paid professionals" to use Norman Freeman's term. Admittedly, some kinds of specialization have yet to catch on: the child as incipient hairdresser, "folk" secondhand-car salesman, or intuitive telephone sanitizer. Nevertheless, the child as *scientist*, or as *theorist*, is now very much part of psychology's theoretical furniture, along with the child, more specifically, as physicist, biologist, or psychologist.

Norman Freeman proposes that we should regard the developing child as an intuitive art critic. It is undoubtedly true that even very young children engage with pictures, including their own drawings and paintings, in terms of not simply the quality of their execution and content but also what we might take as their expressive or aesthetic properties: The picture looks nice, ugly, funny, scary, and so on. But what is the developmental point in making reference to the paid professional art critics given that their values are, as Freeman himself admits, widely distrusted as precious, if not downright phony? Freeman identifies several reasons for studying the development of art criticism in children. Yet are any of these aims seriously advanced, in any positive way, by a comparison of children to professional art critics?

Freeman's first reason for studying children's art criticism sounds very much like the famous explanation once given for climbing Mount

Everest. As Freeman himself puts it, "If it's there, study it." However, there surely has to be some good reason for being interested in children other than that they are simply *there*. After all, as a 19th-century commentator on the new developmental psychology observed, children had been around for an awfully long time before "thoughtful men" bothered to study them (Bryan, 1896, p. 432).

In fact, Norman Freeman does identify three more definite purposes for studying children's art criticisms: (a) understanding the nature of *children* better, (b) understanding the nature of *adults* better, and (c) throwing more light upon *cognitive science in general* "by elucidating principles governing how the mind is organized."[1]

So one possibility raised by Freeman is that we might get a better grasp of children's art criticism by "work[ing] backward" from an adult "role model." But this option seems to be firmly closed down by Freeman himself. It is not just that most children do not end up looking or sounding very much like the paid professionals but also that they are not even aspiring to be like them. The "end role" of art critic is, as Freeman himself puts it, no "role model" for the child.

So is the purpose, instead, to help us get a firmer epistemological grip on where the professional art critics "come from"? Again, according to Freeman, apparently not, and for the same reason. There is no developmental trajectory, not even a curtailed one, between what most children are engaged in and the adult experts. Very few children end up as modernist art critics, and those children who do so rely upon a highly specialized training that, it would seem, serves to subvert rather than extend their commonsense judgments.

This leaves us with Freeman's fourth option: "elucidating principles governing how the mind is organized." Here Freeman adopts the standard "theory theory" approach. On the one hand, there is a preestablished domain of "artworks," and, on the other hand, there is the child destined to become a theorist about that domain, albeit an intuitive and unsalaried theorist:

> As in any other domain of judgment, young children come to develop *something of a theory* of how the domain works. ... [W]hereas art-critical conceptualization evidently needs exogenous cultural support, it may be safe to regard major aspects of early art-critical development as being endogenously driven in their pacing. (Freeman, this volume; emphasis added)

As far as I can see, the research Norman Freeman draws upon to convince us that even young children are theorizing presupposes what it claims to prove, namely, that children *must* be *theorizing*—and, furthermore, that they *must* be theorizing about *art*—if they show any kind of discernment in relation to what most adults deem to be artworks. Take Freeman's summary of an interview with a 16-year-old girl, Wendy, about the picture *Into the World Came a Soul Called Ida*. There is certainly thoughtfulness, interpretation, and justification in her comments but no articulation of any theory. Furthermore, in her evaluation of the picture, she makes no explicit appeal to general principles at all but only references to the specific content of the picture and the specific intentions of the artist. It is possible, of course, that this girl is nevertheless resorting to an unstated *theory* that guides her criticism, namely, that, in general, comments about artworks should refer to content, intentions of the artist, and the like. But that is an article of faith, not a compelling conclusion to be drawn from the evidence. Wendy might just as well be dealing with the artwork on its own individual terms. And why shouldn't she?

Now I am not suggesting that children are inherently incapable of theorizing. If I were an art teacher, I would certainly be perplexed if a "child," certainly one as old as 16, were to prove completely unable to engage in serious theorizing; for example, when working on a school project on the nature of Cubism, by drawing on not only the pictures themselves but also the relevant literature, including Cubists' own conflicting attempts at theorizing their own practice (Fry, 1978). Nevertheless, I do not see that it follows that children, whenever they engage in critically evaluating a picture, must *always* be engaging in theorizing—even in what Freeman refers to as, "something-of-a-theory theorizing."

In my view, the wide appeal to "theory" within developmental theory has got seriously out of hand. Initially, the metaphor of the child as theorist was playful and provocative. But now it is taken too literally, and the metaphor has died.[2] The effect is deeply paradoxical. In its appeal to historically situated practices, such as science, physics, biology, or psychology, "theory theory" keeps managing to eliminate history from developmental theory.[3] By abstracting various historically situated expert practices from their historical contexts, these practices, along with their corresponding "domains," come to appear as natural "givens" that, in some cases, even qualify for their own specially designed neural modules.

In the case of art criticism, there is less risk of losing sight of this historical dimension. There is such a lack of consensus, and there is also so much susceptibility to fashion. Furthermore, professional art criticism, as we now know it, has a relatively short past, having as its pioneers such recent figures as Diderot and Baudelaire. And it is not as though the world beyond that of art criticism is overly impressed by the formalist values espoused in modern art criticism (Bourdieu, 1986). For most people, art criticism does not look much like serious expertise.

So is art criticism a special case? Can this explain why, according to Freeman, there seems to be no continuity between children's and the professionals' versions of art criticism—no developmental *telos* heading toward modernist formalism? I do not think so. There has been plenty of disagreement within the other fields of expertise invoked by the "theory theorists," even within physics, and notoriously within psychology. Furthermore, these other expert practices, as we now understand them, also have surprisingly short pasts. The modern notion of science as a secular movement—"scientific naturalism"—is largely a 19th-century invention, as is the very term *scientist* (Turner, 1974). According to the textbook histories of psychology, the modern discipline began as recently as 1879. And even the domain of physics— Kuhn's ideal of a paradigmatic science and his standard against which to disparage the disorganized state of the social sciences—did not itself achieve any degree of unity until recently. As Kuhn himself (1970) had to concede in his postscript to the second edition of *The Structure of Scientific Revolutions*,

> There was ... no physics community before the mid-nineteenth century.... What is today the subject matter for a single broad community has been variously distributed among diverse communities in the past. Other narrower subjects, for example heat and the theory of matter, have existed for long periods without becoming the special province of any single scientific community. (p. 179)

If we focus exclusively on domains of expertise rather than the *process*—the ongoing practices of experts—we can quickly lose sight of the important fact that such domains are not just self-evidently *there*. The domains are not definable independently of the relevant practices. They have not been waiting from the beginning of time, as it were, for their relevant experts to come along.

BUT IS IT ART?

As Freeman himself emphasizes, the term *art critic* is unusual in comparison to related terms such as *film critic*, *literary critic*, or *music critic*. The term does not serve to specify its corresponding "objects" of criticism. It can be taken to include all objects of art, the visual arts in general (including, say, sculptures and even unmade beds), or else just painting and other related "images." Freeman, and much of the research he cites, appears to restrict the objects of "art criticism" to *representational* images. Certainly, Freeman's proposed criterion of "recognizability" would hardly apply to many paintings from the last century that have nevertheless found an honored place in our art galleries. However, even if we restrict the domain of art criticism to *pictures*, even representational pictures, there still remains further need for specification, for not all pictures seriously count as *art*, not even *mediocre* art (Gallie, 1956), certainly not the majority of efforts one encounters in amateur art exhibitions.

Freeman, along with the other researchers he cites, seems to take the *child's conception of the domain of art* (the range of objects to which art criticism applies) largely for granted. Instead, the issue for these researchers is whether and how children theorize about this domain. Thus the researchers present children with what they, and many other adults, would accept as canonical examples of representational art. But it does not follow, for this reason alone, that the child's criticisms of the artworks they are shown necessarily count as *art* criticism in the adults' sense. To make such an assumption would be to commit what William James called "the psychologist's fallacy": imposing our current—and historically contingent—categories upon the people we are studying. Children may well apply the same kinds of evaluative judgments they are making in the existing research to pictures that the children themselves may not regard as art at all: family or newspaper photographs, comic book images, or advertisements. Alternatively, the children might indeed extend their conceptions of what counts as art to objects well beyond the currently recognized canon, for example, to well-designed or well-crafted artifacts, such as mountain bikes, iPods, cameras, computers (well, at least Macs), and so on. And why not? As the philosopher William Gallie (1956) put it, art is an essentially contested concept, and this is true, I suggest, for both children and adults. Think again about my examples of news photographs, comic book images, or advertisements, and then recall the work, for example, of Andy Warhol, Ray Lichtenstein, or Richard Hamilton. The "domain" of art will never be defined conclusively, once-and-for-all. So, rather than treating children as a separate species of incipient adults, why not include them in the conversation about what counts as art, especially given that "child art" itself has already had such an important say (Fineberg, 1997).

PUTTING DEVELOPMENT BACK INTO DEVELOPMENTAL THEORY

I have never thought of myself as a developmental psychologist. In my view, developmental psychology puts too much emphasis upon the child as a prospective adult, as though *being a child* were not itself a pressing enough issue for children. Yet, as a long-standing outsider, I am also struck by how any serious sense of development has disappeared from developmental theory. Chomsky's version of preformationism has surely triumphed over Piaget's constructivism. Starting from a dualism of organism and environment, the sources of formation are deemed to be internal to the organism. According to this view, the role of the environment is not itself formative, but restricted merely to triggering or nurturing an essentially endogenous process of development. Preformationism is often confused with a commitment to linear stage theories. But linear stage theories do not have to be preformationist (see Costall, 2001, on Luquet), and despite appearances, theories of multidirectional development can prove to be so. In place of an entirely "closed" preprogrammed development, all the incorrigible preformationist has to do instead is opt for a model of development that is equally preprogrammed but now "open" to the input of environmental parameters that merely select between various preordained developmental trajectories.

Theory theory, given its neo-Piagetian origins, was meant, of course, to provide an alternative to nativist accounts of development. It was the child's own efforts to make sense of his or her experience, rather than a subpersonal realm of innate modules, that were supposed to be the driving force of development. Nevertheless, theory theory has come largely to share the same attitude as the nativists in relation to "domains of expertise." These are, in effect, regarded as timeless, Platonic essences, if not for the child, then for the wider grown-up community. The "domains" are, in short, preformed, even if theorizing itself is supposed to be an ongoing process.

However, the "domain" of a theory is not defined in advance. A crucial part of theorizing is sorting out, and eventually specifying, what the theory is supposed to be *about*, that is, its "domain of validity" (see Bohm, 1965). In the case of art criticism and, more specifically, art theory, the point is not to provide a "covering theory" of what happens to be the currently accepted canon of artworks. Rather, it is to challenge the existing canon and redefine the boundaries by, for example, rejecting some accepted artworks as kitsch, Victorian sentimentalism, fashionable ephemera, or, indeed, bourgeois, while arguing, on the other hand, that there are good reasons why other, previously unrecognized works really count as art, for example, photographs, video, or abstract expressionism.

Finally, I want to turn to Freeman's concluding point about the developmental significance for the child of becoming aware that there can be differences in taste and trying to understand how this can be. Here is how Freeman (this volume) puts the matter: "To investigate the child as intuitive art critic is to engage with one strand of the child's journey toward a grasp of subjectivity."

I think this is an extremely interesting proposal. But why not "work forward" from the child rather than "working backward" from adult, and historically contingent, categories such as the domain of "artworks"? A good starting point might be along the lines of the serious suggestion of the philosopher C. S. Peirce that we should take the scope of aesthetics as highly inclusive, extending to everything worthy of admiration (Lefebvre, 2007). Matters of "taste" extend well beyond the "domain" of art to friends, clothes, computer games, and, in short, anything that can really matter. And so the research questions then become for any individual child, what are the kinds of things that come to be worthy of admiration; how does that child sort those things out into his or her own categories; and what, for that child, are the most poignant things regarding disagreements in taste? Freeman refers to differences of taste *between* people, but perhaps one of the most painful aspects of growing up is disagreeing with our former selves and putting aside things that once mattered so much.

NOTES

1. Initially, of course, developmental psychology was envisaged as a method, a means of explaining where *adult* human beings come from, and not just ontogenetically but also phylogenetically. On the assumption that ontogeny recapitulates phylogeny, *and* that development ceases at adolescence, *and* also that, in effect, children are not primarily in the serious business of living in this world, developmental psychology could serve as a kind of lazy person's palaeontology (Costall, 1985). And, in its own way, this emphasis upon the outcome of development is also the project of Piaget's genetic epistemology, to elucidate how the adult mind is organized developmentally. Yet given that Piaget's purpose was to appeal to development to help sort out the epistemological condition of adult knowledge, he was remarkably complacent about the epistemological status of "grown-up" knowledge, "as if the thoughts of the adult were self-sufficient and disposed of all contradictions" (Merleau-Ponty, 1962, p. 355).

2. In some cases, at least, characterizing the child as a theorist can amount to little more than passing the theoretical buck. Take the "theory theory of mind." Even the most literal minded of the "theory theorists" admit that they themselves have no idea how scientific theorizing by adults actually works (e.g., Gopnik, 2003, p. 245). Yet they nevertheless invoke the *amateur* theorizing abilities of young children to solve the traditional

"problem of other minds," a problem that has stumped the most expert philosophical minds for a very long time (for an extensive criticism of theory of mind, see Leudar & Costall, 2009).

3. Equally paradoxically, the computer metaphor has served to obscure the place of technology in our lives.

REFERENCES

Bohm, D. (1965). *The special theory of relativity*. New York: Benjamin.

Bourdieu, P. (1986). *Distinction: A social critique of the judgement of taste* (R. Nice, Trans.). London: Routledge.

Bryan, W. L. (1896). Review of James Sully's *Studies of childhood*. *Psychological Review, 3*, 432–433.

Costall, A. (1985). Specious origins? Darwinism and developmental theory. In G. Butterworth, J. Rutkowska, & M. Scaife (Eds.), *Evolution and developmental psychology*. Brighton, UK: Harvester Press.

Costall, A. (2001). A closer look at Luquet. In G. H. Luquet, *Children's drawings* (pp. xii–xxv). [Translated and edited by Alan Costall.] London: Free Associations Press.

Fineberg, J. (1997). *The innocent eye: Children's art and the modern artist*. Princeton, NJ: Princeton University Press.

Fry, E. F. (1978). *Cubism*. New York: Oxford University Press.

Gallie, W. B. (1956). Art as an essentially contested concept. *Philosophical Quarterly, 6*, 97–114.

Gopnik, A. (2003). The theory theory as an alternative to the innateness hypothesis. In L. M. Antony & N. Hornstein (Eds.), *Chomsky and his critics* (pp. 238–254). Oxford: Blackwell.

Kuhn, T. S. (1970). *The structure of scientific revolutions* (2nd ed., enlarged). Chicago: University of Chicago Press.

Lefebvre, M. (2007). Peirce's esthetics: A taste for signs in art. *Transactions of the Charles Peirce Society: A Quarterly Journal in American Philosophy, 43*(2), 319–344.

Leudar, I., & Costall, A. (Eds.). (2009). *Against theory of mind*. London: Macmillan Palgrave.

Merleau-Ponty, M. (1962). *Phenomenology of perception* (C. Smith, Trans.). New York: Humanities Press.

Turner, F. M. (1974). *Between science and religion*. New Haven, CT: Yale University Press.

12

A NEW LENS ON THE DEVELOPMENT
OF SOCIAL COGNITION

The Study of Acting

Thalia Raquel Goldstein and Ellen Winner

It is an odd fact about *Homo sapiens* that we pretend to be another person without any intent to deceive, and for the enjoyment and edification of ourselves and others. This activity goes by the name of *acting, drama*, or *theatre*. Acting has been described as the ability to "live truthfully under false circumstances" (i.e., conveying something deeply true through conveying a fiction) for the enjoyment and knowledge of others (Noice & Noice, 2006). We could not act onstage without the ability to pretend and without the ability to imitate, both skills that develop in the second year of life (Piaget, 1962). Yet clearly pretense and imitation cannot be sufficient to allow us to act: Although researchers have observed pretense and imitation in nonhuman primates (Byrne & Whiten, 1988), no evidence of dramatic acting has ever been reported in nonhumans.

Most people today are somehow involved in the world of acting, typically as audience members. Yet psychologists have not studied acting, and we therefore know little about the psychological components of acting—the prerequisite skills required, the developmental course of acting talent, and the cognitive and affective effects of engaging in acting. This stands in contrast to how much psychologists have learned about the psychological components of engagement in the visual arts (e.g., Arnheim, 1974; Freeman, 1980; Gardner, 1980; Golomb, 2004; Hagen, 1980; Zeki,

1999; for a review, see Winner, 2006) and music (e.g., Bamberger, 1991; Deutsch, 1982; Sloboda, 1986; Trehub, 2003; for a review, see Winner, 2006). In this chapter, we review the scant amount of research on the psychology of acting, and we describe our own program of research, newly initiated and designed to probe the psychological components of acting. Our argument throughout is that acting is possible only because of humans' skills in social cognition; an understanding of how actors learn to act can provide a powerful lens through which to understand human social cognition—its normative development in childhood and its advanced development in adults trained in acting.

It will be useful first to begin with a brief history of Western acting and a discussion of the two major approaches to acting training in the United States and England today, the "Technique" and the "Method" schools.

HISTORY OF WESTERN THEATRE

Preformal theatre in the form of enacted rituals is probably as old as the earliest humans (Frazer, 1993). All cultures watch performances, whether rituals in which actors tell stories in the voice of impersonated characters, or performances of written dramatic texts (Benedetti, 2007). Religious rituals and the telling of myths, many of which take on the air of theatrical performance, are also a central part of most cultures (Malinowski, 1992). The main function of these early human performances was religious rather than for entertainment. The "actors" in these pieces bear little relation to actors we see in the theatre, in movies, and on television today.

Western theatre is said to have begun in ancient Greece in the sixth century B.C., when a chorus member, Thespis, separated himself from the chorus and began to act out the story as a character within the story rather than tell it as a narrator (Brown, 1995). The Greek plays are the oldest Western plays still in existence and continue to be performed today.

Until the plays produced in Elizabethan England, Greek plays were the most important and prolific form of Western theatre (Brown, 1995). However, ancient Greek acting was not realistic and would not be recognized today as great. Greek acting was formalized and ritualized and adhered closely to the rules of rhetoric. The plot and action were more important than the characters, who were assigned inflexible personalities that determined all their actions (Benedetti, 2007). Instead of a realistic portrayal of the inner psychology of a character, which is today regarded as essential to great acting (Stanislavski, 1950), Greek actors used body parts to symbolize psychological reality, such as showing a diseased foot to portray inner suffering (Easterling & Hall, 2002).

Until the Elizabethans in England at the beginning of the 17th century, acting remained closely related to the work of orators, with the art of theatre defined as a species of rhetoric (Roach, 1985), and tied closely to the church (Hayman, 1969). Because of the size of Elizabethan stages and audiences, as well as the lack of footlights, gestures and actions in Shakespeare's time had to be exaggerated (Hayman, 1969). However, the characterizations were based on real life for the first time, and the actors strove to "become" the characters they portrayed. Richard Burbridge, the most famous actor of Shakespeare's time, was said to be so immersed in his part that he would not come out of character in his dressing room in between scenes (Hayman, 1969).

Acting theory may have begun with the work of the 18th-century French philosopher Denis Diderot, who wrote *The Actor's Paradox* (1770/1957). Diderot believed that acting involved a three-stage process in which the actor first observes the "passions" (fear, rage, awe, joy, etc.), then reflects on emotional behavior and its expression, and finally experiments with the appropriate tone and gestures until hitting the right "mark" for a moment onstage. The greatest artist-actors, he argued, continue to experiment with these three steps throughout rehearsal and performance and arrive at true realism without any personal emotional involvement (Roach, 1985). For Diderot the ultimate goal for the actor is to produce real tears without feeling real emotion. Emotion and cognition were meant to split apart (Benedetti, 2007).

Like Diderot, the late-19th-century French actor Constant Coquelin asserted that an actor's job was to understand the psychology of the character from the outside. Coquelin agreed with Diderot that actors must stay in full control of their feelings and thereby avoid taking on the emotions of the character. The actor must not feel the character's emotions but rather must "pull the strings" that make his characters look as though they feel the requisite emotions (Cole & Chinoy, 1949).

Writing at the same time as Coquelin, the Scottish critic and author William Archer (1888/1957) opposed these views, arguing that actors must genuinely feel what they are acting if they are to be effective actors. We see this same disagreement between the 19th-century Russian acting theorist Konstantin Stanislavski and the 20th-century German playwright Bertold Brecht. Stanislavski (1950) taught that realism onstage could be attained only by recognizing and actually experiencing the emotions and memories of the characters. In contrast, Brecht believed that the actor must remain emotionally detached from the character. This detachment, he argued, would cause audience members to think about the relationship of the play to their own lives rather than merely to empathize. Only in this way would audience members react by *thinking* (deeply) about their own emotional lives and come away "purged" of emotion (Benedetti, 2007; Roach, 1985).

MODERN THEORIES OF ACTING: TECHNIQUE VERSUS METHOD

These two competing positions about what it takes to be a good actor—immersion in versus detachment from the character's emotions—can be found again in the two major contemporary western acting theories. "Technique" is sometimes referred to as formalized, external, "outside-in" acting training (Mamet, 1997; Olivier, 1986). The most influential modern American proponents of Technique-based acting are the playwright and acting theorist David Mamet and his students (Bruder et al., 1986). This approach grows out of the concepts of character and actor emotional separation put forth by Diderot (1770/1957), physical acting put forth by Coquelin (Benedetti, 2007), and emotional detachment put forth by Brecht (Benedetti; Wooster, 2004). This view dates back to ancient Greek theatre, with its basis on physicality and rhetoric (Easterling & Hall, 2002), and is mainly used in England today.

"Method" acting, in contrast, is referred to as presentational, internal, "inside-out" training (Chekhov, 1991; Hagen & Frankel, 1973; Hull, 1985; Meisner & Longwell, 1987; Stanislavski, 1950). Method acting originated with Konstantin Stanislavski at the Moscow Art Theatre in Russia. In direct contrast to the Technique approach, Method actors learn to feel the emotions of their characters (Bruder et al., 1986). This view dates back to Aristotle (trans. 1999) and continued with Archer (1888/1957), who believed that to be effective, actors must express real emotions onstage.

Some have insisted that the distinction between these two approaches is a false one (Hayman, 1969), and others argue that there is no sharp distinction (Burgoyne, Pouylin, & Rearden, 1999). Although there is some overlap today between these two approaches, a distinction remains. Method acting was established in the United States through the Actor's Studio in the 1940s and 1950s (Hull, 1985; Stanislavski, 1950) and is the predominant approach in the United States today (Verducci, 2000). Most actors in the United States over the past half century, including Marlon Brando, Robert DeNiro, and Katherine Hepburn, have been trained in a variation of the original Stanislavski "System," the basis for Method acting (Hull, 1985). In contrast, most British acting training is really closer to the Technique approach, with an emphasis on physicality and the outer portrayal of a character (Olivier, 1986).

There are three related areas in which the Technique and Method approaches diverge, and each of these areas has a strong psychological component: (a) the relation of the actor to the character's mental world, (b) the importance of actually feeling the character's emotions, and (c) the importance of exerting control over one's own emotions. Because of the very different emphases these two approaches take on these three issues and the relationship between these issues and social cognition, actors trained in the Technique approach may develop quite different social-cognitive skills than those trained in the Method approach, and all actors, regardless of training, may develop different social-cognitive skills than nonactors.

Relationship of the Actor to the Character's Mental World

When Oscar-winning actor Peter O'Toole was asked by interviewer Charlie Rose to analyze the basis of the gift of acting, he hesitated, protesting that he did not know. But, pressed by Rose, O'Toole finally said that the gift of acting, which he acknowledged to be rare, was allied "to the human gift of mimicry" (Rose, 2008, March 24). That Peter O'Toole, a British actor trained in the Technique approach, stressed the importance of mimicry is not surprising, given that Technique actors are taught to learn their characters from the outside in.

According to the Technique-based approach, the first step for an actor learning a role is to feel and understand the external physicality of the character being enacted—how the character looks, moves, speaks, dresses, styles his hair, and so on (Bruder et al., 1986; Burgoyne et al., 1999; Hayman, 1969). The most important job for an actor who uses Technique is to develop a clear voice and a workable body in order to overcome his or her own physicality and replace it with the physicality of the character (Bruder et al.). Lawrence Olivier (1986), perhaps the world's most celebrated Technique actor, had a deep interest in the voices, mannerisms, and other physical characteristics of people he met, and he copied these and stored them in his memory so he could use them in later portrayals. According to the Technique approach, a complete understanding of the external physicality of the character will allow the actor to convey the character's inner psychological reality.

Although proponents of Technique acting theory believe that acting is above all "the art and craft of presenting a personality to an audience," most of the actor's grasp of the character's personality must come directly from the script rather than via independent analysis of the character done by the actor (Olivier, 1986, p. 357). It is not the job of the Technique actor to predict what Hamlet would do in every different kind of situation. Instead, the actor must simply focus on the lines for the particular scene. A deep psychological analysis of the character is not necessary (Bruder et al., 1986). The Technique approach trains the actor to discover how characters are motivated to act in the specific and immediate situations in the play rather than to come up with a theory of the characters' enduring, stable personalities. Thus, the Technique actor must grasp what psychologists refer to as *situational* rather than *dispositional* traits (Ross, 1977).

In sharp contrast, Method actors are taught to grasp the inner state of the character first; becoming like the character physically will then follow. An understanding of the full physicality of a character is not necessary in Method acting. Rather, the actor is taught to select only a few key physical characteristics and to use these as a basis on which to layer the character's emotions, motivations, and personality (Meisner & Longwell, 1987). Understanding the character's body is a way to understand the character, but this kind of understanding is not considered primary and is useful only to prevent the actor's own physical characteristics from getting in the way of capturing the character, which would create a "violation of physical truth" onstage (Hagen & Frankel, 1973, p. 52).

The "father" of Method acting, Konstantin Stanislavski (1950), argued that good acting means understanding and creating the entire inner life of a character, which means having a well-developed ability to understand and build up the mental states of another. The actor must grasp the character's enduring dispositions, life purpose, and overall objectives and then use this understanding of what motivates the character throughout the play and in each moment (Noice & Noice, 2006).

The strongest proponent of this kind of cognitive understanding and subsequent perspective taking is the Method acting teacher and theorist Michael Chekhov (1991), who believes in using the imagination to find the subtext behind every line of the character—what the character wants and intends and how his mental state differs from that of the actor's mental state. In Chekhov's Method approach, actors must combine their knowledge of the character's behavior over the course of the play with their knowledge of the character's underlying feelings and mental states to create a "Psychological Gesture," which forms the basis of the character's personality. Only by understanding the intricacies of the character's underlying psychology can the actor avoid clichés, which are never believed by the audience. Method actors try to develop a deep understanding of the mind of their characters and in each of the situations in which their characters find themselves, through active imaginary participation in the life behind the words of the script. In

Method acting, actors must work to close the gap between their personal cognitions and emotions and those of their character (they strive to become more and more like their character while onstage), through constant analysis of their character's cognitions, always asking themselves (as the character), "Who am I?" (Hagen & Frankel, 1973).

The Method actor is also taught to go beyond the boundaries of the script and develop an understanding of the stable and enduring dispositions of their character—their typical likes and dislikes and their "back story," or what happened before the play began. The constant use of the questions "What does the character want?" (Hagen & Frankel, p. 142) and "What would motivate me to behave as the character is behaving?" (Hagen & Frankel, p. 161), and knowing the character's attitude toward the world (Hull, 1985), probably lead a Method actor to a deeper conscious understanding of the mental and emotional state of the character compared to the understanding developed by a Technique actor.

Method actors are also taught to evaluate other characters through the minds of the character they are playing rather than from the perspective of the outsider or audience member. They are taught to imagine the entire history of their relationship with others onstage rather than just the interactions in a particular moment. Acting is seen as a direct response to the other persons onstage, so that the actor can have the appropriate impulsive response as the character, based on the character's (unscripted) history with the other characters onstage (Meisner & Longwell, 1987). Actors must make themselves well-defined mentally but also must make the other characters onstage specific and complex (Hagen & Frankel, 1973). Actors must define the mental and emotional aspects of their character's relationship with the other characters, using their imagination as well as their understanding of their own relationships in real life, combining the two to create new relationships with each different character in each play.

The Method approach thus emphasizes the development of what in psychological terms has come to be called *theory of mind*. We will return to a discussion of theory of mind from the perspective of psychology later on.

The Actor's Feeling of the Character's Emotions

The Technique and Method approaches differ in the importance placed on actors feeling the emotions of their characters. In the Technique approach, actually feeling the emotions of a character while rehearsing and playing that character must be avoided. Creating and feeling the emotions of the character is not the job of the actor, and doing so is seen as an unpredictable way to create realism onstage (Bruder et al., 1986).

It is only the illusion of feeling that is important (Mamet, 1997), and there is no need to "whip yourself into a generalized emotional frenzy" (Bruder et al., p. 72). For Technique actors, feeling the same emotions as the character only serves as a distraction or gives the impression of falsity onstage (Mamet; Olivier, 1986).

In contrast, Method actors are taught that feeling the emotions of the character is critical to playing that character fully. Not only must they understand the character's mental life, but also they must feel the character's feelings. Mere understanding of the character's cognitions without matching those emotions is believed to create detachment, and the characterization will not feel alive (Hayman, 1969); to live and exist in a character, to feel his or her emotions, is how real characterizations are built (Stanislavski, 1950). Method acting involves the fusion of an actor's action with the experience of the heightened emotions of the character (Murray, 1996).

In order to feel the character's emotions, Method actors begin studying the script by going through and finding the specific emotions and reactions that occur in each moment, or "beat." They must be able to understand those emotions and reactions and be able to see them through the perspective of the character. Subsequently, actors create the emotional cues that will allow them to generate and experience the same emotions as their character (Chekhov, 1991). However, the actor cannot just pick an emotion and then use it in the play at large, but must focus on the emotions that apply to each moment, determining how they occur and how to use those emotions to understand what is happening to the character (Chekhov).

In preparation for a character, Method actors can spend rehearsal time finding small objects onstage that remind them of a previous emotion that relates to the emotion of their character and can trigger that emotion whenever they think about it. This ensures that the actor is in the same affective state as the character (Hagen & Frankel, 1973). Working on the emotion ahead of time so that in the moment of the play it is fresh and ready to go is the cornerstone of skilled Method acting (Hull, 1985). A sensitivity to emotion and a developed concentration on affective matters are extremely important.

The Method acting theorist who was the strongest promoter of feeling the same emotions as a character is Stanislavski's closest disciple, Lee Strasberg (Hull, 1985). Strasberg claimed that focusing entirely on a momentary objective (as recommended by the Technique approach) would cut off affective perspective taking and prevent the actor from understanding and playing the emotion of a role (Hull). Therefore, the emotional must take precedence over the cognitive. Lawrence Olivier, who relied solely on language and cognition to create a realistic portrayal, was criticized by Method theorists as an actor who cannot "bring down the house" or cause the audience to feel overwhelming emotion because of his lack of "real" emotion onstage (Meisner & Longwell, 1987). Method theorists claim that by recalling an emotional memory and then connecting it to the experience of the character, the actor is able to recreate this feeling personally onstage, thereby moving the audience as well.

The Method approach thus emphasizes the development of empathy. We will return to a discussion of empathy from the perspective of psychology later on.

Exerting Control Over One's Own Emotions

The Technique and Method approaches make very different demands on the actors in terms of how they must learn to generate, shape, and control their own emotions. Although Technique actors must learn to ignore their own emotions, Method actors must learn to create emotions in themselves. The only way in which Technique actors try to exert control over their emotions is in not allowing their emotions to get in the way (Bruder et al., 1986). Technique actors must learn how to communicate but not re-create emotions effectively, regardless of whether they feel or have ever felt those emotions (Mamet, 1997).

Technique theorists claim that creating and controlling real emotions onstage are impossible and even irresponsible (Mamet, 1997), and Technique actors are therefore trained to focus on the outward expressions of the character, ignoring any personal emotion that may arise onstage. Technique theorists believe that an emotion that arises while onstage can be used within the course of the scene but should not be prepared for or relied on. Emotions should be seen as temporary states that are not necessarily adjusted to. Rather, they are accepted and allowed to run their course.

Instead of trying to alter their own emotions, Technique actors are trained to focus on how to increase their emotional impact on the audience. They are encouraged to ignore any personal emotion that comes up onstage and to suppress its expression. Because there is no such thing as the one correct emotion for any one scene, and emotions are not seen as fully within the control of the actor, having an outward-directed focus and continually monitoring how the audience is reacting should keep the actor from becoming weighed down with feeling emotions.

Because Method theorists believe in feeling the emotions of the character, Method actors must learn how to create, craft, and control whatever emotion they need at a particular moment. The emotion is achieved through the use of affective memory (Hagen & Frankel, 1973). The trick is to relive an emotion the actor has felt at another time. The job of the other senses is to prepare the actor to use his or her emotion memory (Stanislavski, 1948). Emotions excited by the imagination are believed to result in realistic emotion onstage (Roach, 1985), although there is debate on this point. True emotion onstage, equivalent to what we actually experience offstage, is extremely difficult to achieve and is considered the most "elusive" aspect of acting (Meisner & Longwell, 1987). However, either imagination or the atmosphere of the play can and should be allowed to create emotion within the actor, and the actor must use that emotion to serve the portrayal (Chekhov, 1991). According to Method theorists, great acting has roots in true emotion, and no matter how talented, actors cannot convincingly portray an emotion they do not really feel (Meisner & Longwell). Consequently, great acting requires stimulating emotions by whatever means necessary and using the result onstage.

There is an enduring question within Method theory about the extent to which the character's emotions and the actor's emotions can coexist within the actor during a performance. External indication of emotion may cause the internal aspects of emotion to arise, which then makes it impossible for the actor's emotion to differ from that of the character (Metcalf, 1931). However, even when playing the most emotional of characters, the actor still must keep a level of control onstage in order to keep from devolving into "hysteria" (Hagen & Frankel, 1973). Diderot (1770/1957) wrote extensively about the dual consciousness that an actor must inhabit: that of himself, and that of his character. However, Hull (1985) pointed out that an actor who is looking at his character while playing his character at the same time cannot be effective. Actors must learn to use their emotions so that they can feel and express a character's emotional state without forgetting their lines or position onstage. Actors should be more knowledgeable and more accepting of their emotions, a skill analogous to adaptive forms of "emotion regulation" as discussed below.

Both schools of acting emphasize, but in different ways, the development of what in psychological terms has come to be called *emotion regulation*. We will return to a discussion of emotion regulation from the perspective of psychology below.

ACTING AS A LENS ON SOCIAL COGNITION: THEORY AND EVIDENCE

The domain of acting can provide a fertile means by which to study advanced levels of theory of mind, empathy, and emotion regulation, as well as other forms of cognition that have a particularly important role in acting. By studying the kinds of social-cognitive and emotional skills that acting fosters, we can learn about expertise in these skills as well as about how these skills can be trained. Despite this rich psychological territory of acting, few psychologists have tried to study the psychological components and consequences of acting. The research that has been conducted on the psychology of acting has focused primarily on the effect of acting on verbal memory and literacy skills (see Noice & Noice, 2006; Podzlony, 2000, for reviews).

We examine here what psychologists have discovered, and what they might still discover, about the social-cognitive components of acting: (a) the ability to understand the subtle mental qualities of the character (intentions, desires, motivations, emotions, and beliefs, which we refer to as the having of a *theory of mind*), a skill emphasized differently by Method and Technique acting; (b) the ability to feel the character's emotions and have a concurrent emotional reaction, which we refer to as *empathy*, a skill emphasized most by Method acting; and (c) the ability to control one's personal emotions so as to be able to take on whatever emotion is required, which we refer to as *emotion regulation*, a skill also emphasized differently by Method and Technique acting. Our goal is to demonstrate how the study of actors can shed light on our understanding of the development of expertise in these three components of social cognition: theory of mind, empathy, and emotion regulation.

Psychological Research on Theory of Mind and Acting

Actors must be able to grasp subtle aspects of their character's intentions, desires, motivations, beliefs, and emotions in order to create a realistic portrayal of a complex human on the stage or screen. This "cold" understanding of the character's mental states is what allows the actor to adopt the perspective of the character and see the world through the character's eyes. We use the term *cold* because one can understand another's mental states, including feeling states, without oneself experiencing the other's emotions. In the psychological literature, this is referred to having a "theory of mind" (see Wellman, Cross, & Watson, 2001), "mentalising" (Morton, Frith, & Leslie, 1991), "mind reading" (Whiten, 1991), or "social intelligence" (Baron-Cohen, Jolliffe, Mortimore, & Robertson, 1997), all of which we will refer to below by the umbrella term *theory of mind*.

Because Method actors spend far more time in long-term and background psychological analysis of their characters than do Technique actors, we would expect them to become more psychologically astute, better able to analyze the stable personality and inner worlds of others. However, we would also expect Technique actors and Method actors to have an advantage over those without acting training in the analysis and understanding of others' mental and emotional states.

We hypothesize that actors (both Technique and Method) are drawn to acting because of a heightened ability to infer others' mental states, and that this initial gift is further strengthened into expertise by the continual experience of becoming others. However, Technique actors are likely to focus more on the understanding of others' *situational* mental states, whereas Method actors are likely to focus more on the understanding of others' *dispositional* mental states. Training in either theory should increase the ability to understand and read others' mental states.

The study of actors can thus become a way for psychologists to understand expertise in theory of mind. We know a great deal about the normative development of theory of mind. The most investigated major milestone in theory of mind is the recognition that a belief is just a representation of external reality, and as such it can be a false representation. The acquisition of a representational understanding of mind is demonstrated by the child's understanding of false belief, which emerges somewhere between the ages of 3 and 4 (Gopnik & Astington, 1988; Wimmer & Perner, 1983). This kind of understanding is considered to be a social-cognitive aspect of theory of mind because it is based on the ability to infer what someone knows and does not know on the basis of what that person has seen or not seen (Tager-Flusberg & Sullivan, 2000).

Understanding false belief entails the realization that someone not only lacks access to the truth but also has a false belief about the truth. A later, more sophisticated social-cognitive understanding of subjectivity, referred to as *interpretive theory of mind*, emerges by the age of 7 or 8, when children realize that two people can have different interpretations of the same reality (Carpendale & Chandler, 1996).

In contrast to social-cognitive theory of mind, social-perceptual theory of mind involves understanding what another person thinks and feels by attending to that person's facial or bodily expression (Tager-Flusberg & Sullivan, 2000). This kind of ability has been assessed most commonly in adults by the Reading the Mind in the Eyes Test (Baron-Cohen, Wheelwright, Hill, Raste, & Plumb, 2001), in which one is shown pictures of individuals' eyes taken from movies, television, and magazines and presented with four possible mental or emotional state labels. This measure shows age-related changes through adolescence, and adults do not reach ceiling on this test. Individuals with Asperger's syndrome and autism perform poorly on this test.

Although normative and pathological theory of mind development has been heavily studied, very little research has investigated the possibility of the development of advanced levels of theory of mind past the age of 8. Children reach ceiling levels on false belief and interpretive theory of mind tasks by 4 and 8, respectively, and psychologists seem to have assumed that development of theory of mind stops by age 8. Although it is possible that the kinds of basic theory of mind skills reviewed above may reach ceiling in middle childhood, little thought has been given to the possibility that more subtle forms of theory of mind ability may continue to develop through adolescence, and to the possibility that there may be individual differences in the levels of theory of mind ability reached in adulthood, with some individuals becoming true experts at theory of mind. If one thinks about the kinds of skills required by a psychotherapist, for example, or by a literary critic who analyzes the phenomenology of fictional characters, it is not difficult to conceive of what it might mean to be an expert at making judgments about the inner worlds of others.

There is reason to believe that theory of mind skills continue to develop, at least into adolescence. To begin with, the prefrontal cortex areas underlying social cognition continue to develop in adolescence (Blakemore & Choudhury, 2006). This neural development, combined with hormonal changes and new social interaction changes, makes it plausible to hypothesize that perspective taking and theory of mind are not fully developed by middle childhood. We have been able to locate a few studies showing that theory of mind is a graded ability even in adults, and we review each of these below.

Adults with more close friends show higher levels of theory of mind than those with fewer friends, as measured by the "Imposing Memory Task" in which many mental states must be held in mind at once, referred to as *multiple theory of mind* (Stiller & Dunbar, 2007). Participants heard stories of the following kind:

> Sam wanted to find a Post Office so he could buy a Tax Disc for his car. He asked Henry if he could tell him where to get one. Henry told him that he thought there was a Post Office in Elm Street. When Sam got to Elm Street, he found it was closed. A notice on the door said that it had moved to the new premises in Bold Street. So Sam went to Bold Street and found the new Post Office. When he got to the counter, he discovered that he had left his MOT cer-

tificate at home. He realized that, without an MOT certificate, he could not get a Tax Disc, so he went home empty-handed.

They were then asked to make a judgment between two options such as the following:

1. a. Henry thought Sam would find the Post Office in Elm Street.
   b. Henry thought Sam would find the Post Office in Bold Street.
2. a. Sam thought that Henry knew the Post Office was in Bold Street.
   b. Sam thought that Henry knew the Post Office was in Elm Street.
3. a. Sam thought that Henry believed that Sam wanted to buy a Tax Disc.
   b. Sam thought that Henry did not know that Sam wanted to buy a Tax Disc.

This theory of mind task is one that seems to us to be confounded with working memory: To solve the most complex tasks requires holding in mind nine mental states at a time. Hence it is not clear whether this study tells us about advanced theory of mind or about high-level working memory skills.

Dysphoric adolescents show higher levels of theory of mind than do those without dysphoria and are better able to identify both positively valenced and negatively valenced mental states of others (Harkness, Sabbagh, Jacobson, Chowdrey, & Chen, 2005). High levels of perceptual theory of mind in depression may be due to the kind of ruminative introspection that so often accompanies depression (Nolen-Hoeksema, Morrow, & Fredrickson, 1993).

Adults readers of fiction also score higher than those who prefer non-fiction on the Reading the Mind in the Eyes Task (Mar, Oatley, Hirsch, de la Paz, & Peterson, 2006). This may be due to the kind of interaction with, and comprehension of, characters that occurs when one reads fiction deeply. However, although fiction reading was related to the Reading the Mind in the Eyes Test in this study, it was not related to another social-perceptual theory of mind task called the Interpersonal Perception Task (Costanzo & Archer, 1983). On this Interpersonal Perception Task, participants watch a video and then, using prosodic cues, try to determine the relationships among the characters. Mar et al. (2006) explained this contradiction in terms of the heterogeneity of the concept of empathy, in both its cognitive (theory of mind) and emotional forms.

Choudhury, Blakemore, and Charman (2006) found age-related changes between ages 11 and 14 in an emotional perspective–taking study. Participants were told about a hypothetical situation that would cause an emotional reaction from either the first perspective or the third perspective (i.e., *You/A girl are/is not allowed to go to your/her best friend's party. How do you/she feel(s)?*). Participants were then asked to make a judgment between five faces expressing an emotion. All participants responded more quickly when making first-person judgments as compared to third-person judgments. But, with age, reaction times between first- and third-person judgments decreased. The fact that adolescents' time delay between first- and third-person reasoning decreased meant they were getting better at taking the perspective of another and thus becoming more advanced.

Given the above-described studies that have demonstrated individual differences in theory of mind ability in adolescents and adults, we have begun a program of research to examine the possibility that actors, and particularly those trained in the Method approach, should have advanced levels of theory of mind. Given the similarities between the comprehension of characters by readers and the comprehension of characters by actors, we would expect actors to show levels of theory of mind skill as high as those of fiction readers. Support for the hypothesis that acting can lead to advanced levels of theory of mind comes from two studies showing that role-playing activities increase perspective taking, a skill that follows from an understanding of others' mental states.

Chandler (1973) tested the effect of role playing on perspective taking and social skills in emotionally disturbed, delinquent adolescent boys. Boys in this study were either given experience in role playing different characters in a videotaped skit or taught referential communication skills (the control group). All of the boys began with low social competence and low levels of perspective taking. After 10 weeks, those in the role-playing but not referential communication group improved significantly in cognitive perspective taking. In addition, level of delinquent behavior declined in the group trained in role playing. This study demonstrated that training in acting (or role playing) improves perspective taking in boys with low social competence.

In a second study, Chandler, Greenspan, and Barenboim (1974) gave another group of delinquent boys a similar role-playing task in which they created their own videotaped skits and acted out various characters, thereby adopting different perspectives in the same situation.

These boys were compared to a group that created videos but did not act in them. These antisocial children were not good at stepping outside of their own vantage point and taking others' perspectives. However, after 12 months, those who had acted out roles in their videos had higher perspective-taking scores and lower rates of delinquency than those who had made but not acted in videos.

In our initial study of acting training and theory of mind, we administered Baron-Cohen et al.'s (2001) Reading the Mind in the Eyes Test to two groups of adolescents aged 14 to 17. One group was involved in acting training intensively at an independent arts high school or through extracurricular theatre at their public high school. The acting group was compared to a group of adolescents not involved in theatre but involved in other artistic or other after-school activities. Students also completed a control test of visual memory not predicted to be associated with acting experience. Because these students were being trained in the United States, we can assume that their training had a strong Method component.

As hypothesized, adolescents involved in theatre show advantages on the Reading the Mind in the Eyes Test but not on visual memory (Goldstein & Winner, in press). This skill may have been developed by the training these students received: Acting students in the United States are taught to think deeply about characters' mental states, and they are taught to think about how to convey cognitive and emotional states through their facial expressions. Experience understanding and then showing emotion may then lead to the ability to recognize emotion.

Research on acting and theory of mind requires better measures of theory of mind, ones that can really measure what it might mean to be an expert at adult levels of theory of mind. We need measures that can capture the kinds of skills in understanding other people possessed by gifted therapists and fiction writers. We need measures that capture the ability to "read" opaque behavior in terms of the cognitive and affective states hidden beneath the surface, but leaking out in subtle cues.

Thus far, studies showing individual differences in theory of mind in adolescents and adults have all been correlational, including our own. We are now embarking on a quasi-experimental longitudinal study of children and adolescents involved in acting in order to determine (a) whether they come to an interest in acting with an advanced level of theory of mind compared to their peers and/or (b) whether acting training leads to advanced levels of theory of mind. Through this study we will explore questions of causality, as well as test new measures of advanced theory of mind.

Psychological Research on Empathy and Acting

Psychologists have sometimes confused empathy with theory of mind, calling the understanding of what another is feeling an indication of empathy (Baron-Cohen & Wheelwright, 2004; Davis, 1983; Nettle, 2006). But empathy and theory of mind must be distinguished. *Theory of mind* refers to the cognitive understanding of what another is thinking or feeling; *empathy* refers to the tendency to match one's emotions to the emotions perceived in another. Although theory of mind involves "cold" cognitive understanding of another's beliefs and feelings, empathy requires feeling the other's feelings. Empathy involves actually feeling what someone else is feeling or being emotionally moved by an understanding of what someone else feels (Verducci, 2000). Empathy must also be distinguished from compassion, which involves feeling the other person's emotion *and* taking action to ease another's emotional suffering (Levy, 1997).

Once children are able to differentiate between their own and others' emotions (a form of cognitive perspective taking), they can also begin to empathize with others (Hoffman, 1981). Higher levels of empathy have been associated with higher levels of perspective-taking skills (Eisenberg, Fabes, & Spinard, 2006), and empathy cannot exist without cognitive perspective taking and understanding of emotions (Batson et al., 2003).

Skills in theory of mind and in empathy are not necessarily correlated; however, these skills certainly do not cohere in bullies (Bosacki & Astington, 1999). Bullies are strong in understanding what others are thinking and feeling but weak in empathy: They can understand what the victim may be feeling, but they do not feel the victim's suffering.

Research on empathy and empathic responses in adolescence is mixed. Measured through facial and gestural indices, empathic response actually decreases with age (Eisenberg et al., 2006). However, as measured through self-report (which raises the methodological issue of social desirability), empathy increases with age throughout adolescence (Lennon & Eisenberg, 1987).

Levy (1997, p. 70) suggested that theatre is a "school for feeling" and that involvement in theatre can help children learn about moral values. As children are involved in theatre, they will learn to experience their own emotions more deeply and fully. Educated emotions, Levy argued, respond more morally than uneducated emotions, leading to increases in empathy.

Although many researchers have suggested that acting training should lead to increases in empathy, and although this seems intuitively plausible, there has been little empirical investigation into this question. Metcalf (1931) discussed empathy and acting in a theoretical paper, proposing that empathy plays a more prominent role in theatre than in any other art form. Actors, according to Metcalf, adopt the emotion and personality of anyone around them, portray that person's emotion just as it would appear in real life, and therefore must have a great deal of empathy for all those around them. Verducci (2000) also hypothesized that the experience of acting fosters empathy. Actors must figure out their character's personality by paying special attention to the intricacies of the character's behavior (because the words of the script may not fully reveal the character's inner world), and this heightened attention to details of behavior as a window onto a person's inner world was argued to lead to heightened empathy. But according to the definition of empathy proposed here (the ability to feel another's emotions, not just understand them), what Verducci is really talking about is theory of mind.

Prior to our own newly developing program of research, there have been to our knowledge only two studies on the relation between acting and empathy. One unpublished dissertation examined whether being involved in acting increased empathy levels (Collum, 1976). Although not peer reviewed or published, and indeed with some considerable problems, as mentioned below, this is one of the only attempts at an empirical study of the otherwise theoretically accepted idea that actors are more empathic than nonactors. Collum assessed empathy as measured by the Hogan Empathy Scale (Hogan, 1969), a self-report measure that defines empathy (erroneously, in our view) as an intellectual understanding of another's mind without the experience of that person's feelings (Hogan). This scale includes items measuring far more than empathy: social confidence (e.g., "I usually take an active part in the entertainment at parties"), emotion regulation (e.g., "I am usually calm and not easily upset"), emotional sensitivity (e.g., "I have tried my hand at poetry"), and nonconformity (e.g., "It is the duty of a citizen to support his country, right or wrong"), as well as what would normally be considered empathy (e.g., "I easily become impatient with people"). Eighty-three professional actors, MFA students in acting at the University of Florida, and undergraduate theatre majors were compared to a group of 24 nontheatre majors at the university.

Actors scored significantly higher on this measure than did nonactors. However, empathy scores declined with age in professional actors, with those professional actors who had worked the most as actors in the previous year showing the lowest overall levels of empathy within the actor population. Actors who made 100% of their previous year's income from acting actually had negative correlations with their empathy scores. Collum (1976) hypothesized that actors are drawn to acting because of underlying higher levels of empathy. However, as an actor becomes more involved in the business of professional acting, the harsh difficulties of living one's life in the theatre lead to a decline in empathy. Collum's study did not distinguish between Technique and Method actors, and his findings should be viewed with reservation due to the measure of empathy used.

More recently, using Baron-Cohen and Wheelwright's (2004) Empathizing Quotient (EQ), Nettle (2006) found that professional actors scored higher than a control group. The control group was from an earlier study conducted in the Baron-Cohen lab, recruited to help validate and normalize the EQ for later testing. The EQ measures affective empathy, defined as a parallel or reactive emotional response to the emotions of others (i.e., "I tend to get emotionally involved with a friend's problems"). Actors were recruited and tested via the Internet. Nettle also hypothesized that acting attracts people with high empathy to begin with rather than fostering growth in empathy as a function of acting experience. However, whether acting attracts empathetic individuals to the profession, fosters empathy, or both could be determined only by an experimental study, and no such study has yet been conducted.

We have investigated the relationship between acting and empathy in one study. Goldstein and Winner (in press) not only administered the Reading the Eyes in the Mind Test to adolescents involved in theatre versus a control group but also administered a self-report empathy scale. The measure used was Bryant's (1982) Index of Empathy for Adolescents, a common self-report measure of empathy. This measure asks people to judge themselves on a 7-point Likert-type scale in response to statements such as "I can eat all of my cookies even when I see someone looking at me, wanting one."

We found that the adolescent actors score no higher on this empathy scale than did the adolescent nonactors. We believe this result is explainable as follows. Although actors show and perceive a wide variety of emotions onstage, they may well do so without actually feeling these emotions. In other words, they may be using a Technique approach, despite being taught the Method approach. However, another more likely possibility is that actors defend themselves against feeling empathy for their characters in order to avoid emotional exhaustion. Of course, as in previous studies, we relied only on a self-report measure of empathy, which is of course subject to the problems of social desirability as well as self-understanding. Perhaps another kind of empathy measure might demonstrate higher empathy skills in actors. We are now developing a new measure of empathy that does not rely on self-report. We will use this measure in our above-mentioned intervention study to determine whether individuals are drawn to acting because of high levels of empathic ability and whether acting training trains empathy. Ultimately we hope to include both Method and Technique students to determine whether Method actors, who spend far more time trying to feel the emotions of their characters than do Technique actors, become better able to feel the emotions of their characters and hence perhaps better able to feel the emotions of others offstage.

Psychological Research on Emotion Regulation and Acting

Actors must have knowledge of and control over their emotions in order to portray a character's emotions onstage. Psychologists refer to this skill as *emotion regulation* (Gross, 1998) and define it as the ability to become conscious of one's emotions, and the ability to create, control, and use emotions independent of how or when the emotions were activated (Cole, Martin, & Dennis, 2004). Emotion regulation takes different forms at different points during the duration of a single emotion (Gross, 1998). When emotions are not appropriate we must regulate and change our emotions. To change our emotions, we can engage in reappraisal—which means changing the way we view a situation in order to change the emotional impact of the situation (Gross, 2002). Or we can engage in expressive suppression, which means preventing the outward expression of an emotion. Although emotion regulation is typically used to decrease negative emotions and increase positive ones, instrumental emotion regulation can be used to increase or decrease both positive and negative emotions (Gross, 1999).

Because actors must not show their own emotions onstage and must either replace or blend their emotions with those of their character, they have to be using emotion regulation strategies. Although Method actors spend far more time attempting to create emotions in themselves than do Technique actors, both Method and Technique actors must know and understand emotions in a way that nonactors do not have to. However, the strategies used would seem to differ depending on whether one is trained in Technique or Method.

Technique actors must use emotion regulation to mask their personal emotions. Because technique actors do not need to create emotion onstage, personal emotions may arise that are not helpful or congruous with the emotion of the character. Technique actors must be able to let the emotion "pass through them" (Mamet, 1997), to suppress any expression of the emotion, and to regulate themselves so that they can continue acting their character.

Method actors are trained to feel the emotions of the character so that they lose their own emotions and feel only those of the character. That is, the emotions of the character must be indistinguishable from the emotions of the actor. Many Method actors engage in memory exercises in which they recall and reexperience a previously felt emotion in order to bring up the appropriate emotion for a scene (Hagen & Frankel, 1973). This strategy is no different than the kind of emotion regulation technique psychologists refer to as *attention deployment*, in which one chooses something on which to focus in order to control one's emotions (Gross, 1998).

Although there have been no studies of emotion regulation in actors, there have been several studies that use actors as an "expert" population, assuming that any emotion they create on cue is equivalent to emotions that arise spontaneously. These researchers have asked actors to "create" specific emotions in order to study the facial (Ekman, Levenson, & Friesen, 1983), physiological (Futterman, Kemeny, Shapiro, & Fahey, 1994), and neurological (Pelletier et al., 2003) components of emotional processes.

We were able to locate one study examining the emotional development of adolescents involved in a theatrical show (Larson & Brown, 2007). Larson and Brown used grounded theory analysis to show that the adolescents' experiences with emotions in the context of acting helped them learn about regulating and understanding emotions in general. However, there was no control group comparison or measurement of emotion regulation using validated quantitative measures, and the learning about emotions that occurred was attributed to the group leader's openness about emotions. The researchers did not examine how the process of creating a performance and acting in this performance might have brought about emotional development.

We are now beginning a program of research examining how actors emotionally regulate, and whether their ability to emotionally regulate is more advanced than that of the general population, either because acting provides a place for them to practice their advanced emotion regulation or because acting trains advanced emotion regulation (Goldstein & Tamir, n.d.). Thus far, we have found that when Method-trained actors are onstage, instead of minimizing or suppressing emotions that get in the way of their performance, they report that they focus on and actively express, or vent, these emotions. In contrast, when nonactors find themselves in a performance situation (i.e., giving a class presentation), they report that they try to suppress and deny emotions that get in their way. Thus, our study demonstrates that actors do not control inconvenient emotions via suppression or denial but instead accept and focus on these emotions and thereby achieve control over them. A close study of how actors succeed in regulating their emotions could help us understand the processes involved in emotion regulation.

CONCLUDING THOUGHTS

[T]hrough understanding the acts of others we come to know their souls.

—Meltzoff (2002, p. 24)

[T]he purpose of playing, … is, to hold, as 'twere, the mirror up to nature.

—Shakespeare, *Hamlet* (3.2)

The number and variety of subject areas in psychology into which the study of acting can provide insight are astonishing. Although there is very little literature on the psychology of acting, connections can be drawn to many areas of psychological research. Psychologists can learn a great deal from the major drama theorists: Theatre theory is inherently psychological, and psychologists can learn much from both Technique and Method theorists' understandings about how actors can be trained to develop a more acute theory of mind, about why acting may not be a training ground for empathy, and about how actors succeed so well in regulating their emotions.

The actor must convincingly become another person and at least seem to be feeling emotions that will not be present once the actor drops character. Clearly this is a daunting task, which is why so few people become successful actors and why even fewer are considered great actors. Great acting is a very rare gift, as is genius in any area. Although verbal skills, memory, mimicry, imagination, and pretense are all skills used and developed by actors, we believe that social-cognitive skills are at the heart of acting. Psychological research on how acting trains social-cognitive skills can help us understand the development of these social-cognitive skills and what it means to develop expertise in these skills.

If actors have advantages in theory of mind, empathy, or emotion regulation as a result of their extensive training, we can learn how these skills, so important to social interaction, can be acquired. Such findings would have important implications for remediation of individuals deficient in these social-cognitive skills. Theatre, we believe, might provide a means of teaching social-cognitive skills to individuals with autism (indeed, several books have already been written to this end, even though no research has been conducted!) as well as in individuals with other social problems such as bullies, delinquents, and psychopaths (Mealey, 1995).

In the one piece of acting instruction that is known to have been written by Shakespeare, Hamlet instructs a group of players to "hold … the mirror up to nature": to be as truthful and natural as possible. Only through the study of human behavior, mental processes, and emotional states can one possibly understand and replicate the "nature" of a human truthfully. This is the great challenge of acting. Psychology can learn much from the study of theatre. It is surprising that this connection has not been studied by psychologists. It is our hope that this chapter will serve as a starting point for a new research area discovering what acting and psychology can learn from each other. For both acting and psychology, at their cores, seek to understand what it means to be human.

REFERENCES

Archer, W. (1957). *Masks or faces?* New York: Hill & Wang. (Original work published in 1888)

Aristotle. (1999). *Poetics* (K. McLeish, Trans.). London: Nick Hern.

Arnheim, R. (1974). *Art and visual perception: A psychology of the creative eye. The new version.* Berkeley: University of California Press.

Bamberger, J. (1991). *The mind behind the musical ear.* Cambridge, MA: Harvard University Press.

Baron-Cohen, S., Jolliffe, T., Mortimore, C., & Robertson, M. (1997). Another advanced test of theory of mind: Evidence from very high-functioning adults with autism or Asperger syndrome. *Journal of Child Psychology and Psychiatry, 38,* 813–822.

Baron-Cohen, S., & Wheelwright, S. (2004). The empathy quotient: An investigation of adults with Asperger syndrome or high functioning autism, and normal sex differences. *Journal of Autism and Developmental Disorders, 34*(2), 13–175.

Baron-Cohen, S., Wheelwright, S., Hill, J., Raste, Y., & Plumb, I. (2001). The "Reading the Mind in the Eyes" test revised version: A study with normal adults, and adults with Asperger syndrome or high-functioning autism. *Journal of Child Psychology and Psychiatry and Allied Disciplines, 42,* 241–251.

Batson, C. D., Lishner, D. A., Carpenter, A., Dulin, L., Harjusola-Webb, S., Stocks, E. L., et al. (2003). "… As you would have them do unto you": Does imagining yourself in the other's place simulate moral action? *Personality and Social Psychology Bulletin, 29,* 1190–1201.

Benedetti, J. (2007). *The art of the actor: The essential history of acting, from classical times to the present day.* New York: Taylor & Francis.

Blakemore, S. J., & Choudhury, S. (2006). Development of the adolescent brain: Implications for executive function and social cognition. *Journal of Child Psychology and Psychiatry, 47,* 296–312.

Bosacki, S. L., & Astington, J. (1999). Theory of mind in preadolescence: Relations between social understanding and social competence. *Social Development, 8,* 237–255.

Brown, J. R. (1995). *The Oxford illustrated history of theatre.* New York: Oxford University Press.

Bruder, M., Cohn, L. M., Olnek, M., Pollack, N., Previto, R., & Zigler, S. (1986). *A practical handbook for the actor.* New York: Random House.

Bryant, B. K. (1982). An index of empathy for children and adolescents. *Child Development, 53*(2), 413–425.

Burgoyne, S., Pouylin, K., & Rearden, A. (1999). The impact of acting on student actors: Boundary blurring, growth, and emotional distress. *Theatre Topics, 9*(2), 157–179.

Byrne, R., & Whiten, A. (Eds.). (1988). *Machiavellian intelligence: Social expertise and the evolution of intellect in monkeys, apes, and humans.* New York: Oxford University Press.

Carpendale, J., & Chandler, M. (1996). On the distinction between false belief understanding and subscribing to an interpretative theory of mind. *Child Development, 67,* 1686–1706.

Chandler, M. (1973). Egocentrism and antisocial behavior: The assessment and training of social perspective taking skills. *Developmental Psychology, 9*(3), 326–332.

Chandler, M., Greenspan, S., & Barenboim, C. (1974). Assessment and training of role-taking and referential communications skills in institutionalized emotionally disturbed children. *Developmental Psychology, 10*(4), 546–553.

Chekhov, M. (1991). *On the technique of acting* (M. Powers & M. Gordon, Eds.). New York: HarperCollins.

Choudhury, S., Blakemore, S., & Charman, T. (2006). Social cognitive development during adolescence. *SCAN, 1,* 165–174.

Cole, P. M., Martin, S. E., & Dennis, T. A. (2004). Emotion regulation as a scientific construct: Methodological challenges and directions for child development research. *Child Development, 75*(2), 317–333.

Cole, T., & Chinoy, H. K. (1949). *Actors on acting: The theories, techniques and practices of the world's great actors, told in their own words.* New York: Crown.

Collum, D. K. (1976). *The empathic ability of actors: A behavioral study.* Unpublished doctoral dissertation, Florida State University.

Costanzo, M., & Archer, D. (1993). *The interpersonal perception task.* Berkeley, CA: Berkeley Media.

Davis, M. (1983). Measuring individual differences in empathy: Evidence for a multidimensional approach. *Journal of Personality and Social Psychology, 44,* 113–126.

Deutsch, D. (Ed.). (1982). *The psychology of music.* New York: Academic Press.

Diderot, D. (1957). *The paradox of the actor* (L. Strasberg, Intro; H. Irving, Preface). New York: Hill & Wang. (Original work published in 1770)

Easterling, P., & Hall, E. (2002). *Greek and Roman actors: Aspects of an ancient profession.* Cambridge: Cambridge University Press.

Eisenberg, N., Fabes, R. A., & Spinrad, T. L. (2006). Pro social development. In N. Eisenberg (Ed.), *Handbook of child psychology: Vol, 3. Social, emotional and personality development*. New York: Wiley & Sons.

Ekman, R., Levenson, R. W., & Friesen, W. V. (1983). Autonomic nervous system activity distinguishes among emotions. *Science, 221*(4616), 1208–1210.

Frazer, J. G. (1993). *The golden bough*. Oxford: Oxford University Press.

Freeman, N. H. (1980). *Strategies of representation*. London: Academic Press.

Futterman, A. D., Kemeny, M. E., Shapiro, D., & Fahey, J. L. (1994). Immunological and physiological changes associated with induced positive and negative mood. *Psychosomatic Medicine, 56*, 499–511.

Gardner, H. (1980). *Artful scribbles: The significance of children's drawings*. New York: Basic Books.

Goldstein, T. R., & Tamir, M. (N.d.). When emotions are tools of the trade: Acting and emotion regulation.

Goldstein, T. R., & Winner, E. (in press). Actors are skilled in theory of mind but not empathy. *Imagination, Cognition, and Personality*.

Golomb, C. (2004). *The child's creation of a pictorial world* (2nd ed,). Mahwah, NJ: Lawrence Erlbaum.

Gopnik, A., & Astington, J. W. (1988). Children's understanding of representational change and its relation to the understanding of false belief and the appearance-reality distinction. *Child Development, 59*, 26–37.

Gross, J. J. (1998). The emerging field of emotion regulation: An integrative review. *Review of General Psychology, 2*(3), 271–299.

Gross, J. J. (1999). Emotion regulation: Past, present, future. *Cognitive and Emotion, 13*(5), 551–573.

Gross, J. J. (2002). Emotion regulation: Affective, cognitive, and social consequences. *Psychophysiology, 39*, 281–291.

Hagen, M. (1980). *The perception of pictures*. London: Academic Press.

Hagen, U., & Frankel, H. (1973). *Respect for acting*. New York: Macmillan.

Harkness, K. L., Sabbagh, M. A., Jacobson, J. A., Chowdrey, N. K., & Chen, T. (2005). Enhanced accuracy of mental state decoding in dysphoric college students. *Cognition and Emotion, 19*(7), 999–1025.

Hayman, R. (1969). *Techniques of acting*. London: Methuen.

Hoffman, M. L. (1981). Is altruism part of human nature? *Journal of Personality and Social Psychology, 40*, 121–137.

Hogan, R. (1969). Development of an empathy scale. *Journal of Consulting and Clinical Psychology, 33*(3), 307–316.

Hull, L. S. (1985). *Strasberg's method: As taught by Lorrie Hull*. Woodbridge, CT: Ox Bow.

Larson, R. W., & Brown, J. R. (2007). Emotional development in adolescence: What can be learned from a high school theater program? *Child Development, 78*(4), 1083–1099.

Lennon, R., & Eisenberg, N. (1987). Gender and age differences in empathy and sympathy. In N. Eisenberg & J. Strayer (Eds.), *Empathy and its development* (pp. 195–217). New York: Cambridge University Press.

Levy, J. (1997). Theatre and moral education. *Journal of Aesthetic Education, 31* (3), 65–75.

Malinowski, B. (1992). *Malinowski and the work of myth* (I. Strenski, Ed.). Princeton, NJ: Princeton University Press.

Mamet, D. (1997). *True and false: Heresy and common sense for the actor.* New York: Vintage.

Mar, R. A., Oatley, K., Hirsh, J., de la Paz, J., & Peterson, J. B. (2006) Bookworms versus nerds: Exposure to fiction versus non-fiction, divergent associations with social ability, and the simulation of fictional social worlds. *Journal of Research in Personality, 40*, 694–712.

Mealey, L. (1995). The sociobiology of sociopathy: An integrated evolutionary model. *Behavioral and Brain Sciences, 18*(3), 523–599.

Meisner, S., & Longwell, D. (1987). *On acting.* New York: Vintage.

Meltzoff, A. (2002). Imitation as a mechanism of social cognition: Origins of empathy, theory of mind, and the representation of action. In U. Goswami (Ed.), *Blackwell handbook of childhood cognitive development.* Cambridge, MA: Blackwell.

Metcalf, J. T. (1931). Empathy and the actor's emotion. *Journal of Social Psychology, 2*(2), 235–239.

Morton, J., Frith, U., & Leslie, A. (1991). The cognitive basis of a biological disorder: Autism. *Trends in Neurosciences, 14*, 434–438.

Murray, P. B. (1996). *Shakespeare's imagined persons: The psychology of role-playing and acting.* Annapolis, MD: Barnes and Noble Books.

Nettle, D. (2006). Psychological profiles of professional actors. *Personality and Individual Differences, 40*, 375–383.

Noice, T., & Noice, H. (2006). What studies of actors and acting can tell us about memory and cognitive functioning. *Current Directions in Psychological Science, 15*(1), 14–18.

Nolen-Hoeksema, S., Morrow, J., & Fredrickson, B. L. (1993). Response styles and the duration of episodes of depressed mood. *Journal of Abnormal Psychology, 102*(1), 20–28.

Olivier, L. (1986). *On acting.* New York: Simon & Schuster.

Pelletier, M., Bouthillier, A., Levesque, J., Carrier, S., Breault, C., Paquette, V., et al. (2003). Separate neural circuits for primary emotions? Brain activity during self induced sadness and happiness in professional actors. *NeuroReport, 14*(8), 1111–1116.

Piaget, J. (1962). *Play, dreams, and imitation in childhood* (C. Gettegno & F. M. Hodgson, Trans.). New York: Norton.

Podzlony, A. (2000). Strengthening verbal skills through the use of classroom drama: A clear link. *The Journal of Aesthetic Education, 34*, 239–275.

Roach, J. R. (1985). *The player's passion: Studies in the science of acting.* Ann Arbor: University of Michigan Press.

Rose, C. (Exec. Prod.). (2008, March 24). *The Charlie Rose Show* [television broadcast]. New York: Public Broadcasting Service.

Ross, L. (1977). The intuitive psychologist and his shortcomings: Distortions in the attribution process. In L. Berkoqitz (Ed.), *Advances in experimental social psychology* (Vol. 10, pp. 174–221). New York: Academic Press.

Sloboda, J. A. (1986). *The musical mind: The cognitive psychology of music.* New York: Oxford University Press.

Stanislavski, K. (1948). *An actor prepares* (E. R. Hapgood, Trans.). New York: Theatre Arts. (Original work published in 1936)

Stanislavski, K. (1950). *My life in art.* Moscow: Foreign Languages Publishing House.

Stiller, J., & Dunbar, R. I. M. (2007). Perspective-taking and memory capacity predict social network size. *Social Networks, 29,* 93–104.

Tager-Flusberg, H., & Sullivan, K. (2000). A componential view of theory of mind: Evidence from Williams' syndrome. *Cognition, 76*(1), 59–90.

Trehub, S. E. (2003). Toward a developmental psychology of music. *Annals of the New York Academy of Sciences, 999,* 402–413.

Verducci, S. (2000). A moral method? Thoughts on cultivating empathy through method acting. *Journal of Moral Education, 29*(1), 87–99.

Wellman, H., Cross, D., & Watson, J. (2001). Meta-analysis of theory-of-mind development: The truth about false belief. *Child Development, 72*(3), 655–684.

Whiten, A. (1991). *Natural theories of mind.* Oxford: Basil Blackwell.

Wimmer, H., & Perner, J. (1983). Beliefs about beliefs: Representation and constraining function of false beliefs in young children's understanding of deception. *Cognition, 13,* 103–128.

Winner, E. (2006). Development in the arts: Drawing and music. In W. Damon (Ed.), *Handbook of child psychology* (6th ed.). New York: Wiley.

Wooster, R. (2004, Summer). Emotion involvement or critical detachment? Heathcote's links with the ideas of Stanislavski, Brecht and Boal. *Drama Magazine,* 14–20.

Zeki, S. (1999). *Inner vision: An exploration of art and the brain.* Oxford: Oxford University Press.

13

COMMENTARY

Advanced Social Cognition in the Literary Arts

Joan Peskin, Raymond A. Mar, and Theanna Bischoff

For the last two decades, studies on theory of mind (ToM) have almost exclusively examined 3- to 5-year-old children's ability to represent other people's mental states. Only recently have a few studies on the mentalistic understandings of 6- to 8-year-olds been published. Goldstein and Winner's chapter is an admirable attempt to begin examining the development of an advanced ToM and social cognition in older adolescents and adults. In light of their empirical research on actors in the genre of theatre, combined with recent theoretical analyses of adult ToM in the genre of fiction (Keen, 2007; Zunshine, 2006), it can be said that ToM is coming of age within the realm of the literary arts.

There is a notable difference between early ToM and the development of an advanced ToM as needed by, for instance, Method actors. Although the former develops naturally and appears to be intuitive for most children, the latter requires effortfully evaluating other characters as if through the mind of another (i.e., the character one is playing). In studying advanced ToM, we are looking at the development of expertise, which involves the extended effects of time spent in goal-directed and effortful "deliberate practice" guided by a coach or teacher (Ericsson, 2006). Goldstein and Winner frequently allude to the development of expertise and the need for better measures that will capture such expertise in adult ToM; perhaps it is research on expertise that might provide important insights and, most importantly, methodologies for the examination of advanced ToM in the literary arts.

At present, for adolescents or adults there is no standard measure of social cognitive ToM; that is, a test that taps thoughts and predictions about someone's mental states or behavior based on that person's traits or previous actions and experiences. In the absence of such a measure, there is only the limited testing of an individual's social-perceptual ToM by means of the Reading the Mind in the Eyes Test, which assesses mental state recognition based on perceptions of a person's expression portrayed in his or her eyes (Baron-Cohen, Wheelwright, Hill, Raste, & Plumb, 2001). In the study of expertise, on the other hand, the primary methodology is an expert–novice comparison in which experts and relative novices in a particular domain are provided with tasks that require effortful processing, and participants are required to think aloud as they make sense of the problem (e.g., Azevedo, Faremo, & Lajoie, 2007; Peskin, 1998; Sabers, Cushing, & Berliner, 1991; Tabatabai & Shore, 2005; Wineburg, 1991). Researchers then conduct qualitative analyses of the resulting protocols from both groups. It seems that this methodology might be useful for tapping thoughts indicative of social cognitive ToM by comparing expert and novice actors thinking aloud about a new and undelineated character that they must portray.

Another difference between investigations of early ToM and later expertise in advanced ToM is that the former appears to be more domain general, whereas the latter might be somewhat more domain specific. For young children, there appears to be conceptual coherence in the development of mentalistic representational ability that results in the acquisition of a whole host of related understandings and concomitant behaviors at approximately the same time (Schneider, Schumann-Hengsteler, & Sodian, 2005). For instance, when young children begin to represent that someone might not know what the child knows, they also begin to demonstrate related behaviors and abilities: understanding the point of deception in story books (Peskin, 1996; Sodian, 1991), assigning roles during pretend play (Astington & Jenkins, 1995; Jenkins & Astington, 2000), and demonstrating the ability to keep a secret and the ability to play hide and seek (Peskin & Ardino, 2008).

Expertise, on the other hand, has been shown to be mostly domain specific. It involves the development of a cohesive semantic network of concepts that have many strong links within and between them, allowing experts to see large and meaningful patterns. Studies on expertise have shown that chess experts, for example, with their remarkable memory for chess positions, do not have a better memory in general (Schneider, Gruber, Gold, & Opwis, 1993). Their structured set of concepts enables them to recognize patterns specific to their domain of expertise and thereby extract a level of meaning that a relative novice is not able to do. These findings might provide reason to question Goldstein and Winner's implication that by studying the kinds of advanced levels of ToM that are fostered in acting, we can learn about expertise in sociocognitive skills and how these skills can be trained, for it might be that advanced sociocognitive skills are context dependent. For instance, Wineburg (1991) has shown that history experts, but not novices, represent the mental states of the author of a historical document, and similarly, Zunshine (2006) suggested the importance of representing the mental state of the narrator when reading fiction, in particular the unreliable narrator, such as Humbert in Vladimir Nabokov's *Lolita* (1955). In both of these domains, effortfully representing the perspective of the source of the information is an important component of developing expertise. However, does this mean that the trained historian will be more likely to represent the mental state of Humbert when reading fiction? Or that after actors have had intensive Method training in thinking about the mental states of various characters, they will be more likely to represent the mental states of the author of a historical text?

These are important questions stimulated by Goldstein and Winner's chapter, and they extend well beyond the domain of acting into social cognition in the literary arts in general. Goldstein and Winner examined just one genre, theatre, and within that genre only studied the perspective of the "agent," or actor. But what about the minds of the playwright and the audience? Or, in different genres, the writer and the reader? In the remainder of this commentary, we will pose questions and discuss the somewhat limited research on social cognition in the literary arts by first examining writers, then audiences, and then finally returning to actors.

WRITERS

The crucial role played by mental state attribution in constructing a story or play was elucidated by Bruner (1986):

> [A] story must construct two landscapes simultaneously. One is the landscape of action: agent, intention or goal, instrument, something corresponding to a "story grammar." The other landscape is the landscape of consciousness: what those involved in the action think, know, or feel, or do not know, think, or feel. The two landscapes are essential and distinct: it is the difference between

Oedipus sharing Jocasta's bed before and after he learns that she is his mother. (p. 14)

Constructing an effective landscape of consciousness requires the representation of many characters' mental states. Fiction writers are, essentially, inventing people whose beliefs, thoughts, values, and so on are dissimilar from their own. Authors cannot possibly have experienced every situation that their protagonists, however similar to themselves, have encountered (otherwise the text would be not fiction but, rather, autobiography). For many writers of fiction, the narrator or central protagonist is very different from the author, for example Timothy Findley's *Not Wanted on the Voyage* (1996) and Anna Sewell's *Black Beauty* (1877), narrated by a cat and a horse, respectively. The male author Wally Lamb published his famous novel *She's Come Undone* (1992) at age 42, which describes the coming of age of a young woman. Additionally, novels, short stories, and plays usually consist of multiple characters, and fiction writers must write considering the perspective of each of them, crafting not only appropriate actions but also reactions. They must take into account shifts in characteristics such as age, experience, character traits, knowledge, gender, sexual orientation, socioeconomic status, and political orientation for each and every character in their text.

Fiction writers not only have to consider the mental states of their characters but also must predict and understand the minds or thoughts of readers as they encounter the text. Although writing instruction is not as cleanly delineated as the Technique versus Method schools in acting instruction, a common way of teaching writing is the Workshop method, in which a group of writers exchanges texts and then each text is discussed individually. In some versions of the Workshop method, writers are not allowed to speak during the discussion of their own texts, the rationale being that, unlike with spoken communication, published writers cannot change their message to be better understood. In this way, writers are forced to see whether readers interpret the text in the way it was intended. This method of teaching writing may actually help develop ToM in fiction writers, as authors become conscious of discrepancies between what they meant and what they said, and what they intended and how it was received.

Furthermore, just as Method actors are taught to evaluate other characters through the minds of their own particular character—not only in terms of their immediate interaction but also in terms of the entire history of these relationships—so must effective writers think about their characters in a multitude of situations. In creative writing classes, one commonly used exercise is having writers complete a "questionnaire" of facts about their characters (Gotham Writer's Workshop, 2003). They must provide details possibly absent from the text but that help develop the character in the mind of the author such that he or she knows the character intimately. For both writers and Method actors, this involves time spent engaging in a long-term psychological analysis of their characters and their dispositional mental states. In a novel recently published by Theanna Bischoff (2008), one of the authors of the present commentary, the protagonist has breast cancer, and Bischoff interviewed numerous women diagnosed with cancer in order to construct the complexities involved in her protagonist's perspectives, beliefs, desires, and emotions.

Possibly because this psychological analysis is effortful, authors sometimes "reuse" characters, for example in a book series, or a supporting character from a previous novel may become a more central character in another. In a recent media interview, author Jodi Picoult commented that "it's always great fun to bring a character back, because you get to catch up on his/her life; and you don't have to reinvent the wheel—you already know how he speaks, acts, thinks" (Allen & Unwin, n.d.).

Goldstein and Winner predict that actors in general have more advanced ToM, but that this difference is likely even greater for Method actors. This may be similar for writers, as well—all may have more advanced ToM than the general population, but certain kinds of writers, that is, writers of certain genres, may be *most* adept. Leaving questions of causal directionality aside, one might hypothesize more developed social cognition in writers of genres in which characterization is paramount, for instance novelists, playwrights, and screenwriters, as opposed to poets. However, although most poets spend less time on characterization, they also might be more dysphoric than writers of other genres (Kohányi, 2005), and, as noted by Goldstein and Winner, dysphoric adolescents are better able to identify the mental states of others (Harkness, Sabbagh, Jacobson, Chowdrey, & Chen, 2005), as assessed by performance on the Reading the Mind in the Eyes test (Baron-Cohen et al., 2001). This might be because dysphoric adults are more sensitive to stimuli, including social cues, and are inclined to ruminative introspection (Gleicher & Weary, 1991). Thus, it is possible that poets may outperform other writers on this task. Fiction writers, however, appear to be more driven by negative emotions than other successful professionals (i.e., scientists), and could thus possibly outperform matched nonwriters (Djikic, Oatley, & Peterson, 2006). These remain open avenues for future research.

In addition, different subgenres may require more ToM demands on the part of writers than others. For instance, within the genre of fiction, detective or crime stories often involve an unexpected ending, and writers must be acutely aware of their readers' knowledge states and biases and the inferences that the readers are likely to make in order to purposefully lead them in the wrong direction. The hallmark of other subgenres, typically those involving humor or horror, is that they are written so that the reader is aware of something that a protagonist does not know. And, finally, another subgenre with huge demands for perspective taking is that of the novel written with shifting points of view. For instance, Barbara Kingsolver in *The Poisonwood Bible* (1999) shifted narration between five female family members.

Empirical research exists to support the idea that fiction writers might possess an elevated capacity for social understanding. Taylor, Hodges, and Kohányi (2002) collected a sample of 50 fiction writers who had been writing for at least 5 years and administered a variety of measures including a self-report measure of empathy, the Interpersonal Reactivity Index (Davis, 1983). This measure includes four subscales: Empathic Concern (emotional empathy), Perspective-Taking (cognitive empathy), Fantasy (projection of the self into fiction), and Personal Distress (vulnerability to negative affect). Fiction writers reported higher scores on all of these subscales compared to the population norms, and by a large margin. Fantasy exhibited by far the largest difference, with both male and female writers reporting scores over two standard deviations higher than the norm. Fantasy was closely followed by Perspective-Taking and Empathic Concern, with Personal Distress scores the least different from the norm. Personal Distress, however, is also the subscale that is least likely to measure something traditionally considered to be a component of empathy (Mar, Oatley, Hirsch, de la Paz, & Peterson, 2006). A weakness of this study, of course, is that it relies on self-report. An interesting follow-up would be to replicate these results using an established paradigm for the study of individual differences in social cognition or social perception (Ickes, 1997). Of course, as with many of the previous studies mentioned before, the design precludes any causal inferences. Even if it is the case that it is highly empathic individuals who tend to later become fiction writers, this still seems to be an interesting result, one that tells us something about the psychological richness of the writing craft and of literary works.

AUDIENCES (READERS AND VIEWERS)

Bruner (1986) wrote that literary texts

are about events in a "real" world, but they render that world newly strange, rescue it from obviousness, fill it with gaps that call upon the reader, in Barthes' sense, to become a writer, a composer of virtual text in response to the actual. (p. 24)

Filling in the gaps has been seen as the writers' exploitation of the reader's readiness to attribute mental states (Zunshine, 2006). For example, in Virginia Woolf's *Mrs. Dalloway* (1925), the reader is told that Peter thinks that Clarissa has "grown older" but then later that Clarissa notices that Peter is "positively trembling." Readers are forced to construct their own meaning, in this instance, inferring that "he must be excited to see her again" in order to create emotional cohesion in the narrative (Zunshine, p. 22). Zunshine argued that with our evolved cognitive capacity to represent the mental states of others in our social interactions, as we read books we are "intuitively" connecting people's behavior to their mental states (see also Mar & Oatley, 2008; Mar et al., 2006).

There are interesting questions about when this process is intuitive and effortless and when it is not. The creation of what Bruner (1986) called "gaps" or spaces for the reader appears to be effortful for writers. A commonly repeated phrase in Bischoff's writing classes, for example, was "Show, don't tell." It is better, for example, to show a character behaving in an angry manner than to merely tell one's reader, "X was angry." There may be many instances when such processes are effortful for readers, too. Considerations about an unreliable narrator, for instance, or having to track characters' embedded mental states, or think about what the author is intending us to think or feel, involve metarepresentational ability and concomitant effort. For instance, the following comments were made by 17-year-old students thinking aloud when reading a poem: "Maybe the poet is indirectly disturbing the reader by cutting the word in half," or "I think the author does want the reader to take note of how it's broken up, because it is very, very unusually broken up" (Peskin, in press).

Just as readers represent the mental states of characters and occasionally the intentions of the writer, so must theatre audiences engage in mindreading as they view the actions of the characters. One could argue that a hallmark of many plays is that the characters find themselves in some sort of predicament or misunderstanding that requires resolution. For instance, in the play *Cyrano de Bergerac* (Rostand, 1897), the female lead Roxane remains unaware that the man wooing her, who she believes to be the nobleman Christian, is actually Cyrano, whom Christian has hired. Likewise, Christian remains unaware that Cyrano has fallen for Roxane and wants her for himself. Keeping track of disparities between what each of the different characters is thinking is also the hallmark of many situational comedies on television. Park (2001) claimed, "Even television comedy programs are based on metacognition.... For instance, I was watching a popular American sitcom and heard sentences such as 'Well, they don't know we know that they know,' and 'Do you want me to want you to want it?'" (p. 73). This involves several layers of understanding of mind; viewers must track not only the minds of different characters but also different characters' understandings of other characters' minds. What do characters A and B each know about the situation? What does the viewer know about the situation? What does character A know about what B knows, and vice versa? And how are these understandings different?

A question for future empirical work on the social cognition of consumers of the literary arts is whether it is more cognitively demanding to think about characters' mental states when viewing a drama or when reading fiction. In fiction, although readers must make inferences when writers "show" rather than "tell," there are also frequent instances of "voiceovers" when the mental states of the protagonists—their beliefs, intentions, emotions, and desires—are explained to the reader. For theatre audiences, on the other hand, these explanations are absent, except when actually stated by the characters or the occasional times when a play incorporates a narrator or a chorus. In theatre, however, actors mediate between playwright and consumer. Theatre audiences are able to "read" the facial expressions and body language of the actors, visual embodiments that are not available to the reader of a novel or a play.

Goldstein and Winner mention that adult fiction readers score higher on the Reading the Mind in the Eyes Test than nonfiction readers (Mar et al., 2006), but there is also research that has some bearing on the social cognition of film- and theatregoers. Viewing a dramatic production is somewhat akin to viewing someone pretending to carry out an action, and neuroimaging research has demonstrated that the viewing of pretense engages the brain differently than when simply watching human action. German and colleagues (German, Niehaus, Roarty, Giesbrecht, & Miller, 2004) examined neural responses in participants using functional magnetic resonance imaging (fMRI) as they viewed videos of people either engaging in simple actions (e.g., placing a book on a shelf) or miming that same action (e.g., pretending to put an invisible book on a shelf). Importantly, no specific instructions were given to participants; they were not directed to engage in mental inference or empathy. Compared to watching real actions, watching pretend actions led to greater engagement of a number of components of the social cognitive brain network. This implies that, as an audience member, watching actors play out a fiction may actually lead to more intense social processing than watching the actions of real persons.

A study by Mar and colleagues (Mar, Kelley, Heatherton, & Macrae, 2007), however, seems to suggest quite the opposite. Participants in this study viewed either real people or cartoon versions of the same people engaging in the exact same actions. The cartoon footage was digitally "painted" directly onto the live footage so that the biological motion being portrayed was identical for both cases. Using fMRI, it was determined that during the viewing of real persons (without instructions to engage in mentalization), certain components of the social cognitive network were more active compared to the viewing of cartoon persons (including those areas identified by German et al., 2004). Thus, in this study, the more fictive presentation of action (i.e., the cartoon actors) led to less engagement of social-processing brain areas. This appears to contradict the findings of German and colleagues, in which the more fictive actions (i.e., pretense behaviors) resulted in greater social processing. There are, however, key differences between these two studies. To begin, in the study by Mar and colleagues (2007) both conditions (cartoon and real) involved actors (the footage was derived from a film, *Waking Life*; Linklater, 2001). Also, although a cartoon actor is certainly more "pretend" than a real actor, it does not necessarily involve a greater degree of pretense in the same way as watching a real person mime an action. It may be that the social-processing network in our brain is specifically attuned to the actions of real persons (Mar et al., 2007) and must work harder to understand the behaviors of these persons when they are based on pretense (German et al.). What both of these studies demonstrate is that activation of the social-processing network spontaneously occurs during the viewing of actors, without instruction or guidance. An interesting question is whether an audience's social-processing abilities might be taxed to a lesser degree when watching more proficient actors, whose behaviors may be less obviously an act of pretense.

ACTORS

Finally, to return to the social cognition of the actors themselves, evidence that actors may have elevated social skills (cognitive and emotion based) can be found throughout the developmental literature. Children who engage in pretense or pretend play are known to have better ToM abilities and social competence, even after taking into account verbal intelligence and socioeconomic factors (Garner, Curenton, & Taylor, 2005; Seja & Russ, 1999; Taylor & Carlson, 1997).

These studies, however, like much of the research cited by Goldstein and Winner, do not allow for causal inferences, that is, we cannot conclude that this sort of play is what drives better social competence. It could easily be that socially skilled children are simply more likely to act out fantasy play.

There is, however, an experimental study that does not suffer from the aforementioned shortcoming and that lends support to the notion that training in drama results in social growth. Schellenberg (2004) randomly assigned 6-year-old children to an intensive 36-week program in either music (keyboard or voice) or drama, or to a no-lesson wait-list control (this group received keyboard lessons the following year). Class sizes were small (six children per class), and each child had one instructor for the duration of the course. Their instructors were professional music or drama teachers, whose primary income came from teaching. Prior to beginning the course, all children were evaluated by their parents using the Parent Rating Scale of the Behavioral Assessment System for Children (BASC; Reynolds & Kampaus, 1992). The BASC measures both maladaptive behaviors (hyperactivity, aggression, anxiety, depression, atypicality, and attention problems) and adaptive behaviors (adaptability, social skills, and leadership). This measure was then administered a second time, following the course, to evaluate changes in these behaviors as a result of random assignment to the different types of lessons. Schellenberg (2004) found that children who completed the drama lessons exhibited an improvement in adaptive social behavior, but those who took music lessons (or had no lessons) experienced no such improvement. The amount of improvement seen in children who completed the drama lessons over those in the other groups was not small, but moderate in magnitude, equivalent to roughly half a standard deviation (Cohen's $d = .57$). No differences in maladaptive behaviors were observed.

The fact that drama lessons led to an increase in adaptive social behaviors, including social skills, is certainly supportive of the hypotheses put forth by Goldstein and Winner. This study, however, does not test Goldstein and Winner's more refined hypotheses regarding different methods for drama instruction (Technique versus Method) and different forms of social growth (ToM versus empathy). Given the age of the participants, it seems unlikely that the drama instruction in this study involved any explication of the Method approach. A final question that remains unanswered is how age might interact with the hypotheses of Goldstein and Winner. It may well be that the differential facilitation of ToM versus empathy based on different forms of drama instruction may pertain only to adults.

In the above sections we have primarily discussed social cognition in terms of the representation of others' mental states. But in describing actors, Goldstein and Winner also examine social cognition in terms of emotion, in particular empathy. As Goldstein and Winner discuss, it is questionable whether actors exhibit greater empathy, and a recent study might have some relevance for this discussion. In a study of celebrities by Young and Pinsky (2006), successful actors ($N = 59$) were found to score higher than the general population on an established measure of narcissism. Because narcissism is known to be negatively associated with empathy (e.g., Watson & Morris, 1991), this places any possible elevated empathic ability of actors into question. It is important to note, however, that this study examined only successful actors, and their finding of narcissistic tendencies may not apply to less successful practitioners.

CONCLUSION

The relationship between acting and advanced social cognition is not only an unexplored area but also one that exists at the intersection of various other research topics that are similarly uncharted. How writers, audiences, and actors consider the mentalistic states of characters in negotiating Bruner's "gaps" and how these often effortful considerations might foster advanced social cognition (in both the cognitive and emotional domains) are still unclear. Building on Goldstein and Winner's chapter, we have attempted to provide questions, suggest alternative methodologies, and point out directions for future exploration in the hope that advanced ToM and the study of emotion in the literary arts might become a robust area of research in the future.

REFERENCES

Allen & Unwin. (N.d.). [Interview with Jodi Picoult, author of *Nineteen minutes.*] Retrieved September 8, 2008, from http://www.jodipicoult.com.au/nineteenminutes.html

Astington, J. W., & Jenkins, J. M. (1995). Theory of mind development and social understanding. *Cognition & Emotion, 9,* 151–165.

Azevedo, R., Faremo, S., & Lajoie, S. P. (2007). Expert-novice differences in mammogram interpretation. In D. S. McNamara & J. G. Trafton (Eds.), *Proceedings of the 29th annual cognitive science society* (pp. 65–70). Austin, TX: Cognitive Science Society.

Baron-Cohen, S., Wheelwright, S., Hill, J., Raste, Y., & Plumb, I. (2001). The "Reading the Mind in the Eyes" test revised version: A study with normal adults, and adults with Asperger syndrome or high functioning autism. *Journal of Child Psychiatry and Psychiatry, 42,* 241–252.

Bischoff, T. (2008). *Cleavage*. Edmonton, AB: NeWest Press.

Bruner, J. S. (1986). *Actual minds, possible worlds*. Cambridge, MA: Harvard University Press.

Davis, M. H. (1983). Measuring individual differences in empathy: Evidence for a multidimensional approach. *Journal of Personality and Social Psychology, 44*, 113–126.

Djikic, M., Oatley, K., & Peterson, J. B. (2006). The bitter-sweet labor of emoting: The linguistic comparison of writers and physicists. *Creativity Research Journal, 18*, 195–201.

Ericsson, K. (2006). The influence of experience and deliberate practice on the development of superior expert performance. In K. A. Ericsson, N. Charness, P. J. Feltovich, & R. R. Hoffman (Eds.). *The Cambridge handbook of expertise and expert performance* (pp. 683–704). New York: Cambridge University Press.

Findley, T. (1996). *Not wanted on the voyage*. Toronto: Penguin Canada.

Garner, P. W., Curenton, S. M., & Taylor, K. (2005). Predictors of mental state understanding in preschoolers of varying socioeconomic backgrounds. *International Journal of Behavioral Development, 29*, 271–281.

German, T. P., Niehaus, J. L., Roarty, M. P., Giesbrecht, B., & Miller, M. B. (2004). Neural correlates of detecting pretense: Automatic engagement of the intentional stance under covert conditions. *Journal of Cognitive Neuroscience, 16*, 1805–1817.

Gleicher, F., & Weary, G. (1991). The effect of depression on the quantity and quality of social inferences. *Journal of Personality and Social Psychology, 51*, 140–148.

Gotham Writer's Workshop. (2003). *Writing fiction: The practical guide from New York's acclaimed creative writing school*. New York: Bloomsbury USA.

Ickes, W. (Ed.). (1997). *Empathic accuracy*. New York: Guilford Press.

Jenkins, J. M., & Astington, J. W. (2000). Theory of mind and social behavior: Causal models tested in a longitudinal study. *Merrill Palmer Quarterly, 46*, 203–220.

Keen, S. (2007). *Empathy and the novel*. New York: Oxford University Press.

Kingsolver, B. (1999). *The poisonwood bible*. New York: Harper Perennial.

Kohányi, A. (2005). Four factors that may predict the emergence of creative writing: A proposed model. *Creativity Research Journal, 17*, 195–205.

Lamb, W. (1992). *She's come undone*. New York: Pocket Books.

Linklater, R. (2001). *Waking Life*. Los Angeles: Fox Searchlight Pictures.

Mar, R. A., Kelley, W. M., Heatherton, T. F., & Macrae, C. N. (2007). Detecting agency from the biological motion of veridical versus animated agents. *Social Cognitive and Affective Neuroscience, 2*, 199–205.

Mar, R. A., & Oatley, K. (2008). The function of fiction is the abstraction and simulation of social experience. *Perspectives on Psychological Science, 3*, 173–192.

Mar, R. A., Oatley, K., Hirsh, J., de la Paz, J., & Peterson, J. B. (2006). Re: Bookworms versus Nerds: Exposure to fiction versus non-fiction, divergent associations with social ability and the simulation of fictional social worlds. *Journal of Research in Personality, 40,* 694–712.

Nabokov, V. (1955). *Lolita.* New York: G. P. Putnam's Sons.

Park, S. (2001). *Theory of mind dynamics in children's play: A qualitative inquiry in a preschool classroom.* Unpublished doctoral dissertation, Virginia Polytechnic and State University, Virginia.

Peskin, J. (1996). Guise and guile: Children's understanding of narratives in which the purpose of pretense is deception. *Child Development, 67,* 1735–1751.

Peskin, J. (1998). Constructing meaning when reading poetry: An expert-novice study. *Cognition and Instruction, 16,* 235–263.

Peskin, J. (In press). The development of poetic literacy through the school years. *Discourse Processes.*

Peskin, J., & Ardino, V. (2008). Representing the mental world in children's social behaviour: Playing hide-and-seek and keeping a secret. *Social Development, 12,* 496–512.

Reynolds, C. R., & Kamphaus, R. W. (1992). *Behavior assessment system for children.* Circle Pines, MN: American Guidance Service.

Rostand, E. (1897). *Cyrano de Bergerac.* Retrieved February 17, 2009, from http://etext.lib.virginia.edu/etcbin/toccer-new2?id=RosCyra. xml&images=images/modeng&data=/texts/english/modeng/ parsed&tag=public&part=all

Sabers, D. S., Cushing, K. S., & Berliner, D. C. (1991). Differences among teachers in a task characterized by simultaneity, multidimensionality, and immediacy. *American Educational Research Journal, 28,* 63–88.

Schellenberg, E. G. (2004). Music lessons enhance IQ. *Psychological Science, 15,* 511–514.

Schneider, W., Gruber, H., Gold, H., & Opwis, K. (1993). Chess expertise and memory for chess positions in children and adults. *Journal of Experimental Child Psychology, 56,* 328–349.

Schneider, W., Schumann-Hengsteler, R., & Sodian, B. (2005). *Young children's cognitive development: Interrelationships among working memory, verbal ability, and theory of mind.* New York: Routledge.

Seja, A. L., & Russ, S. W. (1999). Children's fantasy play and emotional understanding. *Journal of Clinical Child Psychology, 28,* 269–277.

Sewell, A. (1877). *Black Beauty: The autobiography of a horse.* London: Jarrolds & Sons.

Sodian, B. (1991). The development of deception in young children. *British Journal of Developmental Psychology, 9,* 173–188.

Tabatabai, D., & Shore, B. M. (2005). How experts and novices search the web. *Library & Information Science Research, 27,* 222–248.

Taylor, M., & Carlson, S. M. (1997). The relationship between individual differences in fantasy and theory of mind. *Child Development, 68,* 436–455.

Taylor, M., Hodges, S. D., & Kohányi, A. (2002). The illusion of independent agency: Do adult fiction writers experience their characters as having minds of their own? *Imagination, Cognition and Personality, 22,* 361–380.

Watson, P. J., & Morris, R. J. (1991). Narcissism, empathy and social desirability. *Personality and Individual Differences, 12,* 575–579.

Wineburg, S. (1991). Historical problem solving: A study of the cognitive processes used in the evaluation of documentary and pictorial evidence. *Journal of Education Psychology, 83,* 73–87.

Woolf, V. (1925). *Mrs. Dalloway.* Richmond, UK: Hogarth.

Young, M. S., & Pinsky, D. (2006). Narcissism and celebrity. *Journal of Research in Personality, 40,* 463–471.

Zunshine, L. (2006). *Why we read fiction: Theory of mind and the novel.* Columbus: Ohio State University Press.

AUTHOR INDEX

A

Adajian, L. B., 142, 165
Adi-Japha, E., 185, 197, 209
Allain, J., 14, 38
Allen & Unwin, 253, 259
Allison, K., 154, 161
Altran, S., 142, 161
Anderson, S. E., 143, 160
Appadurai, A., 68, 80
Archer, D., 234, 244
Archer, W., 223, 224, 243
Ardino, V., 250, 261
Aristotle, 224, 243
Arnheim, R., 221, 243
Ascher, M., 142, 160
Astington, J., 237, 244
Astington, J. W., 232, 245, 250, 259, 260
Aujoulat, N., 14, 37
Azevedo, R., 250, 259

B

Bahn, P., 43, 55
Bahn, P. G., 43, 55
Baldwin, J. M., 2, 8, 44, 54
Ball, A. F., 178, 180
Ballenger, C., 142, 160, 165
Bamberger, J., 135, 137, 222, 243

Bang, M., 142, 161
Baquedano-Lopez, P., 141, 162
Barenboim, C., 235, 244
Baron-Cohen, S., 231, 232, 236, 237, 239,
    243, 250, 253, 259
Barton, C. M,, 48–49, 49, 54
Batson, C. D., 237, 243
Beardsley, M. C., 196, 208
Bednarick, R. G., 41, 42, 54
Benedetti, J., 222, 223, 224, 243
Bennet, L., 142, 161
Bereiter, C., 142, 161
Berliner, D. C., 250, 261
Bhatia, S., 172, 173, 180
Biesele, M., 23, 37
Bischoff, T., 253, 260
Blades, M., 205, 211
Blakemore, S., 233, 235, 244
Blakemore, S. J., 233, 243
Blakeslee, S., 11, 21, 39
Bleek, D. F., 25, 37
Bleek, W. H. I., 25, 37
Bleich, S., 85, 96
Bloom, P., 197, 208
Blum, D., 130, 137
Blustein, D. L., 93, 96
Bohm, D., 218, 220
Borkum, J., 187, 211
Bosacki, S. L., 237, 244

SUBJECT INDEX

C

Campbell, Clive, 64
Cam'ron, 78
Canadian Aboriginal music, 73
Canonical knowledge, 143
Canonical literature, 144, 145, 148
Canonical narrative, 145ff
Cape Verdean youths' cultural identity, 67
Carl, Robert, 125
Cave art; *see also* Rock paintings; Upper Palaeolithic cave art
    aesthetics in, 50–52
    Australian Laura region, 52
    bestiary animals depicted in, 29
    biases in interpretation, 42
    chiaroscuro in cave art, 53
    choice of imaged subjects, 29–30
    cognitive processes and, 43
    dating, 52
    emergence, 3–4
    evolution, 12–16, 52–53
    figure-ground reversal in , 51
    hallucinations seen on cave walls, 32
    as memory storage device, 50
    optical tricks in, 51
    planning in creation of, 52–53
    population dispersals and, 47
    preservation of after-images, 33
    reason for creating, 14
    religious elements in, 35–36
    shimmering in, 51
    social practices and, 43
    sociopolitical significance, 52
    sophisticated level of, 15–16
    structuralism influence on interpretation, 41–42
    underworld inhabitants depicted, 29–30
Caves, 24
Channels of Rage, 74
Characters' mental states, 252
Characters reused, 253
Character understanding, 226–227
Chauvet Cave
    discovery, 15–16
    Panel of Horses, 52
Child as expert, 195
Child as scientist, 194, 213

Child as theorist, 215, 219–220
    in domains of knowledge, 194
Childhood development, xii
    adolescent interpretation of feedback, 84
    mirrored in evolutionary changes, 14
    plays as transitional space, 2
    range of variation, 140–141
Children as art critics, 185, 187, 208; *see also* Art critics
    art critical stance, 201–202, 207
    compared to art critics, 197
    diversity in evaluations, 199, 205–206
    domain of art, 217
    evaluation of pictures,199, 202, 203–205
    expect consensus, 206
    nature of development, 200–201
    nature of evaluations, 201–202
    purpose of study of development, 213–214
    stages of, 199–200
    standards considered, 207
Christian Church effects, 35
Chuck D, 65, 73
Civil Rights Movement, 96
Cladistic analyses, 43–44
Classical philosophical aesthetics, 197
Classificatory development in primate species, 44–46
Classroom culture development, 157
Climatic shifts, 46–47
Close listening, 128
Clothing and self-expression, 69; *see also* Hip-hop wear/clothing
Cognition mapping, 46
Cognitive apprenticeship, 175
Cognitive development
    vs. human development, 173–174
    primate species experimental comparison, 44–46
Cognitive empathy, 254
Cognitive perspective taking, 237
Coherence, imposing, 148
Color Purple, The, 155
Commercialization of hip-hop, 70–71
Common, 72
Communication
    art as medium, , 49
    intergenerational, 86